# Jaguar Books on Latin America

## Series Editors

WILLIAM H. BEEZLEY, Neville G. Penrose Chair of Latin
American Studies, Texas Christian University
COLIN M. MACLACHLAN, Professor and Chair, Department
of History, Tulane University

## Volumes Published

John E. Kicza, ed., *The Indian in Latin American History: Resistance, Resilience, and Acculturation* (1993). Cloth ISBN 0-8420-2421-2
Paper ISBN 0-8420-2425-5

Susan E. Place, ed., *Tropical Rainforests: Latin American Nature and Society in Transition* (1993). Cloth ISBN 0-8420-2423-9  Paper ISBN 0-8420-2427-1

Paul W. Drake, ed., *Money Doctors, Foreign Debts, and Economic Reforms in Latin America from the 1890s to the Present* (1994).
Cloth ISBN 0-8420-2434-4  Paper ISBN 0-8420-2435-2

John A. Britton, ed., *Molding the Hearts and Minds: Education, Communications, and Social Change in Latin America* (1994).
Cloth ISBN 0-8420-2489-1  Paper ISBN 0-8420-2490-5

Darién J. Davis, ed., *Slavery and Beyond: The African Impact on Latin America and the Caribbean* (1994). Cloth ISBN 0-8420-2484-0
Paper ISBN 0-8420-2485-9

David J. Weber and Jane M. Rausch, eds., *Where Cultures Meet: Frontiers in Latin American History* (1994). Cloth ISBN 0-8420-2477-8
Paper ISBN 0-8420-2478-6

Gertrude M. Yeager, ed., *Confronting Change, Challenging Tradition: Women in Latin American History* (1994). Cloth ISBN 0-8420-2479-4
Paper ISBN 0-8420-2480-8

Linda Alexander Rodríguez, ed., *Rank and Privilege: The Military and Society in Latin America* (1994). Cloth ISBN 0-8420-2432-8
Paper ISBN 0-8420-2433-6

D1482572

Confronting
Change,
Challenging
Tradition

# Confronting Change, Challenging Tradition

## Women in Latin American History

Gertrude M. Yeager
Editor

Jaguar Books on Latin America
Number 7

A Scholarly Resources Inc. Imprint
Wilmington, Delaware

Scholarly Resources Inc.
104 Greenhill Avenue
Wilmington, DE 19805-1897

**Library of Congress Cataloging-in-Publication Data**

Confronting change, challenging tradition : women in Latin American
  history / Gertrude M. Yeager, editor.
      p.    cm. — (Jaguar books on Latin America ; no. 7)
   Includes bibliographical references.
   ISBN 0-8420-2479-4 (cloth). — ISBN 0-8420-2480-8 (pbk.)
      1. Women—Latin America—History. 2. Feminism—Latin America.
3. Women in politics—Latin America.  I. Yeager, Gertrude Matyoka.
II. Series.
HQ1460.5.C66    1994
305.4'098—dc20                                                94-17441
                                                                   CIP

⊗The paper used in this publication meets the minimum requirements of
the American National Standard for permanence of paper for printed
library materials, Z39.48, 1984.

# Acknowledgments

Graduate students enrolled in several interdisciplinary seminars on Latin American women and their history deserve a great deal of credit for developing the general synthesis of material on this topic as presented here. I used the preparation of a textbook as a teaching device, and they responded enthusiastically, ferreting out and condensing the extensive literature in existence on Latin America's female population into a framework suitable for introducing undergraduates to the history of Latin American women. They brought with them the tools of their respective disciplines: literature, development studies, international studies, public health, rural sociology, religious studies, and anthropology, as well as history, and the insights gleaned from considerable field experience. Special thanks go to Jennifer Accettola, Laura Boland, Richard Browning, Suzanne Corley, Andrea Hamilton, James Huck, Nick Robins, Lisa Petrov, Dee Mitchell, Heather Thiessen, Elizabeth Van Sant, Laura Podalsky, Linda Curcio-Van Nagy, Kim Wargo, and Lisa Zimmerman.

Sue Ingles and Tammy Walker prepared most of the manuscript and my husband, Gene Yeager, provided much-appreciated editorial assistance. The staff at Scholarly Resources, especially Laura Huey Cunningham, Linda Pote Musumeci, Ann Morris Aydelotte, and Sharon L. Beck, has been helpful, professional, and patient throughout this project.

# About the Editor

Gertrude M. Yeager is an associate professor of Latin American history at Tulane University and received her doctoral training at Texas Christian University. She has published books and articles on Chilean, Peruvian, and Bolivian history. Her current research interests are in women's studies.

# Contents

# Introduction

Interpreting Latin American history from a feminine perspective entails more than simply recounting women's participation in wars, social upheavals, and other events that have been designated as traditional benchmarks. It demands an exploration of women's activity—or lack thereof—in the political, economic, and domestic spheres. Essential to a woman-centered history is a knowledge of how women perceive themselves, their roles, obligations, and limitations as dictated by society, and how these perceptions have changed over time.

Continuity rather than change best characterizes the history of Latin American women. This is not to say that change did not occur but, rather, that it evolved at a snail's pace until the 1970s because of the constraints of culture. Part I of this volume explores how Latin American culture has portrayed and defined woman, from the time of Columbus to the present, and kept her in her place. It examines the images of Latin American women created by traditional practices, political ideology, intellectual prescriptions, and popular culture. The selections in Part II describe and analyze the conditions that actually shaped the lives of Latin American women, be they the elite, peasants, or urban workers, in the past and present century.

Home. Family. Honor. These are the guiding principles of female-male relations that have remained constant from 1492 to the present. The typical Latin American family is portrayed as patriarchal in structure with an authoritarian male head, bilateral kinship, and a submissive mother and wife concerned with the domestic sphere. In Spanish the verb "to marry," *casarse*, literally means "to put oneself into a house." A married woman is referred to as *casada* (housed in) not only because of a perceived biological tie to childrearing or because she may not be physically or mentally suited for other labor, but also because, under the patriarchal system, family honor resides within her.[1] As a daughter her virginity must be preserved so that she will make an acceptable wife, thus giving the family the opportunity to extend and strengthen its business and social networks; as a wife her sexual faithfulness to her husband ensures racial purity and continuity of lineage. A wife or daughter's sexual transgression is thought to dishonor the family and sabotage the patriarchal order. In Latin America, a society where the cult of personalism reigns, business and social ties are based on trust.[2] While a husband has to trust his wife and daughters, he also has to control them. His prestige—and therefore the confidence and trust that potential business and social partners might bestow upon him—would diminish if he could not control his "subjects" or guarantee their purity. The models of the Virgin Mary and of the saints help to instill self-denial, humility, suffering, obedience, and religious piety in women. The woman who violates the ideal may suffer serious consequences.

While Spanish culture empowered the "good" woman with moral authority, it also recognized her capacity for sin. Woman represented Eve the temptress, the handmaiden of treachery who could not be trusted. To preserve her virtue, society severely limited her domain to the private or domestic sphere of the home. Spaniards rationalized their behavior, arguing that if men philandered, they did so because women led them astray. Songs served as teaching devices in preliterate cultures. For example, "Corrida de Elena" was one of the traditional narrative ballads or romances found throughout the region from the Strait of Magellan to the American Southwest during the colonial period. In this *corrida* the text plays out the traditional female-male relationship. Elena is Eve, the bad woman who dishonors her husband, and for that transgression he has the right to kill her. The tale is full of movement, violence, and dramatic contrast. Benito, the husband, disguises himself as Elena's lover, Fernando, to force her to confess. Although she pleads for mercy and admits her guilt, he must avenge his honor. The ballad's didactic function is clear when Elena says "all young matrons . . . listen and learn from my wicked deeds" just before Benito strips off her clothes and fires five bullets into her heart.[3]

In colonial culture, honor—that is, family honor—was a highly valued commodity to be preserved at all costs. This emphasis on family honor prevailed throughout Mediterranean culture, but in Latin America it often existed in an exaggerated form. Its double standard of behavior permitted unlimited sexual license for males and severely limited the behavior of women. Philandering men did not dishonor their families; rather, their behavior contributed positively to their sexual reputations. The dishonor went to the family of their female partner and the males who did not prevent it. The centrality of the family to Latin American life has not diminished, and in some areas codes of honor remain.[4]

Other forms of oral tradition also helped inscribe gender roles. A Mexican folktale entitled "Why Women Are Like Cats" establishes the basis for female inferiority by humorously playing with the creation myth from Genesis. Such stories offer valuable clues to the social historian because they often contain the intuitive truths of a culture. The tale begins with women "gabbing," wasting time in the kitchen, their domain. Tío Aurelio uses science to refute "La Cabezona's" (Miss Know-It-All) religiously based and, therefore, inferior knowledge. She claims that women are equal to men because they were created from Adam's rib, but Tío Aurelio disagrees—women were formed from the tail of a cat. In traditional folktales the cat symbolizes evil, treachery, and cunning. Woman is clearly depicted as the ultimate "Other," for she was denied her humanity.[5]

Throughout history the state has helped define the woman's role. In the colonial period it supported the patriarchal family and imposed strict gender roles that limited a woman's actions to the domestic sphere as wife and mother. Not until the Enlightenment (1700s) did definitions of the woman's role in society begin to change in Western European culture. In France the *philosophes'* emphasis on the social utility of a woman in childrearing led them to focus on her education. In the upper class, education would prepare women to manage their homes, while vocational instruction would provide lower-class women with jobs and keep them from falling into a life of prostitution.

Enlightenment ideas, more broadly, formed the intellectual basis for the Latin American independence movement in the early 1800s. Despite the fact that women participated in the wars of liberation as spies, quartermasters, and warriors, most of the new republics did not formally recognize their contributions; for example, women were not granted citizenship. The first government of the Río de la Plata, today's Argentina, created a quasi-public function for women. Although placing women in charge of an institution of public charity may seem like a small step by today's standards, Argentina was fifty years ahead of Chile and one hundred years ahead of Peru in sponsoring such legislation. Most important, the woman's issue entered politics for the first time, where it would remain until the present.

Intellectuals continued to espouse liberal ideas introduced by the Enlightenment, including individualism and popular sovereignty. By 1825 many of the new nations had abolished slavery and ended legal discrimination against Indians, mulattoes, and mestizos. However positive post-Independence society may have appeared, the gap between image and reality was wide. In reality independence affected only a minority of Latin America's inhabitants because, although the majority of the people participated in warfare, the problems at hand concerned the formation and control of governments and the dictation of commercial policy, issues that were to be resolved by planters, merchants, and other individuals who enjoyed social prestige and power. Throughout Latin America victorious elites associated progress with European and North American culture and identified the welfare of their own class with that of the nation. Their flagrant disregard for local culture and traditions, as well as for the rights and well-being of the masses, has resulted in a general condemnation of the liberalism they adopted by many noted scholars and literary figures, among them Carlos Fuentes, who writes in *The Buried Mirror*:

> The resistance of ancient traditions, both Indian and colonial, to sudden change no matter how democratically inspired that change was, could not be underestimated. Like the Crown before them, the new republics seemed remote from the everyday concerns of the workers and peasants.[6]

Although class structure opened somewhat, post-Independence society was not egalitarian. Creole elites inherited political and economic power that had been held by the Spanish upper class.

If Independence did not lead to the creation of the republican governments that intellectuals had envisioned, it did provide women with a symbolic opening that allowed them to engage in debate over their rights and desired roles in the newly created states. Having fought, in many instances, alongside their male kin in the wars, some women felt justified in demanding political rights. In 1824 in the Mexican state of Zacatecas, women petitioned for full citizenship.[7] Their struggle for equality was eclipsed by the political turmoil that arose. Political elites concluded that women would serve their nations best as wives and mothers and should leave politics to men.

Although denied political equality, the sociopolitical importance of women as mothers was a subject frequently addressed by men. Since a woman's primary responsibility was the education of her children, how women should be trained to best perform this function was debated at length. Liberals condemned religious education because it "encouraged irrationality" in women, while secular education made them "emotionally stable . . . better mothers and fit companions for . . . men."[8]

By midcentury, women were participating in the debate about their fate. Realizing that suffrage and the citizenship it conferred were unrealizable, these early women writers narrowed their focus to the right to an education and the reform of family law that regulated the domestic sphere. The literary *tertulia*, or salon, was a source of intellectual liberation for women because it permitted them to write and present their works in public. As a rule, it is within their literature that the most progressive ideas about women appeared because literary devices allowed an author to express her discontent in a subtle manner.

Within the peasant economy, women have always played an indispensable role in subsistence agriculture, which remained family centered, was limited to small acreage, and followed a strict division of labor based on gender. In field work, tasks varied regionally, but women generally were limited to sowing and sometimes harvesting. With the introduction of hacienda agriculture, peasant families many times became tied to the large landed estates that often produced a cash crop for an internal market or, more frequently, for export. The crops varied from wheat in temperate areas to sugar, bananas, and cotton in tropical zones and coffee at higher altitudes. On haciendas, peasants were allowed to plant subsistence plots and pay their rent in labor, and women and men became part of the hacienda labor force. Women performed agricultural work but also did the field cooking and washing and supplied the hacendado's family with a small army of servants.

In cities and towns, women worked as servants, sellers, and artisans before industrialization. The marketplace in particular has been a traditional workplace for Latin American women from pre-Columbian times to the present. Like domestic work, selling is considered essentially an extension of women's work.[9] Street vending and marketing are second only to domestic service as a source of female urban employment. Their popularity stems in part from the flexibility they offer to women who balance household, child care, and income-generating activities. Often the only work available to women who need to supplement the family income, such activities generate little profit, so the goal of most market women is to earn a steady income. Economic necessity dictated that cultural norms be abandoned, and for the majority of Latin American women, conflict did not develop between the private and public spheres. (According to the code of honor upon which the patriarchal family rested, women were confined to the private, or home, sphere while men functioned in the public sphere, representing the family outside the home. Of course, for poor women who had to work, such culturally scripted gender roles remained moot.)

As the nineteenth century drew to a close, much of Latin America experienced profound socioeconomic change, which had an impact on the lives of women. In the era of "order and progress," stability and economic growth ranked high on the political agenda of ruling elites. Governments reinvested profits earned from the growing export sector and established public programs that gave unprecedented numbers of women access to education. For the first time, large numbers of women entered the workplace and educational institutions.

Industrialization was accompanied by migration from rural to urban areas where women entered the developing factory work force while continuing to perform traditional female jobs. As their educational opportunities increased, women became teachers, nurses, office workers, doctors, telegraph and telephone operators, lawyers, and academics. This contact resulted in a proliferation of women's groups and organized efforts to articulate a feminist position on "the woman question."

Positivism was the most widely accepted philosophy at the turn of the century. When positivists applied their scientific outlook to "the woman question," two camps emerged. One group emphasized women's physical and mental inferiority as justification for them to remain in traditional roles. Other positivists urged women to use their moral superiority as a tool to reform society. Many women took advantage of this perceived moral superiority and dedicated themselves to philanthropic work and social reform. The best-known advocate for women's education was the Puerto Rican Eugenio María de Hostos. He believed that women were worthy of education not only because of the social importance of motherhood but also because they possessed sharp mental keenness as well as powerful intuition. He asserted that to deny a woman an education was to deny her "the integrity of her being and freedom of conscience"—in short, he argued that education was essential to her psychological development.

Modernization, which began in the late 1800s, continued at a steady rate in the early twentieth century. Some Latin American nations experienced industrialization and developed a large urban working class. In the Southern Cone region (Argentina, Chile, and Uruguay), industrialization was accompanied by a wave of European immigration that brought with it new political ideologies, most notably socialism and anarchism. Until this point Latin American feminist thought appeared monolithic, as most women based their demands for improved status on female moral superiority and the great sociopolitical significance of motherhood. As feminists became involved in a nascent leftist movement, this consensus shattered.

After 1925 the Latin American women's movement witnessed the creation of two distinct feminist agendas. Liberal or reformist feminists continued to work for women's advancement within the political system, emphasizing modification rather than subversion of existing laws and customs. According to Asunción Lavrin, they "attempted to blend traditional social values with the new social realities, to allow men, and women themselves, to accept and assimilate the changes that were becoming an intrinsic part of their changing reality."[10]

Women socialists (they rejected the label feminist) believed that emancipation could never be achieved under capitalism. Peruvian Magda Portal is probably the best-known female activist within the emerging political left of the 1920s. A founding member of the Alianza Popular Revolucionaria Americana (APRA), a party that advocated the restructuring of Peruvian society to allow for the integration of the Indian majority, Portal did not initially view sexism as one of the social ills that her party had to rectify. In fact she often condemned the aims of Peruvian feminists: "The aprista woman . . . does not want to conquer her rights through an open fight against men, as *feministas* do, but to collaborate with him as her companion."[11]

Although the majority of women socialists agreed with Portal's idea that women and men must work together to achieve social justice, not all of them condemned the agenda of liberal feminists. Alicia Moreau de Justo, wife of the founder of the Argentine Socialist Party, did not find feminism to be incompatible with socialism. Although she disapproved of the individualistic stance of liberal feminists, she supported their struggle for civil and political rights. She also clearly understood that women's suffrage did not signify social change.

The alienation that women experienced served as the impetus for the articulation of a socialist feminist theory that sought to examine the connection between capitalism and patriarchy. Through this period, literature continued to serve as a principal vehicle for the expression of feminist ideas. Literary historians have argued, for example, that Alfonsina Storni represents the first generation of professional women to be affected by the emerging feminist movement of the 1920s.[12] Storni, an Argentine poet and journalist, has attracted the attention of scholars at least in part because of her dramatic and unconventional life. She came from an immigrant and lower-middle-class background, was an unwed mother, and eventually committed suicide. As a writer in the 1920s she, like many others of her generation, attempted to find an alternative feminine literary tradition. Although her poetry is well known, her activities as a journalist, teacher, and dramatist are only now beginning to be studied. Much of Storni's work contains a condemnation, be it implicit or explicit, of the hypocrisy of patriarchal society. Her poem "Tu me quieres blanca" ("You want me pure") is perhaps one of the strongest poetic indictments against the macho attitude of the Spanish American male who, being a libertine, wants the object of his affection to be "pure." She expresses similar disdain for the subordination of women in "Hombre pequenito" ("Little man") in which she writes:

> Little man, little man
> set free your canary that wants to fly
> I am the canary, little man,
> let me go free. . . .[13]

As much of Latin America underwent rapid urbanization in the second half of the twentieth century, the pace of industrialization did not keep up, which created a large economically marginalized population. There are three schools of thought concerning the effects of modernization and industrialization upon women and their work.[14] The integrationalist approach believes that modernization is essential to economic development and that industrialization involves women in public life by integrating them into the labor force. A woman's financial independence increases with integration, and, through her incorporation into the industrial structure on an equal basis with men, she can achieve true emancipation. The marginalist school disagrees with the proposition that industrialization has a positive effect on a woman; rather, it marginalizes her. Industrialization separates the public and private spheres and creates the "double shift" day because women's responsibilities remain the same in the home. The third school advances the exploitative theory and sees industrialization as exploiting poor women. Through gender-categorizing work, industrialization reinforces women's subordination within the labor force and family.

The Cuban Revolution introduced a Marxist definition of women into Latin America. Established in 1960, the National Federation of Cuban Women (FMC) advocated the full and equal incorporation of women into national life. In its first decade the FMC made substantial improvements in women's education and incorporation into the work force and counted about 70 percent of Cuban women as members. Moreover, it became an institution that women in other countries sought to emulate as it took a leadership role in the international woman's movement.

The 1972 Managua earthquake, the 1973 ousting of Salvador Allende, and the 1975 United Nations-sponsored Conference on Women in Mexico City made the seventies an important decade in the history of Latin American women. It is generally accepted that the December 1972 earthquake marked the beginning of the end of the Somoza dictatorship in Nicaragua. While Somoza embezzled international aid and his National Guard looted, the earthquake forced ordinary Nicaraguans to assume the burden of restructuring their lives. As the Frente Sandinista de Liberación Nacional (Sandinista National Liberation Front—FSLN) organized to topple Somoza, Nicaraguan women voiced their own protests. The total destruction of the capital, which had followed on the heels of a two-year drought, created massive unemployment and food shortages. Working-class women in Managua, many of whom were the sole providers for their families, began meeting in Mothers' Clubs to discuss housing, health care, food distribution, and other similar problems. Some groups, such as the Asociación de Mujeres Ante la Problemática Nacional (Association of Nicaraguan Women Confronting the National Problem—AMPRONAC), eventually associated themselves with the FSLN. Other women turned to the Roman Catholic Church for solace and honed their organizational and political skills in Christian base communities (CEB).

A year later, in 1973, the socialist experiment of Salvador Allende ended in Chile's bloodiest coup and was followed by the repressive dictatorship of Augusto Pinochet. Irma Muller was transformed from an ordinary housewife into a political activist when the government "disappeared" her child. Muller, who learned her first political lessons in a neighborhood *arpillera* workshop, eventually became the leader of the Association of Relatives of Detained-Missing Persons. The group demanded information on the whereabouts of the approximately ten thousand persons reported missing between 1973 and 1986. The Nicaraguan and Chilean cases demonstrate that national political events contain a gender dimension; they forced the ordinary woman to become political. The women did not participate, however, in traditional political parties but in grass-roots movements that brought people together to protest certain specific conditions. Grass-roots movements neither have to institutionalize themselves nor achieve their stated goal to be successful. The organizational effort itself is important, especially in the case of women.

Between June 19 and July 2, 1975, the World Conference of the International Women's Year met in Mexico City. It consisted of two main meetings: the United Nations Conference on Women, which was attended by delegates from 133 countries; and the tribune, where representatives of nongovernmental agencies and interested individuals came together. The conference drafted a World Plan of Action for the UN Decade for Women, 1976–1985, with three central themes: equality, development, and peace. The UN conference demonstrated that the differences between feminists were as wide as they were deep and produced a thorough exchange of ideas. In Latin America the debates resulted in a time of introspection followed by a redefinition of feminism.[15]

The period since the 1970s can be considered one of consolidation and reorientation of Latin American feminist thought. The time had come in which neither liberal nor socialist feminism alone could provide a solution to "the woman question." Gender issues were often dismissed as irrelevant even in countries where socialism was achieved. Rather than discard the fundamental ideas of the reformist and socialist traditions, the feminists of the 1970s merged the two and created a doctrine that was both more radical and more flexible than either of the parent versions. Contemporary feminist thought, then, is centered around a number of themes, all of which are open to interpretation. For example, contemporary feminists differ from their socialist predecessors in that they believe that the subversion of the patriarchy must occur before a truly classless society can be established. Another pivotal idea is that "the personal is political." This concept gained popularity among Latin Americans as a result of the influence of the international women's movement. Many feminists interpreted this theme to mean that oppressive political systems are dependent on the traditional family. As Lourdes Azripze explained in the Mexican feminist magazine *Fem*:

> The authoritarianism of the father [*padre-macho*] at the heart of the family in hispanic families responds to a political necessity. Children learn to tolerate a paternal despot in the family, who obliges them to fear and to obey. Thus, they are converted into citizens who will tolerate the same type of despotism in a dictator or political leader.[16]

The writings of Azripze and Rosario Castellanos, probably Latin America's most famous contemporary feminist writer, return to the two central themes of the region's culture that comprise the heart of "the woman question": family and marianismo. Castellanos stands out as a pioneer in the world of feminist literature. Her portrayal of women reveals the extent to which they have been both marginalized and isolated, even in the late twentieth century. In an effort to demystify marianismo, she writes:

> In Mexico, when we utter the word *woman*, we refer to a creature who is dependent upon male authority: be it her father's, her brother's, her husband's or her priest's. . . . The Mexican woman does not consider herself nor do others consider her to be a woman who has reached fulfillment if she has not produced children, if the halo of maternity does not shine above her.[17]

The conditions that led Castellanos to write "Self-Sacrifice Is a Mad Virtue" in 1971 are alive and thriving in Latin America today. The woman who sacrifices all for her children can been seen nightly in the telenovelas churned out in the mass-media centers of Mexico, Venezuela, Brazil, and Argentina and available here on the Univision channel. But Castellanos partially blames women for the conditions in which they live. By practicing "the code of self-sacrifice" demanded by the marianismo model of femininity they perpetuate their inferior status. Unfortunately, life as melodrama is not confined to books or the television in Latin America.

## Notes

1. Quoted in Glen Dealy, *Latin America: The Spirit and Ethos* (Boulder, CO: Westview Press, 1992), 14. See also Richard Browning, "Gender and Family in Latin America," unpublished manuscript.

2. Glen Dealy, *The Public Man: An Interpretation of Latin American and Other Catholic Countries*, 1989.

3. "Corrida de Elena," in John Donald Robb, ed., *Hispanic Folk Songs of New Mexico* (Albuquerque: University of New Mexico Press, 1954), 44–47 (quote from p. 47).

4. Alan Riding, *Distant Neighbors: A Portrait of the Mexicans* (New York: Vintage Press, 1989). For a case-study approach to the various expressions of the Latin American family today, see Man Singh Das and Clinton J. Jesser, eds., *The Family in Latin America* (New Delhi: Vikas Publishing House, 1980).

5. "Why Women Are Like Cats," in Riley Aiken, *Mexican Folktales from the Borderland* (Dallas: Southern Methodist University Press, 1980), 111–13. For a general discussion of the value of folklore and children's games to women's studies see Inez Cardozo-Freeman, "Games Mexican Girls Play," in *Women and Folklore Images and Genres,* ed. Claire R. Farrer (Prospect Heights, IL: Waveland Press, 1986), 12–23.

6. Carlos Fuentes, *The Buried Mirror: Reflections on Spain and the New World* (New York: Houghton Mifflin, 1992), 262. Lisa Zimmerman, a program coordinator with the Nicaragua Network Education Fund, discussed this summary of the region's feminism in a seminar paper, "Latin American Feminist Thought: A Historical Perspective," while a graduate student at Tulane University.

7. Francesca Miller, *Latin American Women and the Search for Social Justice* (Hanover: University of New England Press, 1991), 32.

8. Marifran Carlson, *Feminismo: The Woman's Movement in Argentina from Its Beginnings to Eva Perón* (Chicago: Academy Chicago Publishers, 1988), 13.

9. Ximena Bunster and Elsa M. Chaney, *Sellers and Servants: Working Women in Lima, Peru* (Boston: Bergin and Garvey, 1989), 107. Heather Thiessen explored this synthesis in a seminar paper, "Between Myth and Reality: The Historical Omnipresence of Latin American Women's Labour," while a graduate student at Tulane University.

10. Asunción Lavrin, "The Ideology of Feminism in the Southern Cone, 1910–1940," working paper, The Wilson Center, Washington, DC, 1986, 2.

11. Miller, *Latin American Women*, 101.

12. Gwen Kirkpatrick, "The Journalism of Alfonsina Storni: A New Approach to Women's History in Argentina," in *Women, Culture, and Politics: Seminar on Feminism and Culture in Latin America* (Berkeley: University of California Press, 1990); and Maria A. Salgodo, "Alfonsina Storni," in *Spanish American Women Writers: A Bio-Bibliographical Source Book*, ed. Diane Marting (New York: Glenwood Press, 1990), 504.

13. Alfonsina Storni, "Hombre pequenito," in *Voces de Hispanoaméricas*, ed. Raquel Chang-Rodriques and Malva E. Filer (Boston: Heinle and Heinle, 1988), 353.

14. See Susan Tiano's "Women and Industrial Development in Latin America," *Latin American Research Review* 21, no. 3 (1986): 157–70.

15. Miller, *Latin American Women*, 197–202.

16. Lourdes Azripze, "Familia, Desarrollo, y Autoritarianismo," *Fem* 7 (April–June 1978), reprinted in *Fem: 10 años del periodismo feminista* (México: Planeta, 1988), 87.

17. Maureen Ahern, ed. and trans., *A Rosario Castellanos Reader* (Austin: University of Texas Press, 1988), 49.

# I Culture and the Status of Women

The selections in Part I sample perceptions of Latin American women in modern times. What soon becomes clear is that scholars, novelists, essayists, and musicians frame their questions in terms of the prevailing theories of their times and that even contemporaries disagree. Evelyn Stevens and Josefina Zoraida Vásquez present different interpretations of the evolution of Latin American women. In "Marianismo: The Other Face of Machismo" (Selection 1) Stevens interprets gender roles as two sides of a culturally prescribed and unchanging symbiotic relationship, while an excerpt from Zoraida Vásquez's "Women's Liberation in Latin America: Toward a History of the Present" (Selection 2) searches the past to create a history for what she sees as a significant women's movement. When taken together these articles demonstrate two basic approaches to women's studies in the 1970s and early 1980s. Stevens, in good social-science fashion, searches the cultural bedrock to locate a universal or generalizing principle to explain the female condition in Latin America. As a Mexican, Zoraida Vásquez dismisses the centrality of marianismo as a force shaping the history of the region's women, and, indeed, the term seems foreign to Latin American women who have come in contact with it in the academic marketplace. To them the Marianist tradition is part of their religious heritage, and they do not view their historical evolution as so remarkably different from that of other women, especially those in France, Italy, or other European nations with a Catholic heritage.

Teresa González de Fanning and Mercedes Cabello de Carbonera were two important nineteenth-century Peruvian women's rights activists whose writings were nearly forgotten until women began recovering their own literary heritage. Both believed that the nineteenth century was the century of progress and that the emancipation of women eventually would be achieved. They saw Latin American culture as an obstacle to change, but not an insurmountable one. These two essays are the only examples of their writing available in English. Contemporary editions of González de Fanning's output do not exist even in Spanish, although she was Peru's most powerful advocate of a woman's right to an education (see

Selection 4). Unlike many of her contemporaries she concerned herself with primary and vocational schooling for poor women as well as university training for those of the elite and middle class. Cabello de Carbonera was more radical and controversial than her friend González de Fanning; she was also more famous, and, although she was not a "feminist" per se—the term was not coined until the twentieth century—she vigorously defended women's equality. In her essay "Concerning Women's Intelligence and Beauty" (Selection 3), she takes a tongue-in-cheek look at men looking at women.

The Mexican Revolution (1910–1917) occurred exactly one hundred years after the wars of independence and is one of the greatest political upheavals in modern Latin American history. Yet despite its commitment to empowering workers, peasants, and indigenous peoples, revolutionary ideology could not overcome the deeply ingrained cultural prejudices toward women and skirted the issue. In Selection 5, Lillian Estelle Fisher, one of the first women scholars to study Latin America, documents how tradition, culture, and history shaped the Mexican Revolution's approach to women, giving them substantial legal gains but leaving them inferior to men.

The final two essays in Part I examine how literature and music created cultural images of women. In "Jorge Amado: Champion of Women's Sexual Freedom" (Selection 6), Daphne Patai examines the career of Jorge Amado, whose depictions of women have made him one of Brazil's most popular authors. Donald Castro, in "Women in the World of the Tango" (Selection 7), examines tango lyrics for an understanding of how gender roles have changed in modern Argentine society.

# 1  Evelyn P. Stevens ◆ Marianismo:
# The Other Face of Machismo

*Marianismo has been the organizing tenet of Latin American women's studies in this country since the appearance of Evelyn Stevens's essay, which examines gender (learned), not sex (biological), roles in terms of machismo and marianismo. In the patriarchal Catholic culture—where God was the father and only men could become priests—the Virgin Mary stood as the most prominent image of what an ideal woman should be. The Virgin Mary was so important to gender education that in Latin America the church often supported distinct images of her to accommodate racial diversity. For example, in Mexico the Virgen de los Remedios was revered by the Europeans, the Virgen de Guadalupe by the mestizo and Indian populations. How well a woman lived up to the example of feminine virtue embodied by the Virgin Mary determined her reputation. While the cult of the Virgin influenced attitudes about women's sexuality, the image of the* mater dolorosa—*the mother Mary grieving for her son— likewise shaped women's attitudes toward their lives. The Virgin of the Seven Sorrows idealized women's sadness and encouraged them to accept sorrow in their lives. If the chief characteristics of machismo, the cult of virility, are exaggerated aggressiveness and intransigence in male- to-male interpersonal relationships and arrogance and sexual aggression in male-to-female relationships, then marianismo is the cult of feminine spiritual superiority, which teaches that women are morally superior to and spiritually stronger than men.*

One of the functional imperatives of human society is a division of labor according to a set of criteria generally accepted by most members of the group. That these criteria correspond to no "natural law" is obvious from the wide variations in the ways in which different cultures parcel out the jobs to be done. The only requirement appears to be that the criteria be regarded as right or good or inevitable by most of the people who act according to their dictates. It does not seem to matter whether a particular system is based on tradition, magic, or "logic" as long as the accompanying rationalization helps to keep confusion and tension at a minimum level.

Some of the most obvious and widely used criteria for deciding who shall do what are age, sex, and class. But these categories may be

From "Marianismo: The Other Face of Machismo in Latin America" in *Female and Male in Latin America: Essays*, ed. Ann Pescatello (Pittsburgh: University of Pittsburgh Press, 1973), 90–101. Reprinted by permission of the University of Pittsburgh Press.

manipulated in different ways by societies in different parts of the world. "Children should be seen and not heard" is a semisacred principle which prevails over a large area of the earth, only to be contradicted by diaper dictatorships in other areas. In some cultures, only the man may carve the meat at mealtime, while in others this task is regarded as "women's work."

In every society we find a pattern of expectations based on real or imagined attributes of the individuals or groups who perform certain tasks. With time, these attributes attain a validity which makes it possible to use them as criteria for value judgments quite unrelated to functional necessity. Uncritical acceptance of such stereotypes can contribute to social or political consequences of great magnitude. In Latin America, the twin phenomena of machismo and marianismo offer us an illustration of this observation. Machismo, a term familiar to area specialists, has passed into the vocabulary of the general public, where it has suffered the same kind of semantic deformation as [Max] Weber's charisma.[1]

In the interest of clarity in the following discussion, the term machismo will be used to designate a way of orientation which can be most succinctly described as the cult of virility. The chief characteristics of this cult are exaggerated aggressiveness and intransigence in male-to-male interpersonal relationships and arrogance and sexual aggression in male-to-female relationships.[2]

It has only been in the quite recent past that any attention has been focused on the other face of the problem. Women generally have maintained a discreet reserve with respect to the subject of marianismo, possibly because a very large segment of that group fears that publicity would endanger their prerogatives. A short time ago, however, a handful of male writers began to focus on this heretofore neglected pattern of attitudes and behavior. In this way, the term *"hembrismo"* ("female-ism") has been introduced by one observer, while *"feminismo"* has been used by another.[3]

Marianismo is just as prevalent as machismo but it is less understood by Latin Americans themselves and almost unknown to foreigners. It is the cult of feminine spiritual superiority, which teaches that women are semidivine, morally superior to and spiritually stronger than men. It is this pattern of attitudes and behavior that will be the principal focus of attention in the present paper, but it will often be necessary to refer to the dynamic interplay between the two phenomena.

**Old World Antecedents**

Both marianismo and machismo are New World phenomena with ancient roots in Old World cultures. Many of the contributing elements can be found even today in Italy and Spain, but the fully developed syndrome occurs only in Latin America.[4]

Concepts of honor and shame associated with notions of manliness can be found in many of the cultures of southern Europe, the Middle East, and North Africa, but a Spanish historian argues that the exaggerated characteristics which we have come to associate with machismo are a degeneration of sixteenth- and seventeenth-century upper-class attitudes toward the concepts. "In the plebeian sector of society," says this author [Julio Caro Baroja], "the equivalent of the gentleman of easily affected honour is the professional bravo, the bullying braggart, the dandified tough."[5] Although the behavior pattern gradually became less important in Spanish culture, it seems to have made its way to America via the soldiers and adventurers who participated in the conquest. The time fit is persuasive. It may even be surmised that the conquest drained Spain of these individuals and provided them with a more propitious atmosphere in America, in which they flourished and assumed the importance which they have today. Samuel Ramos argues that in Mexico typical macho behavior is a low-class phenomenon, but he is drowned out by a chorus of other observers who can see ramifications in every social class and in every country of Latin America.[6]

Although all mestizo social classes are permeated with machismo and marianismo characteristics, the same statement does not hold true with respect to other ethnic groupings. Indigenous communities, while patriarchal in structure and value orientations, do not seem to share the machismo-marianismo attitudes as long as they retain their cultural "purity."

Marianismo is not a religious practice, although the word "Marianism" is sometimes used to describe a movement within the Roman Catholic church which has as its object the special veneration of the figure of the Virgin Mary. That cult, as it is practiced throughout the world, is rooted in very ancient religious observances that have evolved within the church itself, at times with the enthusiastic endorsement of ecclesiastical authorities and at other times with at least the tolerance of those authorities.

Marianism, or Mariology, as most theologians prefer to call the religious movement, has provided a central figure and a convenient set of assumptions around which the practitioners of marianismo have erected a secular edifice of beliefs and practices related to the position of women in society. It is that edifice, rather than the religious phenomenon, which is the object of this study.

The roots of marianismo are both deep and widespread, springing apparently from primitive awe at woman's ability to produce a live human creature from inside her own body. This is the aspect of femininity which attracted the attention of the early artists who fashioned the Gravettian "Venuses" of the upper Paleolithic era. In those small crude sculptures, the figures have enormous breasts and protruding bellies, as though they were pregnant. To the early men and women who posed the ontological question in its simplest terms—"Where did I come from?"—the answer must also have seemed simple, and, on the basis of circumstantial evidence, woman was celebrated as being the sole source of life.

Archaeological research points to southern Russia, to the region around the Caspian Sea, as the source of inspiration for the cult of the mother goddess as we know it in the Western world, but not long afterward traces began to appear in the Fertile Crescent and the Indus Valley, as well as in Crete and the area around the Aegean Sea. During these early stages the female figure appeared alone, unaccompanied by any male figure, and for this reason she is sometimes described as the "unmarried mother."[7]

All around the eastern and northern rim of the Mediterranean, the goddess figure multiplied and appeared in various aspects. In Mesopotamia she took on many names and faces: Ninhursaga, Mah, Ninmah, Innana, Ishtar, Astarte, Nintu, Aruru.[8]

At a somewhat later period, we begin to see indications of a growing consciousness of male individuality; the goddess, while still dominant, is depicted in the company of a young male figure, who is somewhat ambiguously seen as either the son of the goddess or as her consort, more likely as both at the same time. The notion that he, too, might actually be performing an indispensable function in the creation of life seems to have dawned rather slowly on mankind.

As far back as the Mesopotamian culture, we see the young god depicted as suffering and dying, in the regular sequence of changing seasons of the year, and being taken into the underworld. The goddess then appears as the grieving and searching mother. This figure of the *mater dolorosa* is found over a wide geographical area and a long time span, which includes the New Testament account of the death and resurrection of Jesus Christ. In this conscious or unconscious allegory of the seasons, we can see the realization of the importance of man in the creation of new life: while he is gone the earth is barren; the female cannot give birth without his help.

The island of Crete is generally credited with being the cradle of the mother goddess cult in the form in which it spread throughout Italy and southwestern Europe, particularly in Spain. Around the third millennium B.C. statuettes appeared in Crete depicting an earth mother, known variously as Gaea, Rhea, or Cybele. Some of the epithets applied to this goddess were Mountain Mother, Mistress of the Trees, and Lady of the Wild

Beasts. In this latter guise she is familiar to the world as the delicately fashioned "snake goddess" from the Middle Minoan III period, which has been exhibited by the Candia Museum and pictured in many books on art history.

Soon after the earliest Neolithic settlers arrived in Spain, they contributed to the propagation of the cult by producing a large number of female figurines first, apparently, in the area around El Garcel but rapidly diffusing out from that center.

In early Christian worship there was no place for the figure of a woman. The new sect drew heavily on Hebrew sources for its inspiration, since the Jews had long before abolished their primitive pantheon, and in so doing they found it both necessary and politic to expunge all goddesses from their theological structure. The result was a conceptually neat and ideologically powerful monotheism, heralding a patriarchal and nationalistic divine leader.

Earlier, however, the Semitic cultures had provided a rich array of female divinities and personifications, among them the goddess Asherah-Astarte-Anath, the Shekinah (the visible and audible manifestation of God's presence on earth which in late Midrash literature appears as a mediatrix between God and man), and the Matronit—the goddess of the Kabbala, whose figure in many ways resembles that of Mary.[9] In the process of "purifying" their theology, that is, constructing a logically coherent religious system, the Jews successfully argued that the goddess figures were inventions of their enemies, introduced to sow confusion and divide the faithful. By jettisoning their superfluous gods and goddesses, the Jewish prophets were able to weld an efficient instrument for the unification of their tribes.

In spite of this hiatus, the history of men's attempts to expunge the female figure from their pantheon has met with only partial success. In almost every culture of the Mediterranean littoral, woman has returned from doctrinal exile stronger, more appealing, and more influential than before. Even where the doors of Scripture have remained closed to her, who can deny the triumph of the Jewish mother?

The sister disciplines of archaeology and comparative mythology speculate that Christian hagiology manifests a remarkable similarity, at a number of crucial points, to pre-Christian beliefs diffused over the geographic area described above. During the early Christian era, the female figure had no place in religious rites, but this situation was changed by the pronouncement of the Council of Ephesus in A.D. 431. As Theotokos, Mother of God, Mary was integrated into Christian dogma, and the two poles of creative energy, the masculine and feminine, emerged into conscious recognition and received their most sublime expression.[10] After the Council of Ephesus, however, Mariology grew so rapidly that popular adoration of the Mother has threatened at times to eclipse that of the Father and the Son, thus degenerating into what some religious commentators have called Mariolatry. A number of Catholic writers have deplored this "tendency to exalt the cult of the Virgin Mary in a way which exceeds the teaching and the spirit of the Church."[11] In recent times, three popes have cautioned the faithful against Marian excesses.[12]

### New World Development

It is an easy task to trace the migration of the Marian cult to the New World. Church history tells us that within ten years after the conquest of Mexico, an illiterate Indian neophyte who had been baptized with the name of Juan Diego saw an apparition of the "Most Holy Mother of God" on a mound called Tepeyacac, north of Mexico City. The place of the apparition is significant, because Indian tradition had long held it sacred to the worship of a goddess whom they called Tonantzin ("Our Mother"). Archaeologists have identified Tonantzin with the pre-Columbian female Aztec deity known as Coatlicue or Cihuacoatl (serpent woman, mother of the gods, weeping woman).[13]

By the middle of the seventeenth century, tradition recognized Juan Diego's vision as an authentic apparition of the Virgin Mary—the first in the New World—and she was given the name of Our Lady of Guadalupe, in honor of a figure venerated in southwestern Spain.[14] In 1756 the Lady of Guadalupe was declared patroness of New Spain (Mexico) by Pope Benedict XIV.

The religious symbol, accepted by the conquerors and venerated by the native population, became a rallying point for nascent nationalistic sentiments, so that when the war for independence broke out in 1810 it was fitting that Mexico's first mestizo hero, Father Hidalgo [Miguel Hidalgo y Costilla], should lead the rebels with the famous Grito de Dolores: "Viva Nuestra Señora de Guadalupe, muera el mal gobierno, mueran los gachupines!" ("Long live our Lady of Guadalupe, down with bad government, down with the spurred ones [Spaniards resident in Mexico]!").[15] One hundred years later, Pope Pius X declared the Lady to be patroness of all Latin America.

Just how the excessive veneration of women became a distinguishing feature of Latin American secular society is difficult to determine. Two points are clear, however: this veneration parallels that which is rendered to the religious figure of the Virgin Mary, and the secular aspect is different both qualitatively and quantitatively from the attitude toward women which prevails in those very European nations where the religious cult is most prevalent.

Latin American mestizo cultures—from the Río Grande to the Tierra del Fuego—exhibit a well-defined pattern of beliefs and behavior centered on popular acceptance of a stereotype of the ideal woman. This stereotype, like its macho counterpart, is ubiquitous in every social class. There is near universal agreement on what a "real woman" is like and how she should act. Among the characteristics of this ideal are semidivinity, moral superiority, and spiritual strength. This spiritual strength engenders abnegation, that is, an infinite capacity for humility and sacrifice. No self-denial is too great for the Latin American woman, no limit can be divined to her vast store of patience with the men of her world.[16] Although she may be sharp with her daughters—and even cruel to her daughters-in-law—she is and must be complaisant toward her own mother and her mother-in-law for they, too, are reincarnations of the great mother. She is also submissive to the demands of the men: husbands, sons, fathers, brothers.[17]

Beneath the submissiveness, however, lies the strength of her conviction—shared by the entire society—that men must be humored, for, after all, everyone knows that they are *como niños* (like little boys) whose intemperance, foolishness, and obstinacy must be forgiven because "they can't help the way they are." These attitudes are expressed with admirable clarity by the editor of a fashionable women's magazine in Chile. When asked, "Is there any Chilean woman whom you particularly admire?" she answered, "Sincerely, I would mention a humble woman from the slums who did our laundry. She had ten children, and her husband spent his time drunk and out of work. She took in washing and ironing, and gave her children a good start in life. She is the typical Chilean woman of a [certain] sector of our society. She struggles valiantly until the end."[18]

But to the unalterable imperfection of men is attributable another characteristic of Latin American women: their sadness. They know that male sinfulness dooms the entire sex to a prolonged stay in purgatory after death, and even the most diligent prayerfulness of loving female relatives can succeed in sparing them only a few millennia of torture.

The sadness is evidenced in another highly visible characteristic of women. Custom dictates that upon the death of a member of her family, a woman shall adopt a distinctive mourning habit. The periods of mourning and the types of habit are rigidly prescribed. The death of a parent or husband requires lifetime full mourning: inner and outer clothing of solid black, unrelieved by even a white handkerchief. Deaths of brothers, sisters, aunts, and uncles require full mourning for three years, and those of more distant relatives require periods varying from three months to a year. After each period of full mourning ensues a prescribed period of "half-mourning" during which the grieving woman may at first wear touches of white with her black clothes, graduating with the passage of time to gray and lavender dresses.

Mourning is not simply a matter of dress. The affected person must also "show respect" for the deceased by refraining from any outward manifestation of happiness or joviality and to deny herself the company of others who may legitimately indulge in levity. This means abstention from attending parties, going to the cinema, or even watching television. Purists insist that cultural events such as concerts and lectures also fall under the ban.

Of course, these rules are supposed also to apply to men, but as "everybody knows" that they do not possess the spiritual stamina to endure such rigors, they usually render only token compliance with custom, often reduced to the wearing of a black armband for a short period. Although during mourning periods their women-ruled households are gloomy places, their escape to more joyful surroundings is condoned and often encouraged. Mistresses and other female companions "by the left" are not required to mourn.[19]

By the age of thirty-five, there are few women who have escaped the experience of at least a short period of mourning, and by forty-five, a large majority of women are destined to wear black for the rest of their lives. It is thus in the woman of middle age that we finally see all of the characteristics of full-blown marianismo coming into majestic flower. The author is familiar with the rather extreme case of a reputedly saintly Puerto Rican woman who had been widowed in her early twenties and who boasted that she had not attended the cinema since then, had never seen a television program, and had refused to pass the house in which her husband had died. Such exemplary devotion made the woman an object of general admiration, an example held up to the younger generation of more frivolous females.

As a result of this usage, the image of the Latin American woman is almost indistinguishable from the classic religious figure of the *mater dolorosa*, the tear-drenched mother who mourns for her lost son. The precursor of that figure can be found in the myths of many pre-Christian Mediterranean cultures: the earth goddess who laments the seasonal disappearance of her son and who sorrowfully searches for him until the return of spring restores him to her.[20]

Does this mean that all Latin American women conform to the stereotype prescribed by marianismo? Obviously not; as in most human societies, individual behavior often deviates widely from the ideal. But the image of the black-clad mantilla-draped figure, kneeling before the altar, rosary in hand, praying for the souls of her sinful menfolk, dominates the television and cinema screens, the radio programs, and the popular literature, as well as the oral tradition of the whole culture area. This is Latin America's chief export product, according to one native wit.[21]

The same culture provides an alternate model in the image of the "bad woman" who flaunts custom and persists in enjoying herself. Interestingly enough, this kind of individual is thought not to be a "real woman." By publicly deviating from the prescribed norm, she has divested herself of precisely those attributes considered most characteristically feminine and in the process has become somewhat masculine.

This brings us to the question of sexual behavior and here, too, as might be expected, practice frequently deviates from prescription. The ideal dictates not only premarital chastity for all women, but postnuptial frigidity. "Good" women do not enjoy coitus; they endure it when the duties of matrimony require it. A rich lexicon of circumlocutions is available to "real" women who find it necessary to refer to sexual intercourse in speaking with their priest, their physician, or other trusted confidant. "Le hice el servicio," they may say ("I did him [my husband] the service").[22]

The norm of premarital chastity is confined principally to the urban and provincial middle class, as consensual unions predominate among peasants and urban slum dwellers. Nubility and sexual activity are frequently almost simultaneous events, although the latter occasionally precedes the former.[23]

Even in middle- and upper-class society, norms of sexual behavior are often disregarded in practice. Premarital chastity is still highly prized, and many Latin American men take an unconscionable interest in the integrity of their fiancées' hymens. But the popular refrain, *el que hizo la ley hizo la trampa* [he who writes the law includes an escape clause], is particularly applicable in this context. A Peruvian woman writes with convincing authority that a large number of socially prominent young women in that country engage in coitus and then have surgical repair of the hymen performed in private hospitals—a practice that goes back at least to fifteenth-century Spain, when the operation was performed by midwives who often acted in the dual capacity of procuresses and mistresses of houses of assignation (see, for example, the *Tragicomedia de Calixto y Melibea*, the literary classic known popularly as *La Celestina*).[24]

An undetermined number of upper-middle and upper-class young women practice other varieties of sexual activity, calculated to keep the hymen intact. But a girl will usually engage in these variations only with her fiancé, and then largely as a stratagem for maintaining his interest in her until they are married. As long as he feels reasonably certain that his fiancée has not previously engaged in this kind of behavior with another man, a Latin American male may encourage or even insist on her "obliging" him in this way. But he must reassure himself that she is not enjoying it. A Peruvian journalist reveals the male insistence on the fiction of the frigidity of "good" women in such reported remarks as: "So-and-so is a bad woman; once she even made love with her husband in the bathtub," and "American women [*gringas*] are all prostitutes; I know one who *even takes the initiative*" (italics in original).[25]

At first glance, it may seem that these norms are imposed on women by tyrannical men—"male chauvinists," as contemporary English-speaking feminists would call them. But this assumption requires careful scrutiny, especially when it is remembered that during the preschool years the socialization of boys takes place almost entirely through the medium of women: mother, sisters, widowed or spinster aunts who live under one roof as part of the extended family, and female servants. From the women in the family a boy absorbs the attitudinal norms appropriate for his social class; and from the servants, when he reaches adolescence—or often even before—he picks up the principal store of behavioral expertise which will suffice him in adult life. It is common practice for a prudent middle-class mestizo mother of a pubescent boy to hire a young female servant for general housework "and other duties," the latter expression being a euphemism for initiating the boy into adult heterosexual experience. "On such creatures," comments the writer previously cited, "a man lavishes his store of honorable semen and his Christian contempt."[26]

At this juncture it may be useful to ask ourselves a question suggested by the apparent contradiction posed by the foregoing material. On the one hand, our Latin American informants paint us a picture of the ideal woman which would inspire pity in the most sanguine observer. Woman's lot seems to be compounded of sexual frustration, intellectual stagnation, and political futility in a "repressive and *machista* society."[27] On the other hand, it is quite apparent that many women contribute to the perpetuation of the myths which sustain the patterns described. Why would they work against their own interests—if, indeed, they do? Might it not be possible that while employing a distinctive repertory of attitudes, they are as "liberated" as most of them really wish to be?

## Alternative Models

If we picture the options available to women, we can see that they cover a wide range including the ideal prescribed by myth and religion as well

as an earthy and hedonistic life-style, and even occasionally a third variant characterized by an achievement-oriented puritan ethic. Some women
choose to pattern their behavior after the mythical and religious ideal
symbolized by the figure of the Virgin Mary. Others deviate from this
ideal to a greater or lesser degree in order to obtain the satisfaction of
their individual desires or aspirations. The ideal itself is a security blan-
ket which covers all women, giving them a strong sense of identity and
historical continuity.

As culture-bound foreigners, we are not qualified to define the interests of Latin American women. We cannot decide what is good for them
or prescribe how they might achieve that good. If we were to ask whether,
on the whole, Latin American women are happier and better "adjusted"
(adjusted to what?) than, say, North American women, we would be forced
to admit that the measurable data on which to base an answer are not
available and probably never will be. It would appear then that the only
meaningful question is whether the restrictions on individual action are
so ironclad as to preclude any possibility of free choice.

Undeniably, the pattern of attitudes and behavior which we have described puts a distinctive stamp on Latin American society; certainly there
are enormous pressures on individual women to conform to the prescriptions. Sometimes the results are tragic, both for the individual and for the
society, which is deprived of the full benefit of the individual's potential
contribution. A notable example of this kind of tragedy is provided by the
life and death of Sor Juana Inés de la Cruz of Mexico, whose genius was
denied and finally crushed by her ecclesiastical superiors.

But what of Manuela, the mistress of Simón Bolívar? Sublimely un-
concerned with the stereotype of saintliness, she made her own decisions.
The collective judgment of Latin American society accords her a measure of esteem not often associated with women who conform to the
marianismo ideal.

The question of personal identity is much less troublesome to Latin
American women than to their North American sisters. The Latin American always knows who she is; even after marriage she retains her individuality and usually keeps her family name, tacking on her husband's
name and passing both names on to her children. The fiction of unassail-
able purity conferred by the myth on saint and sinner alike makes divorce
on any grounds a rather unlikely possibility, which means that married
women are not often faced with the necessity of "making a new life" for
themselves during middle age. When her husband indulges in infidelity,
as the machismo norm expects and requires him to do, the prejudice
in favor of the wife's saintliness guarantees her the support of the
community.

In developing societies plagued by massive unemployment and widespread underemployment, economists might question the value of throwing larger numbers of women into the already overcrowded labor market. It is hard to assess the extent to which marianismo contributes to the present low participation of women in economically productive endeavors.[28] To assume that all or nearly all women would work outside the home if they were given the opportunity to do so is an example of the kind of thinking that sometimes vitiates the conclusions of militant feminists. My inquiries among a very small sample of women from several Latin American countries indicate that when a woman acquires expertise of a kind that is socially useful, she is quite likely to find a remunerative post in conditions far more favorable than her counterpart in, say, the United States or Western Europe. Expertise in Latin America is at such a premium that she will find little competition for a suitable post.

A Latin American mother is seldom faced with the dilemma, so publicized in the United States, of having to choose between her children or her paid job. When women work outside of their home, marianismo makes it plain that no employer, whether he or she be corporation president, a university dean, or a government official, has the right to ask a mother to neglect a sick child in order to keep a perfect attendance record at the office, classroom, or factory. The granting of sick leave to the mother of a sick child is not so much a matter of women's rights as a matter of the employer's duty to respect the sacredness of motherhood which the individual woman shares with the Virgin Mary and with the great mother goddesses of pre-Christian times.

Middle-class women who have marketable skills also have fewer role conflicts because other female members of the extended family, and an abundant supply of low-cost domestic servants, are available for day-to-day care of dependent children. Nonworking married middle-class women are far more fortunate than their North American counterparts; the Latin American women are free to shop or visit with friends as often as they like, without worrying about their children. The point is that as we simply do not know why only a small proportion of women work outside of the home in Latin America, we must leave open the possibility that a considerable number may have freely chosen to have their marianismo cake and eat it too.

**Conclusion**

This excursion into the realm of Latin American culture has revealed a major variant on the universal theme of male-female relationships. We have traced the major characteristics of these relationships as they have developed over thousands of years and as they are observed today. Our historical perspective enables us to see that far from being an oppressive norm dictated by tyrannical males, marianismo has received considerable impetus from women themselves. This fact makes it possible to regard marianismo as part of a reciprocal arrangement, the other half of which is machismo.

The arrangement is not demonstrably more "unjust" than major variants on the same theme in other parts of the world. While some individuals of both sexes have been "victimized" by the strictures, it appears that many others have been able to shape their own life-styles and derive a measure of satisfaction, sometimes because of and sometimes in spite of the requirements of the system.

It seems unlikely that this pattern of male-female relationships can persist indefinitely without undergoing important modification. The mestizos—precisely that part of Latin American society which is characterized by machismo-marianismo—are not a traditional group, in the sense of that word as used by anthropologists. All observable facets of Latin American mestizo society are experiencing the effects of rapid and far-reaching changes, from which the phenomenon we have described could hardly be exempt. In fact, some signs are already apparent that the current generation of middle-class university students holds somewhat different values with regard to relationships between the sexes than those of their parents. This was particularly evident during the 1968 student strike in Mexico, with reference to male-female role perceptions.

In my opinion, however, marianismo is not for some time yet destined to disappear as a cultural pattern in Latin America. In general, women will not use their vote as a bloc to make divorce more accessible, to abolish sex discrimination (especially preferential treatment for women), or to impose upon themselves some of the onerous tasks traditionally reserved for men. They are not yet ready to relinquish their female chauvinism.

## Notes

1. Interviews with American youths who visited Cuba to assist in the sugar harvest show that they use the term "machismo" as a synonym for "male chauvinism." See Carol Brightman and Sandra Levinson, eds., *The Venceremos Brigade* (New York: Simon and Schuster, 1971), passim.

2. For a discussion of this term and its social and political implications, see Evelyn P. Stevens, "Mexican Machismo: Politics and Value Orientations," *Western Political Quarterly*, 18, no. 4 (December 1965), pp. 848–57.

3. *Mundo Nuevo*, no. 46 (April 1970), pp. 14–50, devotes an entire section to the topic of "Machismo *y feminismo*," in which several authors use the term

"*hembrismo.*" Neither *feminismo* nor *hembrismo* seems to me as satisfactory as my own term "marianismo," for reasons made plain by the text.

4. See, for example, Julian Pitt-Rivers, ed., *Mediterranean Countrymen: Essays in the Social Anthropology of the Mediterranean* (Paris and La Haye: Mouton, 1963).

5. Julio Caro Baroja in *Honour and Shame: The Values of Mediterranean Society*, ed. J. Peristiany (Chicago: University of Chicago Press, 1966), p. 116.

6. Samuel Ramos, *Profile of Man and Culture in Mexico* (Austin: University of Texas Press, 1962).

7. See Edwin Oliver James, *The Cult of the Mother Goddess* (London: Thames and Hudson, 1956); and Erich Neumann, *The Great Mother: An Analysis of the Archetype* (New York: Pantheon Books, 1955).

8. Stephen Herbert Langdon, *Tammuz and Ishtar* (Oxford: Clarendon Press, 1914).

9. Raphael Patai, *The Hebrew Goddess* (New York: Ktav Publishing House, 1967).

10. See especially Jean Danielou and Henri Marrou, *The First Six Hundred Years*, vol. 1, *The Christian Centuries: A New History of the Catholic Church* (New York: McGraw-Hill, 1964); and John Patrick Dolan, *Catholicism: An Historical Survey* (Woodbury, N.Y.: Barron's Educational Series, 1968).

11. One of the best of the ecclesiastically approved criticisms of the Marian cult is René Laurentin's short scholarly treatise, *The Question of Mary* (New York: Holt, Rinehart, and Winston, 1965).

12. Catholic University of America, eds., *New Catholic Encyclopedia* (New York: McGraw-Hill, 1967), vol. 9, p. 368.

13. Alfonso Caso, *The Religion of the Aztecs* (Mexico City: Central News Company, 1937), p. 34.

14. Luis Lasso de la Vega, *Hvei Tlamahvicoltica* (México: Carreño e Hijo, 1926). But for a profane view of the same subject, see also Francisco de la Maza, *El guadalupanismo mexicano* (México: Porrúa y Obregón, 1953). A dramatic treatment of the subject is provided by Rodolfo Usigli, *Corona de Luz* (México: Fondo de Cultura Económica, 1965).

15. See Eric Wolf, "The Virgin of Guadalupe: A Mexican National Symbol," *Journal of American Folklore*, 71 (1958), pp. 34–39. My translation.

16. Carl E. Batt, "Mexican Character: An Adlerian Interpretation," *Journal of Individual Psychology*, 5, no. 2 (November 1969), pp. 183–201. This author refers to the "martyr complex."

17. See Rogelio Díaz-Guerrero, "Neurosis and the Mexican Family Structure," *American Journal of Psychiatry*, 112, no. 6 (December 1955), pp. 411–17; and idem, "Adolescence in Mexico: Some Cultural, Psychological, and Psychiatric Aspects," *International Mental Health Research Newsletter*, 12, no. 4 (Winter 1970), pp. 1, 10–13.

18. Rosa Cruchaga de Walker and Lillian Calm, "¿Quién es la mujer chilena?" *Mundo Nuevo*, no. 46 (April 1970), pp. 33–38. The woman quoted in the interview is the wife of an engineer and the mother of two children. Although she professes to admire the laundress, she obviously does not emulate her life-style.

19. *Por la izquierda*: illicit.

20. James, *Cult of the Mother Goddess*, pp. 49ff.

21. Salvador Reyes Nevares, "El machismo en México," *Mundo Nuevo*, no. 46 (April 1970), pp. 14–19.

22. J. Mayone Stycos, *Family and Fertility in Puerto Rico* (New York: Columbia University Press, 1955). See also Theodore B. Brameld, *The Remaking of a Culture* (New York: Harper and Brothers, 1959).

23. Lloyd H. Roger and August B. Hollingshead, *Trapped* (New York: John Wiley and Sons, 1965), pp. 133–47. See also the publications of Oscar Lewis on Mexico and Puerto Rico.

24. Ana María Portugal, "La peruana ¿'Tapada' sin manto?" *Mundo Nuevo,* no. 46 (April 1970), pp. 20–27.

25. José B. Adolph, "La emancipación masculina en Lima," *Mundo Nuevo,* no. 46 (April 1970), pp. 39–41.

26. Ibid., p. 39.

27. Portugal, "La peruana ¿'Tapada' sin manto?" p. 22.

28. Some representative figures for Mexico and other Latin American countries are given in Ifigenia de Navarrete's *La mujer y los derechos sociales* (México: Ediciones Oasis, 1969).

## 2 Josefina Zoraida Vásquez ◆ Women's Liberation in Latin America: Toward a History of the Present

*Latin American women saw their history evolving differently from the models supplied by foreign social scientists such as Evelyn Stevens. To the Mexican writer Josefina Zoraida Vásquez, the history of Latin American women is complex and evolutionary, and should not be reduced to simple generalizations. Of importance to her are questions such as: If our culture is so repressive toward women, how could it produce a feminist movement or a writer of the stature of Rosario Castellanos? Is the history of Latin American women so very different from that of women elsewhere? For her the Enlightenment was a crucial transition point between the colonial mentality and the development of a woman's movement in the twentieth century.*

The majority of Latin American publications on women are commemorative documents or pamphlets, and hardly any serious work exists. The most serious publications come from North America, though they often distort their interpretation with ideas such as modernization or liberationism or by exaggerating other ideas such as "machismo" or, in some studies, "Marianism," that is, the idea of the spiritual superiority of women.[1] Elsewhere such vague concepts as traditionalism or modernism are invoked. There is no doubt that industrialization and urbanization have had a direct effect on woman's role in society, but factors like education modify this role. In some cases woman's role has been transformed by political revolutions, as in the case of Cuba. In other cases changes in the situation of women have occurred in a generally retrogressive situation, as with the reforms introduced by General [Rafael Leónidas] Trujillo in the Dominican Republic. And the curious thing is that the contradiction exists even in the most developed countries where, despite the rapid evolution in customs, no divorce law yet exists. . . .

The arrival of the Europeans gave rise to a new society composed of various social groups with a complex network of relationships based on a situation of conquest. The process whereby this society was shaped was slow, and it is difficult to isolate and define its stages. In any event, the Europeans brought with them their contradictory medieval Hispanic notions about women with which was mingled the Greek philosophical concept of the inferiority of the female,[2] Roman notions of legal equality,[3]

From *Cultures—Dialogue between the Peoples of the World* 8, no. 4 (UNESCO, 1982): 85–91, 99–102.

the ambivalent Judaeo-Christian idea of a "certain" spiritual superiority in women, and traces of Islamic ideas. . . .

The restrictions imposed on the role of women in the Hispanic colonies in the seventeenth century are illustrated by the case of Sor Juana Inés de la Cruz, whose surprising intelligence and vocation obliged her to seek refuge within the walls of a convent. Her case is interesting as an illustration of some of the contradictions of the Hispanic mentality. Juana was illegitimate, although this did not prevent her from serving in the viceregal court, where she won a brilliant reputation for her knowledge and poetry: after all, New Spanish society was Catholic, so sin was pardonable. Obliged to consider her future, Juana had three possibilities: marriage, spinsterhood, or a religious order. Marriage would have terminated her vocation since it would have been difficult to find a husband who was up to her sensitivity and wisdom. Spinsterhood was impossible for a woman without resources, and it raised the problem of the lack of independence and protection; so taking orders was "the least incongruous and the most decent" thing to do, as she herself admitted. Having taken this basic decision, Juana surrounded herself in her cell with scientific instruments and books, and took as much time off as possible from her religious devotions to increase her general knowledge and write poetry. But her life, apart from the vexations of communal living, was hardly tranquil. Using the pseudonym of Sister Filotea, the Bishop of Puebla accused her of worldly ambition and lack of piety because she was pursuing her intellectual vocation. Her reply is the only instance of a statement on women's problems to survive from the colonial era. But despite her resistance, Sor Juana was eventually obliged to give up her instruments and library. Fortunately an early death freed her from her despair.[4]. . .

But the eighteenth century was to combine external influences with the changes of mentality that accompanied the maturing of colonial society. On the one hand, the worldliness brought into the empire by the Bourbon monarchs to some extent shook the old religious society, and on the other, the Enlightenment and its schemes for social and economic regeneration made its influence felt.

The Enlightenment represented a fundamental change which inevitably influenced ideas about women. The Spaniard Benito Feijóo included in his *Teatro Crítico Universal* (an anthology of essays on diverse matters) a "Defense of Women" which went so far as to reject biblical arguments for the subjection of women to men. Feijóo argued the possibility of translation errors and included a list of notable women which proved that they could excel when given the chance to exercise their talents. Fray Benito insisted on the idea that it was necessary "to persuade humankind of the equality of the sexes in intellectual endowments" so that women could realize their own dignity. He continued: "Let women therefore understand that they are not inferior to men in knowledge: they would then speak out with confidence so as to expose the sophisms of men wherein nonsense is disguised as rational argument."[5]

The Count of Campomanes [Pedro Rodríguez] also defended the intellectual equality of the two sexes and attempted to prove it by providing both with the same education, since experience teaches that "intellectual talents know no sexual distinctions and the well-educated woman is neither less enlightened nor less able than men, although she is much more agile in manual operations than are men."[6] For Campomanes, the deep cause of Spanish economic stagnation was the "pitiful idleness" in which women were kept which could only be overcome by educating girls and eradicating restrictions on women's working.[7] These ideas inspired Charles III's decree of 1784 which abolished the bar on women's exercising certain types of professions. This decree was later extended to Spanish America, and we know that the guilds admitted women and that some women actually went on to become guild masters. By the end of the century, women were following a number of craft trades.

Charles III himself defended the admission of women to the "economic societies," and one of their members, Josefa Amar y Borbón, in her *Discurso sobre la educación física y moral de las mujeres* (Discourse on the moral and physical education of women), 1790, attacked the conditioning of girls whereby they were raised only to be attractive and agreeable to the opposite sex. According to Josefa, this prevented them from becoming true human beings, to the detriment of their husbands and children. As can clearly be seen, Josefa was less of an innovator than Feijóo and Campomanes.

The Enlightenment created an appropriate climate for church, state, and private individuals to look to the establishment of schools where reading and writing were taught on a regular basis. By the second half of the eighteenth century, the French Order of the Company of Mary was collaborating freely in the education of girls. And as a measure of the change of mentality which was taking place, the governor of Guadalajara decreed that the principal surgeon should train midwives in their profession, "so as to avoid the constant evils which the want of skilled midwives inflicts upon mankind."[8]

For part of the eighteenth century, in fact, enlightened thought and the activities of the Bourbons laid down the general lines of what were to become the goals of a liberal education. Thus it was that the early years of the nineteenth century, in fact, really were only an amplification of already formulated ideas and the multiplication of educational establishments where the "three Rs" were taught on a regular basis. Other subjects were added later: religious studies, art, geography, and geometry. Even in colleges for poor Amerindian girls it was argued that pupils would "make progress if they are encouraged to think and reason."[9]

The importance given to education affected large sections of society so that both the liberals of the Cadiz Cortes (parliament) of 1812 and the absolutist Ferdinand VII busied themselves with making it popular. Ferdinand gave orders for an inquiry into the state of schools, and asked the pope for the church's collaboration in granting an increase in teaching orders and the abolition of contemplative orders.

Many political thinkers wrote on the education of the "weaker" sex from the traditional standpoint of woman as wax to be molded in the hands of men. Despite certain differences of emphasis, one can generally say that throughout the nineteenth century the subject of women continued to be treated along the lines laid down by Josefa Amar y Borbón: the education of girls was important for them to be able to perform their parts as mothers. There were those who asked for a broader education for women— for example, Dalmira Regurviasa in 1817,[10] or Ana Josefa Caballero de Borda, who published her *Necesidad de un establecimiento de educación para jóvenes mexicanas* (Need for an educational establishment for young Mexican girls) in 1823. . . .

Latin American women have approached the issue of political and economic equality in a less boisterous way than those of the English-speaking world, although one might well wonder to what extent they have been left at the starting post. The struggle against tradition turned out to be a difficult one in all countries, and not only in Latin America, and this led the General Assembly of the United Nations in 1967 to make a solemn declaration containing eleven articles. . . .

Article 4 calls for the granting to women of the right to vote in all elections, to stand for election, and [to] occupy public positions.[11] In 1970 the Commission on the Legal and Social Condition of Women recommended the General Assembly to undertake a program of international action to advance the condition of women. The objectives approved by the Assembly were to be achieved in the decade following 1970, and the halfway point, 1975, was consequently declared to be the International Women's Year during which results would be evaluated. This decision helped to pressure Latin American countries into applying legal reforms.

Another factor which gave new impetus to old struggles was the feminist movement which was reinaugurated in the United States at the beginning of the 1960s. The communications media ensured that publicity about injustices was effective and results were visible within a decade. Some high-circulation periodicals for female Latin American readers, such as *Claudia, Vanidades,* and *Buenhogar,* gave much attention to the topic.

With the exception of *Claudia*, there was obvious reticence about feminism, but imperceptibly attitudes began to change so that in recent years *Claudia*, *Vanidades*, and *Kena* have become platforms for new attitudes.

Throughout broad layers of today's Latin American society there still exists hostility to the transformation of the family, but the idea is accepted that women should be educated and should work and exercise political rights. Nevertheless, only exceptionally is it recognized that education and socialization should be reformed away from their traditional aims of making good wives and mothers—goals which are so limiting on women's development as human beings.

The legal changes which have taken place in some countries are surprising. Attempts have been made in Mexico to detect every trace of discrimination in order to abolish it; the paternalist character of the Federal Labor Law of 1961, which prevented women from performing dangerous, unhealthy, or abnormal work, was abolished by the new Labor Law of 1970 and the reform of Article 123 of the constitution which now prohibits such work only for pregnant women. In 1974 the legal code was also reformed so as to establish equality of rights and obligations for both parties in both marriage and divorce.

Although progress has not been even for all Latin American women, it has certainly been constant. The curious thing is that, as elsewhere, the contradictions have remained. Equal political rights have been achieved in every country, at least on paper. But there has been successful resistance to effective reform of family structure: in Argentina, Chile, Brazil, and Colombia divorce has still not been legalized.

For similar reasons, despite the monstrous demographic growth of almost the whole of Latin America, the subject of birth control has been a thorny one. More or less timidly, the majority of countries have had to mount campaigns to rouse the population's awareness about the problem of irresponsible growth. Mexico, with many reservations, began a campaign in the mid-1970s with the slogan: "If there are fewer of us, we can live better." Gradually, radio publicity—the most intense forum in Latin America—has been raising more specific subjects like contraceptives, which all government and semiofficial health agencies now supply free. This has made a slight dent in the birthrate figures. More surprising has been open discussion about the need to legalize abortion, although the obstacles are formidable.

The situation of women has certainly come a long way since those not-so-remote times when prejudice condemned them to an inferior position because of their biological role as mothers. Some argued that this role, as well as emphasizing woman's emotive nature, limited part of her rational faculties and hindered her from performing tasks which required cold calculation and logic. Other more romantic arguments claimed that women had the potential to behave like men, but if this potential was developed they would lose their most valuable assets: emotivity, tenderness, capacity for sacrifice, etc. Some old clichés still recall these times, such as "Women think with their wombs," or "If they have the same potential, why are there no women Einsteins?" However, women like Margaret Thatcher and Indira Gandhi have neutralized part of this argument since they have demonstrated that they can be cold, calculating, clever, and hard when they get into power.

The conquests made by Latin American women are to some extent impressive: the law gives them equality of rights, maternity is protected, they have work and educational opportunities and have gained access to responsible posts. Yet the situation leaves much to be desired. In the first place, society still conditions Latin American women to think of self-fulfillment only in terms of children. The changed situation is allowing an increasingly large group of women to devise broader programs for their own lives, but often with negative results because of the absence of an accompanying adjustment of male psychology to the new role of women. This is having disastrous effects on the family since the percentage of divorces is now starting to rival that of developed countries. On the other hand, the progress made is to a large extent benefiting only a small group of educated women, since the majority of working women in Latin America are employed in domestic service and other minor chores. In the cities, two out of five working women are in service,[12] while in the countryside opportunities for reasonably paid work for women are nonexistent, and this conditions women into greater passivity and dependence than elsewhere. Only 13 percent of the work force is female, compared with 41.4 percent in the USSR, 27.6 percent in Europe, and 21.3 percent in the United States.[13]

According to data supplied by the United Nations, women make full use of their voting rights in some Latin American countries. For example, in the mid-1960s 46 percent of registered voters in Chile were women, and 37 percent in Peru. In Argentina the same percentage of women as of men voters (80 percent) actually voted in 1973.[14] There are women's sections in the majority of political parties and trade unions in Latin America, which implies that women are totally dependent on male leadership. And there are, of course, few women in important posts. . . .

The explanation for this general situation lies in a complex intermeshing of elusive factors which are aggravated by underdevelopment. Nevertheless, it is my opinion that the heart of the matter lies in education, formal and informal. Formal education has always discriminated against women from elementary school to universities. Except for countries like Chile, Argentina, and Cuba, the female illiteracy rate is much higher than that of the male, and men dominate the universities absolutely. In Mexico, for example, there are more seventeen-year-old girls with children than there are at school.

But it is perhaps informal education which weighs most heavily in perpetuating the inferior position of women. Family, religious institutions, radio, television, advertising, cinema, comic strips, and textbooks continue to transmit messages about the role and goals of women, their behavior and possibilities, etc. Traditional ideas and beliefs survive behind reforms granting rights and wider work and educational opportunities and effectively hinder the successful development of most women's lives. This is why the main struggle now consists of combating many nuances of vocabulary, imagery, and stereotypes which seem inoffensive but are effective instruments of control. Obviously, increased educational opportunities will allow women to choose motherhood responsibly and not put up with it as something accidental and inevitable as has usually happened among our working classes.

Latin American society is in a state of transition between two value systems, and this generates contradictions. But the idea that women's liberation must be fully realized as a necessary step toward achieving a more just and responsible society is already strong enough on the continent to allow us to hope that the process will be completed in the not-too-distant future.

**Notes**

1. Evelyn P. Stevens, "Marianismo: The Other Face of Machismo in Latin America," in Ann Pescatello (ed.), *Female and Male in Latin America*, pp. 89–101, Pittsburgh, Pa., 1973. [See Selection 1, this volume.]

2. Aristotle, *Politics*.

3. *La condición jurídica de la mujer en México*, p. 25, note 12, Mexico City, UNAM, 1975.

4. See A. J. R. Russell-Wood, "Female and Family in the Economy and Society of Colonial Brazil," in Asunción Lavrin (ed.), *Latin-American Women: Historical Perspectives*, pp. 60–100, Westport, Conn., Greenwood Press, 1978.

5. Benito Feijóo, "Defensa de las mujeres," in *Teatro Critico Universal: Discursos varios en todo género de materias para desengaño de errores comunes*, Vol. I, pp. 388 and 390, Madrid, Joaquín Ibarra, 1723.

6. Pedro R. Campomanes, *Discurso sobre la educación popular de los artesanos*, p. 290, Madrid, Fábrica Nacional de Moneda y Timbre, 1975.

7. Ibid., p. 295.

8. Carmen Castaneda, "La educación en la Nueva Galicia," p. 179, Mexico City, El Colegio de México, 1975 (doctoral thesis).

9. Elisa Luque Alcaide, *La educación en Nueva España*, p. 290, Seville, Consejo Superior de Investigaciones Científicas, Escuela de Estudios Hispanoamericanos de Sevilla, 1970.

10. Patricia Echevarría, "Mexican Education in the Press and the Spanish Cortes, 1810–1821," p. 88, Austin, University of Texas, 1969 (doctoral thesis).

11. United Nations, *Tendencias y cambios actuales*, p. 8, New York, United Nations, July 1975 (doc. E/CONF 66/3).

12. Elsa Chaney, "Women in Latin-American Politics: The Case of Peru and Chile," in Pescatello, *Female and Male*, p. 106.

13. Ibid.

14. United Nations, *Tendencias y cambios actuales*, p. 11.

## 3  Mercedes Cabello de Carbonera ◆ Concerning Women's Intelligence and Beauty

*How little things have changed for women since Mercedes Cabello de Carbonera first read this essay in 1876 at the literary salon sponsored by Juana Manuela Gorriti! More than any of the other women who gathered regularly in Gorriti's parlor, doña Mercedes was openly dissatisfied with the role society assigned to women and she used the salon to articulate a feminist agenda. She refused to accept the inequality of men and women. Her confrontational style and aggressive prose, unusual for the time, won her the pejorative nickname "la doctora". She is particularly famous for her stinging characterizations of upper-class Lima women. The writings of Cabello de Carbonera, especially her novels, the most famous of which are* Blanca sol *and* Las consecuencias, *have been recovered by students of women's literature, and, although they have not been translated into English, contemporary Spanish editions of them are readily available.*

The eminent and illustrious writer [Juana Manuela Gorriti], to whom I have the honor of dedicating this work, suggested this beautiful and difficult theme, making me commit to talk about it during this meeting. She knows well that her wishes, even the smallest ones, are commands which I fulfill with delight. Her inspired words will always act as a powerful incentive for my pen.

Thus, after this brief explanation offered as an excuse about my interpretation of the subject, I will attempt to satisfy the friend while fulfilling a commitment at the same time.

Because of necessity, my treatment of the subject will be light and superficial; otherwise, it would be necessary, when speaking of beauty, to write a whole treatise on aesthetics in order to express the relativity of the ideal of beauty. It is subject to a thousand interpretations; sometimes it is related to the fashion and the traditions of one country, at other times it is dependent on many other circumstances that make it difficult and almost impossible to establish a general principle of beauty applicable throughout all times to all people. A writer has stated, with good reason, that what Pascal said about justice can also be said of beauty: "What to this side of the Pyrenees is beauty, to the other side is ugliness." Prozer Collard has stated that "what is beautiful is felt, not defined."

From "Estudio comparativo de la inteligencia y la belleza en la mujer, trabajo de la señora Mercedes Cabello de Carbonera leido por su autora," in *Veladas literarias* (Buenos Aires, 1902), 207–12, trans. Daniel Castro.

For instance, among the southern people, where the tropical sun would seem to have dyed with dark colors the eyes and the hair, and toasted with its warmth the skin of the inhabitants, the preferred type of beauty is that of the women whose golden hair resembles golden threads and whose light blue eyes are seen as the reflection of our limpid blue sky. The opposite is true among the people far away from the equator, where the shadows of a cloudy and opaque sky make the sun stingy with its heat and its light; there, black-eyed women with jet black hair are the models of beauty. Thus, we find that the Greeks, those masters of artistry, painted their Venuses with blonde hair, and Byron, the immortal singer of beauty, celebrated Spanish women with their dark skin and their ebony hair, finding them far superior to the colorless tones of English women.

I will not speak of the people unreached by the benefits of civilization and have educated their taste to formulate an ideal of beauty. It is among them that the greatest aberrations are found. For instance, there are some wild tribes where it is customary to dye one's teeth black with herbs, and according to them it is very ugly and only characteristic of dogs or other animals to have white teeth.

This theme will be even lighter and more superficial, considering that in order to establish a comparison between beauty and intelligence, we must regard the seductive and smiling face that a woman exhibits in the salons, considering her primarily as an ornament, or a little jewel, or, if the qualifier is allowed, like a fairy of enrapturing beauty and enchanting talent.

It will be necessary to forget the great mission entrusted to her by nature, the exalted and sublime mission of being a wife and a mother, a case in which beauty counts little and intelligence a great deal. If it were necessary to consider this last aspect, it would be a great absurdity to establish a comparison between the importance of beauty and intelligence.

In comparing beauty with intelligence, I will talk about beauty according to our type, that is, about the one with the sky-blue eyes, the golden hair, the alabaster skin, and the supple and delicately shaped body.

Will it be necessary for me to present a type for the intelligent woman? No, talent has only one type, and it can never be mistaken, nor can it be hidden; although, among the multitude of intelligences there are many forms and gradations, true talent has only one form, a unique and eternal form because it is modeled on God.

To judge the power of one or the other, let us imagine two types, opposite to each other: one possessing a perfect and dazzling beauty without any intelligence, the other possessing a powerful and clear intellect and no beauty.

A beautiful woman! These words seem to us to symbolize the other: A perfect woman! Beauty is the most eloquent manifestation that nature uses to awaken in our soul the idea of a great, perfect, and infinite Being. This is why, in every noble heart, there exists a fervent cult of everything beautiful; this is the reason that a beautiful woman inspires admiration and sympathy in us.

Beauty has a language, an eloquence of its own which is peculiar to it. A beautiful woman speaks with her eyes, with her smile; she even speaks with her motionless, smooth brow. Admirable language which lends itself to be translated according to each person's desire: the dreamy, spiritual man translates it with his soul, just as the material and vulgar man will interpret it in his own way. These are the reasons why beauty has the privilege of seducing and fascinating all men.

This is not the case with intelligence, which only seduces the very talented man. The great Voltaire has said: "Only a genius can understand a genius."

The merit of an intelligent woman is like that of a beautiful painting. Show a dull, vulgar man a painting of great merit where amidst vague and dark tones there shines the creator's idea, that is, the soul of the painting. After looking at it for a long time, the dull man will be convinced that the painting says nothing; nevertheless, there is an idea there, a great idea that only an intelligent man can understand.

Many times I have asked myself: Why is it that beauty is not always linked to intelligence? Why is it that the woman who fascinates us with her beauty disappoints us with her intelligence, and why is it that what is a delight to the eyes is usually a disappointment to the soul?

How many women I know whose beauty would gain a great deal if they became silent; that way they would have only the symbolic language of beauty, that language which as I have said already has the privilege of being interpreted differently by each person. Thus, her lips would not reveal at every turn that her brain is as imperfectly drawn as the line of her features is perfect.

Beauty without intelligence is an illusion that is close to disenchantment. It is like a fairy that fascinates us, as long as we look at her through the enchanting prism of her beauty. However, it disappears as soon as the light of reason penetrates beyond the place where the eyes can see.

Intelligence without beauty is like a rich treasure hidden in the ruggedness of a mountainous and arid terrain; it is hidden to enrich the happy man who will finally find it. It can be said that it is a magnificent book with a rustic cover, something that fools choose to ignore, because they only look at the outside.

The country violet is betrayed by her perfume, despite its attempts to hide itself. The intelligent woman is that way; the only one that cannot find her is the one unable to understand her.

A talented man can be made to conceive happiness thanks to a beautiful woman, but only an intelligent woman can make him realize it. The first will make him dream, the other will make him think and feel.

In the turbulent and stormy sea of passions, to dream is to navigate without a compass or a rudder, at the mercy of the storm. That is why every dream has a sad and bitter awakening. To feel and to think is to travel safely protected from the cliffs and the dangers, crossing the enchanted and smiling paradise inhabited by the sweet emotions where true happiness lives.

Here, at last, having come to the moment of resolving the problem of the importance of beauty and intelligence, we have to ascribe supremacy to one of the two. You must have guessed my opinion. I would have liked not to let it be known but, rather, to promote a discussion and to submit this problem to your illustrious opinion. But how do we establish a parallel between two things so essentially different? How do we compare that which constitutes the beauty of the soul with that which constitutes the perfection of external forms? How do we equate intelligence, which shines and perfumes the whole of existence, with beauty, that spring flower which is born, takes on color, and shines only once during one period of life?

How do we compare that which is as ephemeral and fleeting as a falling star that passes without leaving behind not even a vestige of its clarity, with a source of pure light that irradiates our whole existence and that of all the people who surround us?

Being an enthusiastic admirer of everything beautiful, I pay fervent homage to it, but I have not been able to even find a way of establishing a comparison between the merits of beauty and those of intelligence. I do not believe I am mistaken in recognizing the superiority that a woman's intelligence holds over her beauty.

## 4  Teresa González de Fanning ◆
## Concerning the Education of Women

*Teresa González de Fanning exemplifies the nineteenth-century woman writer who, although she participated actively in Lima's intellectual life during the last quarter of the nineteenth century, won many awards, and was elected to the Ateneo de Lima, Peru's most prestigious literary circle, fell into oblivion in the intellectual history of Latin America. She is re-membered as a champion of a woman's right to an education, a theme she hammered away at for over three decades in essays and the press. She even tied Peru's humiliating defeat in the War of the Pacific (1879–1884) to the faulty education of its women. After the war she established a school for girls where she tested her pedagogical theories; the school was an immediate success and became a favorite with liberal elite families.*

Selected by the president of the Moral Science Department to present to you a work about the importance of women's education, I have hesitated a great deal before deciding to accept such an honorable task because I was conscious of the difficulty of fulfilling this commitment so far above my limited strength.

I have been persuaded to present this imperfect paper by two rea-sons: in the first place, your indulgence, which I ask you to grant me; and then, the conviction I feel that all of us are obligated to contribute to build the edifice of the common good, even if it is only with a little grain of sand.

The dismal war, which took away my lifelong companion, my natu-ral support, placed me in the situation of having to feed the interest that had always inspired me: the education of children.

As the principal of a girls' school, I have been able to observe the defects from which the education of women suffers in our country; and I am going to take the liberty of pointing out the most significant ones. I hope that the illustrious ladies who make up this respectable audience will take note of my observations and will correct, if they find them just, the dark blemishes which darken the moral beauty of the Peruvian woman.

Nations, like individuals, are exposed to terrible commotions, both in their physical and moral natures. These commotions consume their vi-tal sap and their vigor and endanger their existence. The last war has been for Peru one of those terrible cataclysms that shook the social edifice.

From *Sobre la educación de la mujer* (Lima, 1876), trans. Daniel Castro.

In addition to the loss of so many of its good offspring, a loss that will never be felt enough or mourned enough, a profound malaise has come over the nation, almost a total unhinging of society that alarms the thinkers and the patriots. It seems that defeat, taking away the laurels to which we were entitled—given the justice of our cause—also has taken away our confidence in the highest expectations of the country as well as the energy necessary to realize them.

Dismay and skepticism have taken the place of the faith that multiplies our strength. Like the Orientals we have given in to a fatalism that borders on inertia, which will lead us into a fathomless abyss unless an energetic effort can save us from the vortex. But where will the impulse which will lift this prostrated society, which will restore faith to the faithless, and which will resuscitate this Lazarus, come from?

It will seem to you a great audacity that I, small among the lesser ones, will dare to point out a remedy to such a tremendous malady, and that I would raise my voice in this sanctuary of knowledge, in the presence of such eminent patricians, philosophers, and statesmen. But the wisdom of history has shown us how many times Providence has made use of feeble instruments to realize its loftiest goals.

France, victimized by internal dissent and an external war, was on the verge of losing its autonomy when a humble and ignorant shepherdess [Joan of Arc], inspired by the one who conducts the destiny of nations, and sustained by that unbreakable faith, capable of moving mountains, gave new energy to the strong warriors who were beginning to despair in the face of such imminent danger, and . . . France was saved.

Ladies and gentlemen, forgive, then, my audacity; excuse it in the name of the good intention that guides me, and allow me to ask you: Do you want to regenerate society? Do you want Peru to rise up powerful and vigorous, supported by its citizens who will enrich it with their virtue and make it occupy the place that it deserves among nations? Well, if you want it, then educate women. As long as there are mothers who do not understand the magnitude of their mission, you will not have citizens who will be able to lift the motherland from the cruel prostration to which it has been reduced by its maladies. And their influence is so significant that you must observe that always, behind a great man, you will find a great woman—call her mother, wife, or sister—who has assisted and encouraged him along the way.

The family is to the state what the waves are to the sea, the roots to the tree, the molecules to the body. Do away with the family and the state will disappear. Thus, it is mandatory that its regeneration should begin with the family. Educate the woman, raise her moral level to make her understand that she is the priestess of good, the worker of the future, and, like a sound wave, her harmonious echo will reverberate in the family and in society, and Peru will be saved.

For many centuries, woman has been the pariah of society. She was considered an agent of the evil genius, an inferior being; it was even doubted that she had a soul, and, consequently, she was found to be the annex of man.

In ancient countries the birth of a son was a happy event worthy of being celebrated with canticles and solemn ceremonies; yet, the birth of a daughter was the total opposite—it was a curse of affliction and opprobrium for her parents.

In India, according to the sacred book of the Hindu, the woman who only gave birth to girls could be repudiated by her husband. In enlightened Athens, the father to whom a daughter was born manifested his sorrow by hanging on the door of his house a fleece of wool instead of the olive wreath with which he so happily would announce the birth of a son.

The humiliations suffered by a woman at birth were only the prelude to what was to come for the rest of her life, living like a serf, always subject to her father, to her husband, and even to her sons. The day of emancipation never dawned for her.

The Gospel, that wise code of love and fraternity, repaired that secular injustice, replacing woman's dignity as the companion of man, where she had been placed by the Creator. But it is not enough to have broken the chains of the serf to complete her redemption; it is necessary for her to learn the duties that her position demands.

Much has been done in this sense. The most illustrious thinkers of this and the past centuries have given the matter a great deal of thought. The philosopher from Geneva [Rousseau] states in his *Emile*: "Men will always be whatever women want; whoever desires to see great and virtuous men must educate women about greatness and beauty." A noteworthy contemporary writer has said: "The spirit of a people, as well as its traditions, its preoccupations, its virtues, and, better yet, the civilization of humankind—they all rest in the maternal breast."

But why accumulate quotations to convince you of a truth that exists in everybody's conscience? Fortunately, the time when women were considered almost like pieces of furniture has passed. Aside from the barest social rudiments, women were taught the duties of housekeeping when it was thought that the pen would be a dangerous instrument in their hands. An odd aberration made ignorance the safeguard of their innocence.

The time of obscurantism has passed, and today the culture of nations is measured by the degree of prestige enjoyed by women. Witness to this is the Great American Republic, where not only are they regarded with particular respect, but also they find the same opportunity as men for acquiring knowledge.

Peru has followed this civilizing current. As soon as it joined the ranks of the independent nations, it quickly created schools which, without distinction, admitted both sexes to receive an education.

The large number of matrons and young women who exercise the career of the teacher reflects women's response to this call. Despite the fact that due to a lamentable oversight they have been denied access to higher education, they, nevertheless, by their own efforts are widening their sphere of influence.

Thus, we see that some of them have learned telegraphy, and they are rendering useful services in the government offices. We also see that another of our compatriots, after an excellent study of law, has petitioned Congress to authorize her to receive the degree of doctor of law, while yet another has undertaken a higher education for the purpose of studying the science of Hippocrates [medicine].

All this proves, then, that a positive step has been taken concerning women's instruction. However, you know well, ladies and gentlemen, that we cannot confuse instruction with education, and the latter, which we know is the most important, has followed a wrong path, which has led us astray from our objectives in educating our children. This objective we will say, making use of the expression of a well-learned French writer [Descartes], must not be other than to shape men or women: that is, rational creatures, subservient to duty, lovers of truth who will make full use of their faculties to accomplish their own perfection and be of use to the rest of the people.

Unfortunately, this is not the perspective from which most of our matrons have decided to educate the children that heaven has placed under their maternal aegis. Instead, many of them (this is painful to admit) are not even aware of their important mission, nor do they propose a determined objective for their children. They love their children very much, but their love is expressed in a condescendence that becomes outright weakness because of an excess of pernicious indulgence concerning its physical and spiritual development. Let us demonstrate this.

Hygiene prescribes that a child must receive, methodically and regularly, healthy and substantial nutriment, that excessive spices and stimulating beverages, spirits or alcohol, must be avoided, and instead they should be given water and milk as prescribed by nature. The child must also enjoy the fresh morning air and do adequate exercise to develop muscles.

Is this done? Certainly not.

In times past it was accustomed that the children would go to sleep at sundown and would get up at sunrise; today, they stay up like the adults, they get up late, feeling lazy and still half asleep, they come to the table where they refuse to eat and do not agree to eat unless they are cajoled and spoiled, and then, they only eat little bits. Because their mothers love them so much, their wishes are granted. Later they will make up for it by eating sweets and unwholesome treats. The result of this is weak, sickly children whose development will later resent this noxious practice which is already contributing to the degeneration of our race.

If we pass from the physical to spiritual education, the soul is saddened by the spectacle presented by our youth. Children who have not even reached adolescence exhibit the vices of old people. What can a country [expect] from a generation that enters life under such deplorable auspices?

Do not let it be said that we exaggerate the malady, because it is found in the churches as well as on the streets, in the classroom as well as at home. Many believe that children up to the age of seven or eight are unconscious beings who must be abandoned to their own devices because they are not responsible for their acts; to proceed otherwise would be to oppress [them] and to deprive them of the joys of childhood. It is claimed that the day will soon come when they will have to go to school, and with that they will have to be subject to a strict discipline. There the teacher will correct the defects derived from the natural disturbances of childhood.

Whoever thinks this way is making a grievous error. The soul of a child is a blank book, where it is up to the father and, more especially, up to the mother to write the first pages, sketching in the process the general outline of the work. When the principles are sound, the job of the teacher is easy and fruitful. On good soil, the good seed will produce a fresh, vigorous plant which will produce abundant fruit. The opposite is like building on sand.

Education must begin with life, and it is the mother, we insist, who is called to fulfill such a delicate mission. It is she who must shape the men of tomorrow, the future citizens, and those who must succeed them in the august priestliness of motherhood. Even when the child is in diapers and his halting tongue cannot express his thoughts without the help of mimicry, he already harbors little passions that time will ripen. The child is susceptible to wrath and envy, to revenge and jealousy. It is human nature with its vices and virtues in germinal form. These are potential assets that, well combined, will produce a felicitous result. That is the task placed on the mother by nature. She must work so all the notes of the instrument will harmonize to produce a perfect combination.

Through example and perseverance, she must modify bad inclinations and strengthen good tendencies; she must be firm and energetic, without being harsh, sweet and benevolent, without being weak. How can it be expected for a child, whose mirror is his mother, to love the truth if he notices that his mother does not do it? How can he be peaceful and tolerant if he receives examples of impatience and wrath? And how many times, instead of correcting bad inclinations, they are unwittingly fomented! How many times is the child incited to revenge, to anger, to lie, and to deceive?

How many times have we seen the case of the child who commits a small, mischievous act and is candidly told, "Is it not true, my little child, that it was So and So who did that?" The child, full of satisfaction, will hurry to answer in the affirmative. Thus, he receives his first lesson as to how one can avoid telling the truth for one's own benefit. Other times, it happens that he hits himself, and then he is asked to beat the object which he hit; thus, he is allowed to savor the forbidden taste of revenge.

Children raised this way become used not to respect what belongs to others and to impose on others their despotic will. This way they are transformed into petty tyrants whose heavy yoke becomes unbearable when time erases the mirth of childlike grace.

You might say that these are small futilities that must not be taken into consideration. You are wrong, ladies. These little things are the seeds that germinate and bloom, these are the outer edges of the picture of life which time will color and accent more and more. Mothers, take care of those little things, the task will only become easier.

Watch those tender plants entrusted to your maternal vigil, separate from them whatever can harm them, and foment with dedication their moral development without overlooking their physical and intellectual development. Become children like they are, and, through their insatiable childish curiosity, teach them untiringly their duties to God, to themselves, and to their fellow human beings. Educate their senses and cultivate their intelligence.

Each one of their questions can afford you an opportunity to inculcate a moral notion, or to teach them about an object in nature or in art, its component parts, its use or its origins, always taking care to not offend their credulity, because if they become aware that they are being deceived, they will distrust you and you will lose the authority of your word, which must be for them the highest expression of truth.

It is at this time of transition when the discreet mother must gradually transform her authority in order to become the friend and adviser of the son and especially of the daughter. She must concentrate on the education of all her affective faculties. Like the painter, who, having given

tangible form to a beautiful creation of his genius, recreates himself con-
templating his masterpiece, and, correcting little details every day, man-
ages to add new beauty, the mother must perfect every day this copy of
herself, trying to make the moral beauty of the copy to exceed that of the
original. To attain this are necessary, above all, perseverance, observation, and vigilance.

In the past it was customary for girls to remain inside the house, removed from social contact. This made them timid and ill mannered. Today, they associate with adults and they acquire a liberty and a looseness
that make them lose that modest timidity, so enchanting in their early
years. It seems to us that, [in] trying to get away from a mistake, we have
fallen into a worse one.

In effect, they listen to and take part in all conversations, no matter
how simple they might seem (although they are not always this way), and
they begin to peel back the veils of innocence one by one, of that innocence which is to childhood what perfume is to a flower. It is not enough
for the family to abstain from talking about the things that a child should
not hear, because the people on the outside will not be as discreet. Mothers can never exercise enough caution about this matter.

It seems that many times children are not conscious of what is being
said around them, yet at every turn we have proof that the opposite is
true. To this effect, I cannot resist the temptation of telling you a humor-
ous occurrence that recently happened to a lady. She was talking to one
of her friends while a child, apparently intent on his own games, played
nearby. In the course of the conversation, one of the two ladies said, "But
two of them are 'natural children.' " The child interrupted them and asked
vivaciously, "How about the others, are they made of rubber?"* A chorus
of laughter greeted this question, which expressed not only happy ignorance but [also] the interest with which the child had followed the conversation, despite his apparent disinterest.

Any concept that children hear without understanding affects their
imagination, and they ruminate and work it until they can decipher the
enigma. The result of their investigations is not kept to themselves—it is
communicated to their immediate circle which will listen to them with
the interest felt for the unknown and the stimulus of the forbidden truth.
It is in this way that an innocent conversation, a word, or an unplanned
act can affect the innocence of the child who hears it and communicates it
to the ones who surround him.

*The term "natural child" is used in the context of being illegitimate—born
in a natural state rather than according to legal prescriptions.

A good education for women must have, at its base, religion, morality, and home economics. By a religious education, we understand the
practice of a pure and simple Gospel morality, not the exaggerations that
exalt the impressionable imagination of the youth and produce those
mystical occurrences which are manifestations more of intemperate fa-
naticism than of sincere piety. This separates them from society as if from
a danger, and often it weakens the family ties that for the common benefit
must be strengthened more and more every day. "In the spiritual world,
as in the world of matter," says Jules Simon, "there is no progress whose
cost is not too high, if it attacks, even slightly, the sacred ties of the
family."

Applying this thought to religious education, we can say that if this
education attacks the sacred bastion of the family, rending it apart instead
of bringing it together, it has surely deviated from the path prescribed by
the Divine Master. The woman must be the sun of her home, she must
vivify and stimulate it. In order to do this, she must possess a quality that
is innate in her heart, something that mothers must cultivate with particular solicitude: we are talking about *abnegation*.

An egoist man is antipathetic; an egoist woman is a repulsive being,
sort of a phenomenon outside the natural order. It is so much a characteristic of a woman to sacrifice herself for the benefit of her people, to spread
happiness and comfort around her, to suffer as long as she alleviates the
suffering of those close to her, to be the tutelar and providential angel to
her children.

Her mission is to console, and she is never more beautiful or angeli-
cal than when she sacrifices her pleasure and even her necessary rest in
favor of her people. The one who is not ready to sacrifice to fulfill these
duties of elementary and sublime Christian charity does this because the
poisonous plant of egoism germinates in her soul. To avoid egoism from
taking root in the heart of her daughters, those who want to educate them
well will never work too much.

A vice that has become infiltrated among us, just as a virus is infiltrated in the blood, is the passion for luxury. Young girls enjoy silk and
lace in a frightening way. Used to these things from birth, they [silk and
lace] become every day more and more of a necessity. What they now
demand from their parents will be later demanded from their husbands.

A very discreet lady used to say that "every silk dress means one less
boyfriend for the girls." In effect, a young man of modest means who
only enjoys a small income cannot take on the ominous burden of setting
up a home and keep up the trend to which this woman is used. Some
brave souls, who can only see the present, have taken this dangerous road;

however, they have soon fallen like the fabled Icarus, and they have seen their jewels and their rich furnishings pass to the hands of the best bidder.

Others, more prudent, or perhaps more depraved, run away from marriage as if from cholera, and instead they create clandestine unions, harming in this manner public morals. The statistical registers furnish depressing numbers about this fact; of the number of children born, the illegitimate children exceed by far the number of legitimate ones. We do not believe that luxury is the only cause generating this occurrence, but it is definitely one of the main reasons.

It is true that in many cases luxury is more apparent than real. It is true that many young women, through dint of hard work and ingenuity, know how to fix themselves up and how to transform, at little cost, their clothes, giving them an air of elegant novelty. For these we only have applause and congratulations, [but,] unfortunately, they are not the majority.

Ordinarily, those fanatical worshippers of luxury and fashion lack even the most essential notion of home economics. We mothers know that they cannot even conceive of how to fix a dress without going to the dressmaker. They, of course, are incapable of adhering to a budget; and, not having enough with their regular income, they must pawn their possessions, with the subsequent loss of the pawned object and the economic instability that this accrues, thus setting the stage for the ruin of the family. Domestic peace cannot resist this hard test. On the contrary, this originates such profound harm that even considering it is frightening. Let us agree that a bad education is at the root of this problem.

We have said it before and we repeat it now: the mother must be the friend and adviser to her daughter, who must hold no secrets from her. Young girls' secrets can be guessed: when the fruit is ready, it tends to come off the tree that supports it. The magical word, the hidden impulse that agitates her mind and excites her nervous system, is *love.*

Mothers, do not pretend to go against it, but try to direct it. Steam compressed in excess can blow up the machine; well channeled, it can work wonders. Avoid for your daughters the hidden and precocious escapades, [for] they corrupt the heart and hold a thousand dangers. Let them find out through you that they must find a twin soul, a person who will complement their being, for it is a legitimate aspiration, and you will help with your advice.

If you manage to gain their trust, you will save yourselves much grief, and they will avoid many dangers. You will war with the street pirates, that corrupting plague, that leprosy of society that invades avenues and even the divine temples, lying in wait for the innocent. Make them look at love not as the fascinating and romantic mirage that their dreamy fantasy presents to them but as the transcendental act that will decide the happiness or the wretchedness of their whole life. They must not consider themselves the idol that a passionate husband adores perennially but the loving and discreet companion who, with her solicitous and affectionate behavior, will win his love and will make the home thrive.

Prepare them above all so they can face the storms of life. Women do not always get married, and when they get married, because of some predetermined order, they almost always outlive their husbands. In one case or the other, what will be their fate if they do not know how to keep their fortune, if they have it, or to earn a living if they do not?

This is an emergency that must worry parents. Do not raise girls who will grow old without growing up. Educate rational beings, capable of fending for themselves, and capable of facing all types of eventualities. Do not be satisfied with the fact that your daughters know a language halfway, or how to play music, or how to embroider. Put yourself in the situation where they must appeal to their knowledge to take care of their needs. It is a lifesaver which those who cross the stormy sea of life must not lack.

Woman is accused of being frivolous, which does not take into consideration that frivolity is not in her spirit but in the incomplete and superficial education that she receives. For lack of adequate sustenance, her activities and her intelligence are misused in futilities, not unlike the badly prepared vine which is covered with dense foliage, but, instead of the desired fruit, it produces only a few poor clusters of grapes.

I conclude, ladies and gentlemen. Perhaps I have gone on too long, and I have abused your goodwill; however, I have only touched lightly on an issue, as extensive as it is interesting and complex, which the education of women represents—the education of the women called on to operate a social revolution that will heal the wounds of our beloved country.

It is to be hoped that my aspirations, magnified by the clear talent of the people listening to me, would give rise to the regenerating movement which, thanks to the moralizing of the family, will extend its powerful influence throughout society.

## 5  Lillian Estelle Fisher ◆ The Influence of the Present Mexican Revolution upon the Status of Mexican Women

*Originally published in the* Hispanic American Historical Review *in 1942, Lillian Estelle Fisher's report on the status of women in postrevolutionary Mexico has become a useful historical document. Using the narrative analytical style that became her scholarly trademark, Fisher weaves the contributions, the pain, and the sacrifices that ordinary peasant and working women made to the revolution. Of particular interest is the conflict she perceives between unquestioned legal advances and the continued inferior status of women. The Mexican experience demonstrates the limits of liberal reform even when it is achieved within a revolutionary context.*

Women have always played an important part in Mexican history. Their influence has greatly increased since the social revolution of 1910. That revolution, which preceded the Russian Revolution by nearly ten years, was not merely a series of military events, but a great social upheaval. Emphasis was now placed on national values, facing difficult situations, and changing formerly adopted policies. The mass education advocated included [instruction for] women. Even the Indians found that they too had human rights, among them being the right to acquire an education. The intellectual life of the country was quickened. The day of the hidalgo and aristocrat had passed, for the people had asserted themselves. Peonage was practically abolished, and labor unions were permitted to organize and protest against injustice as freely as in any part of the world.

In the recent revolution many women, particularly of the working class and peasantry, were ready to take their place side by side with their men. Some carried the message of [Emiliano] Zapata's agrarian reform to the country people, while others, like Lucrecia Toriz, a textile worker, helped organize the strike of Río Blanco, which was a signal of revolt against the corrupt dictatorship of Porfirio Díaz.[1]

María del Refugio García, the daughter of a village doctor in Uruapan, Michoacán, is an interesting example of a brave woman who dared to defy the dictator. She made her first speech to the country people when she wore short skirts and had braids down her back, urging them to defend themselves against the tyranny of Díaz. The peasants listened to her frequently. Later her reputation as a radical speaker became so well known

From *Hispanic American Historical Review* 22 (1942): 211–28. ©1942 by Duke University Press. Reprinted by permission of Duke University Press.

that her friends took her out of the state for fear that she might fall into the hands of the police. In 1913 she became a Mexico City representative of the Michoacán revolutionary movement, and all her life she has worked for the rights of the country people.[2]

In the revolution from 1910 to 1920, peasant women followed the soldiers onto the battlefields and aided them in military campaigns. On account of the insecurity of the country, women of the upper classes had to leave their homes in small towns and the rural districts. Many went to the United States, where they learned lessons never to be forgotten, because some had to work for their living. Others, going to large cities in their own country, were confronted with rivalry, necessity, and problems unknown before. Women had to study, and great advantages came from this for, as Dr. Puig Casauranc has always said, their emancipation will come through culture.[3]

Women have obtained more rights than ever before in Mexico as a result of the revolution, yet their position is still far inferior to that of men. Within many homes man still reigns supreme—a heritage of the Middle Ages. Daughters are taught absolute obedience not only to their fathers but also to their brothers. If there is little money in the family, sons are educated at the expense of daughters. Sometimes even when the family has plenty of money, parents refuse to educate their daughters because they will have no need for a career when married.[4] In some conservative upper-class families, after the age of fourteen the girl seldom attends school. Her education is considered finished with a few courses in music, painting, and languages. She engages in light conversation, is ambitious to make a favorable impression, and sometimes belongs to philanthropic organizations, generally of a religious origin. On the other hand, girls of the middle class often continue their studies in commercial schools, high schools, and normal schools. The majority of them become enthusiastic teachers. Others with greater ambition attend the universities and remain there until obtaining degrees of doctors in philosophy, letters, chemistry, or pharmacy. A number of them become physicians, attorneys, and engineers.[5]

Formerly the supreme goal of every woman's life was marriage. Although the mother's marriage was a lifelong tragedy, she could imagine no other lot for her daughters, on the theory that any kind of marriage was better than none. The Spanish custom of long engagements still prevails, and many women still marry the men their families select for them.[6]

The Mexican Revolution gave women divorce, and this seemed to be a great boon. In 1917, President Venustiano Carranza decreed in the law on family relations that, with the granting of divorce, it was necessary to reform the family, for it formed the basis of society. To obtain divorce the couple must have lived for one year in the jurisdiction of the judge from whom they obtained it, and the innocent party, when injured by it, had a right to alimony not exceeding one third of the income of the other. Marriage was to be considered a contract and the breaking of it should injure only the breakers, not the children. The age requirement for marriage was increased to sixteen years for the man and fourteen for the woman, but the governor might make exceptions in unusual cases. The authority in the family was to be exercised jointly by husband and wife as equals. The direct care of the home belonged to the wife. She could always demand the income of her husband, which was to be used first of all to maintain the family.

A woman who lived on her own resources or had an establishment for herself, exercised a profession, held an office, or discharged a public obligation, had the right to choose a residence different from that of her family. In case of marriage, she could select and vary her residence with the consent of her husband. She had the privilege of having a different home from that of her husband if he established his habitation in an unhealthy or indecent place or transferred it to a foreign country when not in the service of his country. A woman with a lucrative profession might perform all tasks connected with it and could freely dispose of the products of her work, although she was obliged to contribute proportionally to the maintenance of the home and the education of the children.

The wife might administer her own personal possessions and the income from them, and make any kind of contract concerning them without the consent of her husband. If she gave him the right to administer them, she could demand an account from him at any time and revoke the power granted him whenever she wished. Naturally, common possessions were handled jointly.[7]

In regard to property rights for women, the Spanish laws, upon which the Mexican Constitution of 1917 was based, were always more liberal than the English. The latter gave the husband full control over his wife's antenuptial property, her personal possessions, and inheritance. He kept that right even when the marriage relations ended. In the United States the approach is toward the Latin American theories, and the English laws have had to be modified.[8] The legal standing of man and woman has been equal in Mexico since 1917, for under the constitution woman was not subject by reason of her sex to any restriction in the acquisition and exercise of her civil rights.[9]

The Constitution of 1917 is quite liberal in regard to protection of working women. In Article 123, unhealthy and dangerous occupations and overtime work are forbidden to all women, and children under sixteen years of age; neither are they to be employed in commercial establishments after ten o'clock at night. Women are protected before and after childbirth from excessive physical labor and permitted periods of rest without loss of salary. The same compensation must be paid for the same work, without regard to sex or nationality.[10] Every worker has a living wage, the rate to be determined by special commissions to be appointed in each municipality and enforced by state and federal legislation, but minimum wage was more a matter of legislation than fact. By the fall of 1931 the federal congress had not yet put this proviso into effect, and the constitutional minimum wage was not even operative in the Federal District or applied to industries under federal control, such as cotton, oil, mining, and transportation.[11]

Some of the social laws for women did not immediately accomplish what was expected of them. For example, very few women had the courage to take advantage of the divorce law, because the Catholic tradition was still strong within the family. The woman who divorced her husband did so against the opposition of all her relatives. The man might be a scoundrel, diseased, and morally corrupt, but usually her family would rather see her dead than divorced. If the husband decided to fight the divorce, his wife generally had no chance of winning it, unless her political connections were better than his.[12]

Other labor enactments were soon necessary for women, as the constitution did not meet their needs, and their entrance into industry was an inevitable condition of modern life which had come to stay, for industrial or professional work is no more harmful for women than for men, provided they receive an equitable wage, work in safe and sanitary places, have reasonable hours, and enjoy the benefits of accident, health, retirement, and other insurance. The social legislation of almost every American country includes enactments for "equality of pay for equality of work," yet they were not enforced, and the evils intended to be corrected still exist. The idea is common in Latin America that any organization of working women is opposed to the interests of employers. Until recently, on account of lack of organization, women have not succeeded in obtaining even elementary justice. They are timid before employers who, under threat of dismissal, forbid them to join a union or other group of workers.[13]

Women have, nevertheless, worked for increased privileges and have had considerable success. The first woman's congress was held in Mérida, Yucatán, in January 1916, with seven hundred delegates present. Papers were read and discussions held concerning industries suitable for the employment of women, education, and social problems.[14] On November 6, 1920, a woman's society was founded in Mexico City, similar to the Pan American Round Table of the United States, the purpose of it being to promote closer relations between American nations.[15] The next year a feminist congress met in the capital and was attended by many women. Some were cultured and others lacked education, but all were optimistic and enthusiastic, even though their efforts were ridiculed in the press by the men reporters who attended the meetings.[16] Mexico had a branch of the Pan American Association for the Advancement of Women, which held its first national convention in Mexico City in May of 1923, and the governors of twenty states promised their aid. Women's economic questions, labor conditions, social problems, civic rights, and many timely subjects were discussed.[17] In the same year the Mexican branch of the Young Women's Christian Association [YWCA] and a child welfare society, called the Pestalozzi Froebel Society, were formed.[18] The YWCA has been quite active in Mexico, where, as in many Latin American countries, it is doing most useful work.

The women students in the Medical School, desiring to cooperate with the work of education and the improvement of women, organized a student society in August of 1928 and named it for Rosalia Slaughter Morton, who had visited Mexico in the interest of the Pan American Round Table. The new organization wanted to affiliate with the Pan American Round Table, because the latter provided scholarships for Mexican women doctors and women students of medicine.[19] Two years later the seventh Congress of the Women's International League for Peace and Freedom was held in Mexico City, at which time women's responsibility for peace and various international problems were discussed.[20]

Some effort was made by Mexican women to organize for industrial purposes in 1931, when a cooperative association, known as the Society for the Protection of Mexican Women, was formed in the capital. Its constitution empowered it to establish and operate such commercial, industrial, and agricultural enterprises as were considered necessary to provide employment for women.[21]

The very important Federal Labor Law adopted in 1931 was partly, at least, the result of the influence of various women's organizations. The law provided that women, and minors between the ages of twelve and sixteen, should never be compelled to work overtime; women and minors were not to be employed in night shifts, in places where intoxicating drinks were sold, or in unhealthful or dangerous trades, except where, according to the opinion of competent authorities, sufficient precautions had been taken to protect the workers; and they were not to be permitted to work underground in mines. Expectant mothers were not to be allowed to engage in work involving great physical exertion three months prior to childbirth. They might have a vacation with full pay, consisting of eight days before and one month after the birth of their children and, if still unable to work, could be given leave without pay. When returning, they were to have rest periods during the day to care for their children, and every establishment with more than fifty women was to have a nursery. Women were to work eight hours a day and have one day of rest in seven. Since Article 123 of the constitution had not been enforced, provision was now made for minimum wages and equality of wages between the sexes. While almost all the states passed enforcement laws, in 1932 minimum wage was effective in only one state, San Luis Potosí, and in the chief city of the state of Jalisco. In the other provinces the towns did not establish committees to determine the rates; consequently, the acts remained practically dead-letter laws. Mexico has had public employment agencies for a number of years, relief funds for unemployment, and, in 1934, started projects for better housing of workers.[22]

The Homestead Decree of August 4, 1923, granted widows of Mexican nationality who were heads of families the same rights as men to take up a certain amount of national or uncultivated land not reserved by the government. The amount varied from twenty-five to five hundred hectares, depending upon the location and capacity for irrigation. Title would be given to the land after two years of cultivation or stock raising by the person taking up the claim.[23]

President Emilio Portes Gil believed that women must first be prepared to hold public positions, which had always been monopolized by men; that they must be educated to discharge the functions of such offices efficiently and be collaborators with men; and that they must be educated like men. When the president was given a list of many professional women, doctors, lawyers, and literary women, he read it carefully and said he was glad to know that so many women were ready to work with men for the social advancement of the country.[24]

The interpretation of citizenship for women caused much discussion. The first article of the constitution states that "every person in the United States shall enjoy all guarantees granted by this Constitution." Elodia Cruz believed that the word "all" had nothing restrictive in it and did not include men only. She also maintained that Article 34 on citizenship spoke in a general manner, as did all other parts of the document.[25] Dr. Puig Casauranc was of the same opinion. On the other hand, Licenciado Ignacio García Téllez believed the opposite and said that the constitution did not intend women to vote.[26] President Portes Gil declared: "Our laws were made . . . by men for the benefit of men. . . . When the Constitution was promulgated, certainly it purposed to confine the use of the vote only to men."[27] Some men feared to give women the right of suffrage because of their religion. A gentleman who was a Mason of high degree said: "Twenty-five thousand Mexican women coming before the Chamber [of Congress] to ask the vote for women! How horrible! It means that, if they obtain their object, we shall soon have a bishop as president." Yet it was noticed that some Masons sought wives educated in convents.[28]

Soon after President Lázaro Cárdenas took office, Margarita Robles de Mendoza, a teacher, sociologist, feminist, and delegate to the Inter-American Commission of Women in Washington, asked him whether Article 34 should not be interpreted as giving the right of citizenship to women. On March 20, 1935, the Department of Government answered that, according to its opinion, there were no reasons, technical or otherwise, for denying Mexican women citizenship in the republic. In his message to Congress on September 1 of the same year President Cárdenas also admitted this by saying: "The working woman has the right to take part in elections, since the Constitution puts her on equal footing with man, a fact confirmed by some of the contributory legislation in force: the civil laws, which give her the same prerogatives as man; the labor laws, which grant equal rights; and the agrarian laws, which concede to her equal benefits."[29]

Now, according to law, a foreign woman who has contracted matrimony with a Mexican, and may have established or may establish a residence within national territory, becomes a citizen by naturalization and retains her Mexican nationality even after the matrimonial relationship has been dissolved. Also, the Mexican woman who marries a foreigner does not lose her nationality because of her marriage. The tendency at present on the American continents is to confer independent citizenship on women.[30]

Mexican women today do not think that their sphere is confined to domestic economy only. Despite family opposition and social taboos, they are breaking away from their traditional lives. Probably the first profession open to them was teaching, and in that field they have done pioneer work. As in other countries, they are now intimately connected with public life and have come to participate in all social work from manual labor to intellectual tasks, and new occupations are constantly opening for them. Women have served satisfactorily in the secretariat of public instruction, the tribunal of minors, the council of defense, social positions, and in the administration of justice. Elodia Cruz has made a case for them to take part in elections and hold public offices. Some women are better educated than men, she says, and yet do not vote. They work in offices, shops, and factories, and perform their labor well. Unmarried women frequently support parents, brothers, sisters, and relatives but still do not vote, while unoccupied and vagrant men are not excluded from the suffrage.[31]

Yucatán was among the first Mexican states to give women the vote in local elections, and recently several of them have played prominent parts in its political life.[32] Since 1924, when the revolutionist Rafael Nieto was governor, San Luis Potosí has granted women the privilege of taking part in municipal elections and holding office under certain conditions if they know how to read and write. The next year they were given all the rights of suffrage. This did not apply, however, to members of religious associations and women being educated and cared for by such organizations.[33] A law was also passed in the state of Chiapas in 1925 giving women equal political rights with men.[34] In 1934 a restricted suffrage was granted to women in the state of Guanajuato to vote for local deputies and the governor, but the greater part of them was excluded because only professional women, property owners, or those who had commercial establishments and other industries might vote. Recently, the states of Vera Cruz, Durango, Tamaulipas, and Hidalgo have followed the example of those states in granting women suffrage in local elections.[35] Women were permitted to vote in the primaries held on April 5, 1936, when senators for the national congress, governors of several states, and deputies in local legislatures were chosen to represent the National Revolutionary Party. It was reported that 2,750 women voted in the Federal District at that time.[36]

Nothing definite was done about citizenship of women in 1937, as Elodia Cruz still insisted that Article 34 of the constitution should be reformed or clarified. She said that, if it were interpreted justly, no reform would be needed, but, since it was given a masculine interpretation, reform was necessary to remove future doubts. She, therefore, urged women to organize and petition the governmental authorities to have it changed.[37]

President Cárdenas took a liberal attitude toward women. In 1934 he permitted the women's section of the National Revolutionary Party to begin a nationwide fight for the vote and publicly stated that he would aid the movement. Pressure was immediately placed upon the state governors to help the cause and, as already mentioned, a number of states granted women local suffrage.[38] In 1938, Cárdenas announced to the nation: "Only the Revolution . . . has achieved for the Mexican woman a complete rescue from her social inferiority, obtaining the constitutional reform necessary to grant her rights and functions of citizenship that put her on the same plane of dignity with man."[39]

To improve the situation a constitutional amendment giving women the vote was drafted in 1938. It was passed by the Senate and House and referred to the states for ratification. Although President Cárdenas, in his message to Congress on September 1 of that year, urged that prompt action be taken, the amendment has not yet become law. Since all the states have not ratified it, the revolution has not yet granted woman a complete rescue from her social inferiority.[40]

Without every member of their sex having the vote, Mexican women realize that they cannot obtain all that is needed relative to social legislation, as they do not have a legal weapon. Frequently, Mexican husbands are Marxists outside and feudalists within their homes, and politicians fight tenaciously, with every weapon in their power, the efforts of organized women to secure the vote and obtain really effective laws to protect themselves.[41]

Despite opposition, a strong feminist movement has sprung up in Mexico in recent years. Some masculine writers call it "the bloody struggle between men and women," yet no violence has occurred in this struggle of women to be respected and treated like human beings and conscientious adults.[42] The most important organization is the United Front for Women's Rights, established in 1935. It has had a stormy career in its efforts to centralize the work of hundreds of women's groups throughout the country, which by themselves lacked strength and a definite plan. Today it has a membership of more than fifty thousand women of all social classes, even pure-blooded Indians, and includes some eight hundred organizations.

When Indian women become interested in such work, they are very active. Even their husbands and brothers have approved of their efforts to organize, built meetinghouses for them, and aided them financially. One time, when a protest meeting was held in Tamaulipas against the discrimination shown them by a local politician, the women paraded down the main street with their banners and posters, and behind them came all the men of the village, because they sympathized with them.[43]

The platform of the United Front has been endorsed by the National Council of Women Suffrage. It has a simple program, which even unorganized women are asked to support. It comprises the right to vote and be voted for without restrictions; a modification in the Civil Code so that women may have the same legal rights as men; a change in the Federal Labor Law in the interest of feminine labor; modification in the Agrarian Code to permit all women to receive land under the same conditions as men; the protection of women government employees by statute; incorporation of indigenous women into the social and political life of the nation; establishment of work centers for unemployed women; protection of infancy and children; and a widespread program of cultural education for women.

The success of the United Front depended greatly upon its general secretary, María del Refugio García, who had defied President Díaz when still a child. Active in organizing women, she found Carranza a weak, hesitating liberal, fearing any adequate reforms. In despair she turned to [Alvaro] Obregón. As a woman employee of the government, María realized the need for organizing her sex, because the very politicians who pretended to be revolutionists opposed women's efforts. At that time it had only been possible to form spontaneous groups here and there without any united program.

Obregón and [Plutarco Elías] Calles did not keep their promises. Consequently, in 1931 a woman's congress was called by the National Revolutionary Party [PNR]. María went and publicly accused Calles on account of his puppet president, [Pascual] Ortíz Rubio, and for murdering country people. The police imprisoned her, the news spread rapidly through the city, [and] thousands of women surrounded the jail. The police had to be summoned for fear of a riot, and María was hurriedly released. In 1935 she began a nationwide campaign for the organization of the United Front for Women's Rights. Two years later she ran for federal deputy from her district of Uruapan against four candidates who were supported by the PNR. It was reported from reliable sources that she won the election, but at the last minute the party declared that a woman could not hold such an office until the constitution was revised. María can bring more women together at one time than any other person, and politicians watch her activities.[44]

The executive committee of the National Revolutionary Party recognizes the full rights of women in the economic order. Its program provides for equality of rights and occasions for women to work in the field, shop, or public office; equal remuneration and guarantees for both sexes for equal work of equal quality; equal opportunity for their education in their specialties compatible with their sex and direction of the home; absolute equality of civil rights in connection with the administration and direction of the home; and equal civil rights in popular elections for members of *ayuntamientos*, local chambers, and the national congress. The party fights all attempts to exploit women in any form. It favors the establishment of houses for children of workers, maternity homes, dispensaries for the needy, workhouses for abandoned women, and a legal defender of women to protect their rights. It believes in the privilege of all classes of women to organize—country women, city workers, women teachers, servers of the state, and professional women.[45]

The National Revolutionary Party was reorganized in 1939 and named [the] Party of Mexican Revolution (PRM). It now has a very active section of Feminine Action with delegates and subcommittees over the whole country. As it thinks it is useless to prohibit the organization of women any longer, it recognizes their legal citizenship and right to vote. Yet, in 1939, Congress would not let women go to the polls. Women believed that political intrigue was in back of this; therefore, their fight for the vote still continued. They now intend to appear at the polls every time a national election is held to show their dissatisfaction until the vote is obtained.⁴⁶. . .

For the first time, women took an active part in politics in the 1940 presidential campaign, although they were not permitted to vote. Many of them worked for Juan Andreu Almazán, the conservative candidate, wholeheartedly. On many occasions members of the Partido Feminino Idealista rose long before daybreak to go out and distribute propaganda for the Revolutionary Party of National Unification (PRUN). Some of them were imprisoned for this. They were very active supporters of Almazán in 1940.⁴⁷

Journalism has played a great part in the new freedom for Mexican women—an occupation which they themselves have helped to develop. Mexico can be called the "birthplace of American journalism" because it had the first printing press early in the sixteenth century. There have been women journalists almost continuously since the widow of Pedro Ocharte, the daughter of Juan Pablos, early printer of New Spain, took over the establishment of her husband after his death in 1594. It was not until the present time, however, that journalism existed in the modern sense of the term.

The pioneer among women journalists is Emilia Enríquez de Rivera, who established her well-known magazine for women, *El Hogar* (The home), thus opening a new era in women's periodicals. *El Hogar* compares favorably with the leading magazines of its type in the United States. Señorita Rivera assisted her father, an editor of a small magazine, and after his death was without means and preparation for a career. An old friend of her father's loaned her a small sum of money to start her magazine. In a little dingy room with an old handpress she worked alone and brought out, on September 13, 1913, the first issue of the first modern magazine for women of Mexico. She has seen it grow from a small sheet to a good-sized periodical of fifty-some pages, requiring a staff of sixty to produce it. Among its contributors are the best writers of Mexico. Señorita Rivera, a lady of poise and striking personality, is still the leading Mexican woman journalist and is known in the United States and other countries. . . .

Although Mexican women have been slower to adopt professions than women in the United States, they take their careers very seriously, and every year more are preparing for them. When they hold public posts, no matter how small, they cause improvement. On May 21, 1922, Dolores Arriaga de Buck was elected magistrate of the Supreme Court of Justice of the state of San Luis Potosí. Her candidacy was supported by the governor, who said that he was glad his state had chosen the first woman judge of the republic.[48] The next year two women, Rosa Torre and Eusebia Pérez, were made members of the city council of Mérida and had the support of the Liga Feminista, similar to the League of Women Voters in the United States.[49] Soon, two women councilors appeared in the municipal council of the capital; one was sent there by the press and the other by the mothers' societies of that city. Elvira Carrillo Puerto was the first woman deputy to the national congress.[50]. . .

Mexico has the distinction of being the first Latin American country to honor a woman with the diplomatic appointment of minister, although there have been several women consuls. In 1935, Palma Guillén was chosen minister to Colombia, and was the first female diplomat to serve on an American continent in an American republic.[51]. . .

In 1939, Aurora Mesa was municipal president of the town of Chilpancingo in the state of Guerrero. She is a charming, soft-voiced woman who, during her short term, brought water pipes into the town for the first time, paved the streets, reorganized the schools and hospitals, and left money in a formerly empty treasury.[52]. . .

Since 1912, schools for girls have been established in arts and crafts, vocational education, trade, commerce, and industry. In 1924, Mexico City had five trade schools for young women, and only three for men. The reason that there were only three trade schools for men was that they had a better chance to learn trades outside of schools than women. One of four commercial schools was exclusively for women, and it conducted both day and night classes. Many women attended evening schools where they were taught elementary subjects and instructed in the work of various small industries.[53]. . .

More interest is shown in child welfare and hygiene. In 1922 a family welfare exposition was held, during which villages were visited in two cars provided by the president and talks made on hygiene, child care, food values, and community activities.[54] The next year a Children's Aid Society was organized by a group of women in Mexico City, Señora Obregón, the president's wife, being one of them. A home was established for one hundred newsboys and the society was allied with the Humane Society in the United States.[55]

Campaigns have been carried on against illiteracy, and in 1923 Eulalia Guzmán was director of the committee on illiteracy organized under the Department of Public Education. She was very successful in getting six thousand middle-class men and women and two thousand students to volunteer to teach the illiterate. One young woman taught two hundred of them to read and write.[56]

Women have been very active in the crusade for their own social betterment, and now the government has become interested in it. In

February 1937 the first National Congress on Industrial Hygiene was held in Mexico City. It was attended by 576 delegates, representing all official departments and many organizations. Over four hundred resolutions were adopted and referred to the proper governmental departments for action.[57] On June 21 of the same year a Child Welfare Bureau was established as a department of government, to supervise all social welfare work for mothers and children in public or private institutions.[58] The next year a League of Mental Hygiene was founded in the capital.[59] In July 1939 a National Committee for Mother and Child was established in Mexico City, and Dr. Guillermo Lechuga was made chairman. A hearty response came from all parts of the republic, and the Ministry of Public Health has promised to support the committee's work for the welfare of the Mexican people.[60] Mexico also has a National Department of Education, with a secretary of education in the president's cabinet,[61] and in some respects in the matter of social legislation is ahead of the United States.

Women are now being educated to confront the problems of life, and women's movements, which at first were merely gatherings of higher-class ladies for charitable purposes, have gradually developed considerable independence. Women are now working out their own problems and arousing interest in social betterment, community service, education of the poor, and many other vital questions affecting their country. When they obtain the vote in all parts of the republic, which is at present their chief goal and which, no doubt, is only a matter of time, they will accomplish much for the welfare of their sex and be a decisive factor in human destiny.

**Notes**

1. Verna Carleton Millan, *Mexico Reborn* (Boston, 1939), p. 152.
2. Ibid., p. 166.
3. Margarita Robles de Mendoza, *La evolución de la mujer en México* (Mexico, 1931), pp. 19–20, 29.
4. Millan, *Mexico Reborn*, p. 158.
5. Samuel Guy Inman, "The Feminist Movement in Latin America," *Pan American Union Bulletin*, April 1922, Vol. 54, pp. 353–354.
6. Millan, *Mexico Reborn*, p. 158.
7. C. Venustiano Carranza, *Ley sobre relaciones familiares* (Mexico, 1917), pp. 3–71; Dr. Francisco Cosentini, *Declaración de los derechos y obligaciones civiles de la mujer y del hogar* (Mexico, 1930), arts. 3, 16, 17, 19–22, 24, 27–31, 33, 63, 69, 93.
8. *Pan American Union Bulletin*, March 1925, Vol. 59, pt. I, pp. 232–240.
9. Cosentini, *Declaración*, art. 1; *México código civil*, art. 2.
10. H. N. Branch, "The Mexican Constitution of 1917 Compared with the Constitution of 1857," in the *Annals of the American Academy of Political and Social Sciences* (Philadelphia, 1917), pp. 94–96.

11. Barbara Nachtrieb Armstrong, *Insuring the Essentials* (New York, 1932), p. 111.

12. Millan, *Mexico Reborn*, pp. 161–162.

13. *Pan American Union Bulletin*, March 1927, Vol. 61, pt. I, pp. 259–261.

14. Ibid., January 1916, Vol. 42, pp. 147–148.

15. Ibid., January 1920, Vol. 50, p. 114.

16. Robles de Mendoza, *La evolución de la mujer*, p. 19.

17. *Pan American Union Bulletin*, June 1923, Vol. 56, pp. 630–631.

18. Ibid., August 1923, Vol. 57, p. 211.

19. Ibid., October 1928, Vol. 62, pt. II, p. 1191.

20. Ibid., October 1930, Vol. 64, pt. II, p. 1078.

21. Ibid., January 1931, Vol. 65, p. 105.

22. Ibid., January 1932, Vol. 66, pp. 67–68; ibid., July 1935, Vol. 69, pp. 523–535; Armstrong, *Insuring the Essentials*, p. 111. See Rudolf Broda, "Minimum Wage Laws in Some Mexican States," *International Labor Review*, July 1930. Minimum wage does not work much better in South America, except in Uruguay, where there is an attempt to enforce it for employees of large farms and cattle ranches. Armstrong, *Insuring the Essentials*, pp. 112–113.

23. *Pan American Bulletin*, December 1923, Vol. 57, p. 624.

24. Robles de Mendoza, *La evolución de la mujer*, pp. 58–59, 61.

25. Elodia Cruz, *Los políticos de la mujer en México* (Mexico, 1937), p. 18.

26. Robles de Mendoza, *La evolución de la mujer*, p. 26.

27. Ibid., p. 60.

28. Ibid., pp. 84–85.

29. *Pan American Union Bulletin*, May 1936, Vol. 70, pp. 426–427.

30. *Ley mexicana de nacionalidad*, arts. 2, 4; *Diario oficial*, January 20, 1934, No. 17, p. 238; *Pan American Union Bulletin*, July 1936, Vol. 70, p. 542; ibid., October 1932, Vol. 66, p. 736.

31. Cruz, *Las políticos de la mujer*, p. 19.

32. Millan, *Mexico Reborn*, p. 168.

33. *Pan American Union Bulletin*, March 1923, Vol. 56, p. 309.

34. Ibid., August 1925, Vol. 59, pt. II, pp. 842–843.

35. Millan, *Mexico Reborn*, p. 168.

36. *Pan American Union Bulletin*, May 1936, Vol. 70, p. 427.

37. Cruz, *Las políticos de la mujer*, pp. 19–22.

38. Millan, *Mexico Reborn*, p. 168.

39. Virginia Prewett, *Reportage on Mexico* (New York, 1941), p. 179.

40. *Pan American Union Bulletin*, March 1940, Vol. 7, p. 165; Prewett, *Reportage on Mexico*, p. 179. So far [as of 1942] only six American republics enjoy complete suffrage: the United States (1920), Uruguay (1932), Brazil (1932), Cuba (1934), El Salvador (1939), and Chile (1940). In Peru (1933) women have the right to vote in municipal elections. Women in Panama voted for the provincial councils on October 5, 1941.

41. Millan, *Mexico Reborn*, pp. 160–161.

42. Robles de Mendoza, *La evolución de la mujer*, pp. 97–98.

43. Millan, *Mexico Reborn*, pp. 163–164.

44. Ibid., pp. 164–167.

45. Antonio Luna Arroyo, *La mujer mexicana en la lucha social* (Mexico, 1936), pp. 20, 30–31.

46. Millan, *Mexico Reborn*, pp. 168–169.

47. Prewett, *Reportage on Mexico*, pp. 212, 228.

48. *Pan American Union Bulletin*, August 1922, Vol. 55, p. 199.

49. Ibid., February 1923, Vol. 56, p. 203.

50. Robles de Mendoza, *La evolución de la mujer*, pp. 35, 21

51. *Pan American Union Bulletin*, April 1935, Vol. 69, pp. 356–359.

52. Millan, *Mexico Reborn*, p. 169.

53. *Pan American Union Bulletin*, April 1913, Vol. 36, p. 640; ibid., December 1922, Vol. 55, p. 629; ibid., October and December 1924, Vol. 58, pt. II, pp. 1059, 1275; ibid., December 1916, Vol. 43, p. 805.

54. Ibid., September 1922, Vol. 55, p. 305; ibid., December 1922, Vol. 55, p. 634.

55. Ibid., April 1923, Vol. 56, p. 415.

56. Ibid., September 1922, Vol. 55, p. 305; ibid., June 1923, Vol. 56, pp. 580–581.

57. Ibid., June 1937, Vol. 71, p. 511.

58. Ibid., September 1937, vol. 71, p. 729.

59. Ibid., July 1938, Vol. 72, p. 434.

60. Ibid., May 1940, pp. 415–416.

61. For the work of the department, see Moisés Sáenz and Herbert I. Priestley, *Some Mexican Problems* (Chicago, 1926), p. 64 et seq.

# 6 Daphne Patai ◆ Jorge Amado: Champion of Women's Sexual Freedom

*Through his novels—several of which are available in English transla-tions and are immensely popular in the United States—Jorge Amado cre-ated the image of the Brazilian woman as the sensual* bella mulata *(beautiful mulatto woman). The Amado legacy became flesh when Sonya Braga, one of Brazil's leading actresses, starred in two hit movies based on his stories,* Gabriela, Clove and Cinnamon *and* Dona Flor and Her Two Husbands. *Amado has been hailed a champion of women's sexual rights because his heroines escape the strict behavioral code of marian-ismo and become free through sex. But Daphne Patai, a professor of Por-tuguese and women's studies at the University of Massachusetts, warns that there is more to reading a novel than finding a comfortable chair and a quiet place because even fictional images carry gender-coded mean-ings. In her analysis of Amado's novel* Tereza Batista, *Patai examines how the reading audience comes to accept and even to vicariously par-ticipate in the repeated rape of a twelve-year-old girl.*

Oscillating between sociopolitical criticism and romantic lyricism, Jorge Amado has published more than twenty novels. His works have appeared in numerous translations and he is without doubt the Brazilian novelist most widely read outside of Brazil.

Amado's partisanship is well known, and to this day he considers himself a champion of the oppressed. Not surprisingly, his novels have often been criticized for their biased characterization, their sympathetic treatment of the poor and downtrodden matched by the irony and ridicule heaped on the rich and powerful. Yet in Amado's fictional representation of women, as an analysis of his 1972 best-seller *Tereza Batista* reveals, we have a good example of what Fredric Jameson has called an ideologi-cal double standard.

With the publication of *Gabriela, Clove and Cinnamon* (1958), which was a best-seller not only in Brazil but in the United States as well, Amado's work took an openly humoristic and increasingly romantic turn. *Gabriela* was the first of Amado's four novels (to date) having a female protagonist. Amado continued to focus on women's life in Brazil in *Dona Flor and Her Two Husbands* (1966), and in this novel there is a much

From "Jorge Amado's Heroines and the Ideological Double Standard" in *Women in Latin American Literature: A Symposium* (Amherst, MA: International Area Studies Program, University of Massachusetts, 1979), 15–36. Reprinted by permission of the author.

greater emphasis on magic and a corresponding diminution of social protest and criticism.

In writing a third novel with a female protagonist, Amado himself said: "Gabriela and Dona Flor are characters with whom readers easily identify; hence their popularity. With Tereza Batista I tried to create a third image of the Brazilian woman—sensual, romantic, courageous, long-suffering, decent."[1] This novel, *Tereza Batista: Home from the Wars* (published in the United States in 1975) is more complex than *Gabriela* or *Dona Flor* from the point of view of narrative structure and technique, but its theme is familiar: Amado returns to the depiction of a young girl— twelve years old—who is sold to a man.

In his earlier novels, too, Amado had often adopted the tone and techniques of popular Brazilian poetry (*literatura de cordel*). In *Tereza Batista*, however, the novel is actually given the structure of five more or less separate episodes, or *folhetos*, each of which is a kind of imitation, although of course in prose, of the ballads so popular in Brazil and sold on street corners and in marketplaces, especially in Brazil's poverty-stricken northeastern region.[2]

Although the five episodes that make up the novel do not occur in chronological order in terms of Tereza Batista's life story, for the purpose of summarizing the plot they can be rearranged as follows: Tereza, not yet thirteen years old, is sold by her aunt to Justo, a brutal and crude man, owner of a local store. Justo is wealthy but not a member of the traditional landed aristocracy. Tereza is brave and a fighter, and she resists Justo's efforts to rape and subdue her. In lengthy, detailed scenes the reader witnesses Justo's success in terrorizing and taming Tereza. After two years of constant tyranny and sexual abuse, graphically depicted in the novel, Tereza is seduced by a young student, Dan, and discovers sexual pleasure with him. When they are found together by Justo, to protect herself and the young man from Justo's vengeance, Tereza kills Justo. After this, through the intervention of Emiliano Guedes, a powerful local landowner forty years older than she, Tereza is released from jail. Emiliano sets her up as mistress of his home (in a different home, of course, from the one in which his family lives), slowly "raising her little by little to his level"— as Amado tells us.[3] They live together for six years and, on the verge of a new life, in which Emiliano will openly acknowledge his life with Tereza, he dies in the midst of their lovemaking. Tereza then goes to work as a dancer in a bar in another town (this is the episode with which the novel opens), and she falls in love with Janu, a sailor who is married and feels a bond of loyalty to his wife. They part, and Tereza throws herself into dangerous work. With a group of prostitutes helping her, she inoculates the local population against a smallpox epidemic after the doctor and nurse have fled from the town. Later still, Tereza finally reaches Salvador, the capital of Bahia, where she works in a brothel, under the impression that Janu has died at sea. Here she organizes a strike of the prostitutes—called the closed-basket strike—against some local city officials who wish to move them to slum housing in order to make a killing on the rent. Through a series of adventures, having to do also with the presence of some American battleships in Bahia just at this time, the prostitutes win their strike. At the end of the novel, with Tereza on the verge of marrying one of her suitors (out of sympathy and fatigue), Janu appears and claims her.

*Tereza Batista* contains familiar elements that characterize Amado's work as a whole: the strong emphasis on colloquial Portuguese, lyricism in the treatment of love, social critique, insistence on the magical atmosphere of Bahia, satirical portraits of the upper class and the bourgeoisie contrasted with the sympathetic treatment of the poor, horror and humor, and the graphic depiction of sex.

Although Amado quite rightly insists upon the inevitably political nature of literature,[4] in some ways he claims to be an objective reporter. [He has] said, "I consider myself more of a journalist than a novelist, because I do not add anything to my writing about the people of Bahia that does not already exist in their lives. I simply transfer the reality of their lives to a literary plane and recreate the ambience of Bahia, and that is all."[5] But these words, while clearly indicating Amado's commitment to a mimetic literature, glide smoothly over the serious problem of the writer's relation to his or her material, for a process of selection and construction invariably accompanies the representation of reality in a novel. It has often been pointed out that novels, "in their total value systems, *interpret* . . . reality," and that "reality" in literature is never "merely descriptive or reflective but moral and creative."[6]

When we initially approach a novel, we are prepared to accept, at least provisionally, the world which it will create. But our assent and acceptance are subject to withdrawal as our vision deepens of what the novel is defining as "reality." It happens that the world of *Tereza Batista* is ostensibly one of protest against the oppression of the poor and, especially, of women. But things are not always what they seem in literature. The term "ideological double standard" has been used by Fredric Jameson to describe certain kinds of adventure stories in which the author allows the reader to vicariously experience and satisfy the taste for violence, while ostensibly making the practice of such violence the object of a political and social critique.[7] Lionel Trilling also discusses certain books in which, as he says, "the pleasure in the cruelty is protected and licensed by moral indignation. In other instances, moral indignation, which has been said to be the favorite emotion of the middle class, may be in itself an exquisite pleasure."[8] Other critics too have touched on this problem. Frank O'Connor has asked how, if the writer is not one of the exploited, does he or she describe them without being one of the exploiters?[9]

In *Tereza Batista*, a conflict of this type may be at the heart of many of the contradictions apparent throughout the novel. One of the most blatant instances of the ideological double standard occurs in the extensive rape scenes. Because the novel does not follow Tereza's life chronologically, when we meet her in Part One she is already a vivacious, courageous adult woman—whose sexual attractiveness is especially stressed. This image cannot help but color the reader's experience of Part Two and the way in which the reader views Justo's rape of the twelve-year-old Tereza. In the scenes which depict this ongoing brutalization in great detail, the narrative concentrates not on Tereza, but on Justo's experience—his thoughts, his reactions, his pleasure, his anger. Much more attention is lavished on this grotesque character than on the terror and pain of his victims. While one may defend this on the grounds that Amado characteristically prefers depicting action rather than states of being, it is nonetheless true that narrative focus establishes the important character in a scene.[10] Without a doubt, this character is Justo throughout the most violent chapters of Part One, and it is he who emerges, to some extent, as an individual in these scenes, while Tereza is little more than merely one girl in a long line of his victims, distinguished from the others only by her ability to fight and her efforts to defend herself—efforts which are insufficient.

The narrative perspective, by focusing in this way on Justo, urges a kind of complicity on the reader. "The observation of evil is a fascinating occupation," write [Max] Horkheimer and [Theodor W.] Adorno. "But this observation implies a measure of secret agreement."[11] Bertolt Brecht developed his concept of the alienation effect in drama precisely to prevent the spectator from empathizing so much that a critical reaction would become impossible. Not empathy, but the ability to establish causal relations and thereby deflate the notion of "inexorable fate" is the aim of Brecht's epic theater,[12] and, although we are dealing with a different form, it is worth noting that the novel too may encourage us to view a particular fate as inexorable and unavoidable.

Jorge Amado avoids focusing the same critical light on the treatment Tereza undergoes at the hands of various men that he did bring to bear on his depiction of the deliberate politics of both disease and prostitution. The rape scenes in *Tereza Batista* not only dwell graphically on Justo's sexual pleasure in a way that is bound to stimulate the appetites of certain readers,[13] but, moreover, convey a sense of business as usual in the entire proceedings. The history of Justo's previous rapes reinforces the inevita-

bility of the outcome. In addition, by depicting some of Tereza's predecessors as having insatiable sexual appetites, which Justo presumably
awakened, Amado conforms to the worst clichés used to justify men's
brutality to women.

A still more interesting, if less violent, case of the ideological double
standard appears in the novel. Amado "raises" Tereza's value in the
reader's eyes by insisting on the fact that she alone was different, in some
way unapproachable even when converted into a virtual slave. It is suggested that for this reason she was able to "retain" Justo's interest for
more than two years—and the reader is clearly meant to respond to this
information in a positive way and to take it as a sign of Tereza's unusual
worth. Thus, the very devices used to valorize Tereza Batista in fact have
as their point of departure conventional attitudes which demean women;
that is, Tereza is a heroine to the extent that she is unlike other women (or
female children) who—the implication is inescapable—deserve their fate
at the hands of brutal men and, even more, grow to like this treatment. In
addition, the point of view from which we appreciate Tereza's special
value is, of course, Justo's—that is, we are meant to appreciate that she
*holds* his interest. It is worthwhile pondering Amado's attitude toward
this brutal character whose judgment of Tereza the reader is invited to
share. This is precisely an instance of appearing to criticize certain practices while in fact deriving a value system from them, and it is characteristic of Amado's depiction of the relations between men and women.

The chapter describing Justo's lack of interest in or recognition of
women's capacity for sexual pleasure implies that, were he a more con-
siderate lover, his rapes would not be rapes. Given the fact that he either
buys or merely takes (and in either case rapes) the young girls he wants,
his lack of concern for their sexual enjoyment seems like rather arcane
grounds for subjecting him to criticism. But by even raising the issue,
Amado paves the way for the inference that this is his principal offense;
that is, were he to take these girls and yet show some consideration for
their sexual response, everything would be all right. However, given the
total lack of choice of his victims, it is only degrees of abuse that are
under discussion. One critic has pointed out that "*the opposite of cruelty
is freedom. The victim does not need the ultimately destructive gift of
kindness when offered within the cruel relationship. He [or she] needs
freedom from that relationship.*"[14] Amado has failed to perceive this important distinction, as revealed again in his description of Emiliano, who
takes Tereza out of the whorehouse and then wins her over as well, and
whom the reader is invited to view in a positive light.

Tereza's first love is Dan, cowardly and treacherous, but also a talented seducer hardly of the *machão* type—and consequently so offensive

to Justo's vision of what masculinity should be. Their lovemaking, although described as a mutual discovery, abounds in traditional images of masculinity and femininity. Tereza views Dan as an angel, although hardly a sexless one. He is described, on their first night together, with his "sword upraised," his "gleaming sword"—while Tereza is a "rose" (p. 206). "The flower throbbed, the sword flamed" (p. 207), Amado writes of their lovemaking. Yet the relationship of sword to flower can only be one of destruction—quite apart from the status of these images as clichés. Again, it is only through Dan's ministrations that Tereza, like a phoenix—the image is Amado's—is reborn and finds the courage to rebel against Justo. Thus, although Dan is depicted as a coward and Tereza as a warrior, her courage is seen as a response to his love and, more specifically, as her desire to protect him from the humiliation of having to comply with Justo's demand that Dan perform fellatio on him. Justo's choice of a "punishment" for Dan is interesting too, for it reveals that even if Dan was able to act as a male in relation to Tereza, nonetheless in relation to Justo he is to take the role of the female. Simultaneously, this suggests the hidden degradation attributed to the female role.

Tereza's relationship with Emiliano, the oldest and most powerful of the Guedes family, represents her greatest success in terms of upward social mobility. After this she will return to her own people through her attachment to Janu, the sailor. But once again, in describing Tereza's six years with Emiliano, Amado "valorizes" Tereza by stressing a man's interest in her—a man of high social standing this time. All men want Tereza Batista, as Amado reiterates throughout the novel, but Tereza's good taste, beauty, loyalty, intelligence, and tact all serve to make her an adequate partner for a wealthy and powerful man such as Emiliano.[15] There is, furthermore, something in the description of Tereza's initial reaction to Emiliano which suggests the mythical fascination of the female with the strongest male in the tribe. Amado describes Tereza's recognition that Emiliano is superior to Justo; she appreciates Emiliano's gift for command, his "masterful gestures"; he represents a "proud and lofty vision" to her, contrasting sharply with Justo's sheer animality (pp. 304–5).

But even after six years of life with Emiliano, Amado still has Tereza think in stereotyped female terms: she wonders how she will be able to live, once he has died, now that she can never again hear his "masterful step and lordly voice" (p. 304). Thus, Tereza still responds as an inferior to a superior, a weak woman to a strong man. In addition, Amado regularly falls back on verbs which describe precisely a relationship of ownership and domination, such as "possess," "forbid," and "permit." Throughout their relationship, then, the contrast in status between Tereza and Emiliano is explicit.

As Tereza's "value" was affirmed by Justo's continuing interest in her, so it is once again affirmed through Emiliano's interest—even more valuable given his superior status. But although, unlike Justo, he did not wear a chain of gold rings representing the maidenheads of girls under thirteen who had been his victims, Emiliano was nonetheless Justo's greatest competitor. Amado writes: "The three brothers gave him plenty of competition, especially Emiliano Guedes. No girl ever came out of his sugarmill in one piece. Not a single gold ring on [Justo's] necklace had come out of the Guedes canefields" (p. 120).

Emiliano, a representative of the very powers Amado theoretically criticizes—the rich landowners, industrialists, and other capitalists—is nonetheless sympathetically drawn in the novel, mainly, it seems, as a means of indicating Tereza's special worth and deserved ascension in the social order. Amado's irony and even open sarcasm are not directed against Emiliano, nor against the total control such men have over the lives of women. Where irony is put at the service of social criticism, as it is throughout the novel, a lack of irony tends to act as affirmation, however inadvertent. By inference, the reader comes to see the areas in which Amado accepts and reinforces a particular status quo—and the main area in which this consistently occurs in Amado's novels relates to male dominance.

Two qualities define Tereza Batista from the beginning of the novel to the end: "she was made for love and when it came to loving she didn't fool around"; and "maybe because of what she went through as a child, she never could stand to see a man hit a woman" (p. 5). Yet in this novel we see a heroic figure who is nonetheless assimilated into a traditional male vision of femininity. The book ends with the reassertion of the primal claim of love and biology upon women. Tereza's heroic status (created by the use of epithets such as "Tereza the Fighter" as well as by her struggle against various forms of evil and oppression) makes all the more striking her complete submission to Janu, for it affirms how much of a man he must be to dominate such a woman. Despite Tereza's overt heroism, then, the underlying affirmation within the novel relates to men's continued domination of women, and at the end there is not so much a meeting of equals as a heroine transformed into a mere semitraditional woman whose fate is sealed when she invites Janu to "make a baby" with her.

Is it the case, then, that Amado, devoted as he is to realism, as well as to fantasy, could not have written otherwise? On the contrary, the variety of possible positions in relation to any given reality always implies an "otherwise." Similarly, there is nothing inevitable about the degradation of women by which Amado squeezes some laughter out of his audience.

To reflect the commonly held view of women is one thing, but a writer can both reflect and be critical at the same time. Amado was free to either throw light on or merely caricature the sexual repression of women, and, in this book, he caricatures it. This is apparent, for example, in his description of the fear generated in the city by the prostitutes' strike, given the imminent arrival of two shiploads of American sailors. Amado writes: "Several ladies fainted, and an old woman suffered a heart attack and had to be rushed to the emergency room of the hospital. Old maid Veralice sighed as she resignedly obeyed her sister-in-law's admonition to shut the doors and windows: if only there *would* be an invasion of lustful, woman-hungry sailors! She'd know what to say to a blond, lusty Yankee sailor: Here I am, come and get me!" (pp. 523–24). And further: "The American battleships had steamed away from the port of Bahia after three days and three nights, and with them spinster Veralice's last best hope of being ravished by a blond Yankee with a tool a foot long" (p. 530). Veralice is an insignificant character, clearly brought into the narrative for the sole purpose of providing this crude laugh by being the object of a vulgar joke. In fact, the frustrated old maid is a stock figure in many of Amado's works. Again, the conflict is evident between Amado's social critique (which implies showing the reasons why things are as they are) and his desire to provide "entertainment" at any price, even if it means the acceptance and hence reinforcement of many clichés. Is the reader expected to read Amado's novel as five *folhetos* so separate that this type of "humor" will seem to bear no relationship to the rape scenes described in the second part of the novel? Or, on the contrary, does this constitute merely one more reflection of the ambivalence abounding within the novel?

Jorge Amado, imprisoned as a Communist during the Vargas regime and lionized for more than the past decade, seems to prove once again that the best way to politically disarm an artist is through success and fame within the very world he is attempting (or once attempted) to combat. Amado may be, as Carlos Heitor Cony wryly states, "the only inhabitant of this planet who has managed to believe with the same sincerity in Marx and in [the *candomblé* priestess] Menininha do Gantois,"[16] but the fact is that it is the latter, far more than the former, whose influence is apparent in his recent novels. Could it be that a social critique is palatable only via humor, folklore, and magic? Certainly it is the case that Amado's portrayal of the joys and magic of Bahia is primarily consumed not by the Bahians whom he describes with sympathy and affection. It is unlikely that the workers, prostitutes, and vagabonds have the economic power, not to mention literacy, to make a best-seller.[17] Rather, the success of the novel must come, things currently being as they are, from those who are ostensibly ridiculed and criticized in the work, those who are depicted as villains, exploiters, and fools: landowners, petit bourgeois citizens, civil servants, professionals, and politicians. But, happily, these can avoid recognizing themselves, for their portraits in *Tereza Batista* come packaged in such local color, such richness of "folkloric" detail, as to be substantially defused. One puts down a book such as *Tereza Batista* not disturbed by the brutality and exploitation it describes and ostensibly protests, but diverted by the picturesque life it depicts, and, precisely to that extent, not inclined to take it too seriously.

Even Amado's explicit protests against brutality and poverty are undermined by the basic bonhomie of his vision of life. Laughter, however, has its conciliatory uses too, and "the wrong kind overcomes fear by capitulating to the forces which are to be feared."[18]

Amado's representation of women no doubt plays a vital role in his popularity with the middle and upper classes that must predominantly be his audience. It may be that male readers are reassured by Amado's evident commitment to the status quo in that most fundamental of issues: men's domination of women. It may be that in his treatment of women (whether glorifying some as desirable creatures or poking fun at the rigid morality and bitter frustration of others), men feel Amado appealing to them as fellow males, implicated in the same power structure. In addition, without a doubt Amado's graphic depiction of sex must appeal to some readers. But how, then, does one explain his appeal to women readers, who have power only marginally, if at all? I think here it is important to look again at Amado's consistent championship of women's sexual freedom. By adopting such a stance, Amado makes it difficult for readers to see beyond the appearance to the real relations between men and women depicted in his novels. Once we are aware of the ideological double standard at work in Amado's novels, his attitude becomes clear: he seems to want his women to be ever better, lustier partners to his men. He is interested in establishing, first and foremost, his female characters' sexual desirability, and he depicts them as free agents in this sphere of life alone. His male characters are happiest when they understand and reciprocate sexual pleasure, and Amado seems to be saying that there is no risk here in upsetting the more fundamental domination to which women will continue to submit, if only their sexual needs are recognized.

Amado's prostitutes with hearts of gold, frustrated old maids, tough and admirable madames—all affirm, through the ideological double standard that Amado employs, that some things are constant and stable. And foremost among these, in Amado's works having female protagonists, is women's need for men and acceptance of male dominance.

## Notes

1. *Veja*, 14 December 1972, p. 90.
2. On Brazil's popular poetry, see Mark J. Curran, *A Literatura de Cordel* (Recife: Univ. Federal de Pernambuco, 1973). In his most recent novel, *Tieta do Agreste* (Rio de Janeiro: Record, 1977), Amado goes even further on the pretense that his works are within the tradition of Brazilian popular literature. Thus the novel bears the subtitle: "Shepherdess of Goats, or, the Return of the Prodigal Daughter, Melodramatic *Folhetim* in Five Sensational Episodes and a Moving Epilogue: Emotion and Suspense."
3. Jorge Amado, *Tereza Batista: Home from the Wars*, trans. Barbara Shelby (New York: Alfred A. Knopf, 1975), p. 319. References appearing in the text will be to this English translation.
4. See Amado's "Discurso de posse na Academia Brasileira, Julho 1961," in Roger Bastide et al., *Jorge Amado: Povo e Terra: 40 Anos de Literatura* (São Paulo: Martins, 1972), p. 13.
5. "PW Interviews: Jorge Amado," *Publishers Weekly*, 23 June 1975, p. 20.
6. Joseph Sommers, "Literature and Ideology: Vargas Llosa's Novelistic Evaluation of Militarism," presented at the University of Minnesota meeting on Ideology and the Literature of Latin America (March 1975), p. 47; and Warner Berthoff, "Literature and the Measure of 'Reality,' " in *Fictions and Events: Essays in Criticism and Literary History* (New York: E. P. Dutton, 1971), p. 58.
7. Fredric Jameson, "The Great American Hunter, or, Ideological Content in the Novel," *College English*, 34:2 (1972), p. 182.
8. Lionel Trilling, "Manners, Morals, and the Novel," in *The Liberal Imagination* (New York: Doubleday, 1953), p. 213.
9. Frank O'Connor, *The Lonely Voice* (Cleveland and New York: World Publishing Company, 1963), p. 72.
10. Eric S. Rabkin, *Narrative Suspense* (Ann Arbor: University of Michigan Press, 1973), p. 40.
11. Max Horkheimer and Theodor W. Adorno, *Dialectic of Enlightenment*, trans. John Cumming (New York: Herder and Herder, 1972), p. 230.
12. See *Brecht on Theater: The Development of an Aesthetic*, ed. and trans. John Willett (New York: Hill and Wang, 1964).
13. In his latest novel, *Tieta do Agreste*, Amado opens the book with a comparable scene: a breathless, cursing older man in angry pursuit of a young and agile girl. After a few paragraphs, however, it becomes clear that Tieta is a willing partner (she is described as a young girl in heat, like the she-goats she cares for). Again, Amado stresses sexual appetite. But in opposing the stereotype of the chaste and sexually repressed woman, Amado depicts still another stereotype: women in heat, unable to do without sex. Such women are not, however, real agents, but rather mythical sexual beings. Only their sexual appetites are "free" and unrestrained. In other respects they continue to be dominated by men. Money alone ultimately provides power in Amado's novels, and women participate in this power peripherally. Tieta, for example, exercises her power throughout the novel by virtue of her wealth, which causes the local people to accept her back into their midst despite the disgrace she had suffered in her youth. Her ability to control the lives of the people around her by means of her wealth is taken for granted.

14. Philip P. Hallie, *The Paradox of Cruelty* (Middletown, Conn.: Wesleyan University Press, 1969), p. 159.

15. In this respect she is as atypical as the heroine of Bernardo Guimarães's *A Escrava Isaura* (1875), a slave of white appearance, education, and manners.

16. Carlos Heitor Cony, "Jorge Amado de Todos os Santos e Senhoras," *Manchete*, 16 August 1975, p. 41.

17. According to Décio de Abreu, *Publishers Weekly*, 22 September 1975, p. 65, the illiteracy rate in Brazil is still about 40 percent. This makes all the more extraordinary Amado's continued high sales; he himself reports that his books now sell about five hundred thousand copies a year.

18. Horkheimer and Adorno, *Dialectic of Enlightenment*, p. 140.

## 7 Donald Castro ◆ Women in the World of the Tango

*Tango, the musical expression of argentinidad (Argentineness), is both a type of song and a style of dance. From the onset, Argentine society was profoundly male and, because of the scarcity of women, prostitution was an important part of life in the port city of Buenos Aires. In its early years the tango was associated with brothels and makeshift dance halls. Eventually it moved to cafés where people listened rather than danced to tango bands. Just before World War I (1914), "Tangomania" spread to Europe, where Pope Pius X denounced it as "lubricious and immoral." The tango not only survived papal censure—it flourished and is still a popular musical form throughout South America's Southern Cone. Although the bibliography on the tango is extensive and tango lyrics are concerned primarily with male/female relations, few scholars have subjected this element of popular culture to gender analysis. Donald Castro, a professor of history at California State University–Fullerton, has published extensively on the tango and believes that it reveals much about the evolution of gender roles in Argentine society. He demonstrates that despite the significant progress made in Argentina toward women's rights between 1880 and 1955, depictions of women have remained traditional in the tango.*

A number of Argentine social scientists have found their society characterized by a sense of rootlessness (*desarraigo*). This social malaise is attributed partly to the attempt of the elite to create, through massive immigration, a "Europe in America." Clearly, another factor must be the subservient relationship of women to men in Argentine society. One Argentine sociologist, Julio Mafud, has described this condition as "the masculinization of society" (*machismo social*). Throughout the colonial period, European migration to the La Plata region was preponderantly a movement of single males. Nor was the sex imbalance offset, as in other areas of Latin America, by the presence of large numbers of Amerindian or Afro-Creole women. In the nineteenth and early twentieth centuries, massive European migration only reinforced this demographic imbalance.

Given the scarcity of European women, a double standard defined the two types of women: the ideal, European (white), virginal, and unapproachable for most; and the others who, because of their African or Amerindian origins, were considered a vessel for male pleasure and were viewed as more a species of female animal than as women—*hembra* rather than *mujer*. While sexual relations with the former were conducted in the marital bed, those with the latter were casual, and the products of these unions were what Mafud has called *hijos de nada* (children of nothing).[1] In Argentina, then, the dominant society was one of lonely, rootless, vulnerable men searching for the protection of a mother and an unknown father. In many senses, even during the gender reforms of Juan and Eva Perón (1946–1955) and later under Isabel Perón (1974–1976), the role of women as subservient and as protective mother symbols did not change.

The male-created image of women in the context of Buenos Aires popular culture—the tango and the world of the tango—is the focus of this study, and the gender attitudes outlined here are expressed in eloquent and rich detail in popular cultural forms: the tango, *lunfardo* poetry (in the argot of the city), and the *sainete porteño* (popular theater of Buenos Aires). The tango, in particular, was seen as a sort of mirror into the soul of the *porteños*, who used the form to express pain, joy, frustration, and innermost secrets. As one author observed, "Tango, you are the soulful condition of the masses."

In the world of the *porteño* male, a series of functions is ascribed to the female, who is mother, wife, sister, daughter, lover, or vehicle for pleasure. In these relationships the double standard for acceptable behavior is evident: male indiscretion is forgivable and is the result of being led astray by a female temptress; female indiscretion, however, is due to innate evil and cannot be forgiven because of its betrayal of the role of wife and mother. Clearly, how men view women can be found in the terms they use. *Porteño* Spanish has a richly detailed lexicon to describe women. Often these terms convey very specific meanings. For example, the use of *mujer* or *vieja* to describe one's wife conveys a more affectionate image than that of *esposa*. It is possible to compile an entire catalog of terms used in the "Golden Age" of tango lyrics (1917–1943): *bacana* referred to a kept woman, *china* to a woman of the lower classes, *churra* to a beautiful, desirable woman.[2]

Prostitution, an important part of the life of Buenos Aires, was legal and largely unregulated, with houses of prostitution located in many parts of the city and in the suburbs. The massive immigration of primarily single males, the dominance of Latin-oriented cultural views of male superiority, and the connivance of corrupt immigration officials allowed Buenos Aires to become one of the principal centers of the "white slave" trade.[3] In Argentina, the purported haven for the immigrant, prostitution represented the exploitation of the immigrant by immigrants for the profit of neither. Many of these houses were well known and had famous political and police protectors—for example, the conservative ward leader of the working-class suburb of Avellaneda, Alberto Barceló, and his political ally Juan Ruggiero ("Ruggierito"). Prostitution, its practitioners, the characters associated with the trade, and the sites where it was carried out were all topics for popular culture after 1880. This was true both for the culture originating in the oral tradition (the tango lyrics) and for the expressions of written popular culture (*sainete porteño*). Since prostitution was closely associated with the tango prior to 1917, the world of the tango was viewed as immoral. Women associated with it fulfilled the roles of whore, gangster moll, or girl of loose moral character. Women were portrayed in these negative stereotypes—with the prostitute by far the most common—in the improvised tango lyrics of the period prior to 1917. These early tangos were often warnings to avoid certain prostitutes, because of their lack of hygiene, or were tributes to the talents of others. "Entrada prohibida" ("Forbidden entry"), "Quecho" ("Whorehouse"), "Siete pulgadas" ("Seven inches") and "Dame la lata" ("Give me the chit") were tangos of the period. The last refers to the metal chit, or token, that was given to the person who controlled entry into a brothel's rooms. Prostitution was also a prominent theme in novels, popular poetry, and the theater of the day.

The era after World War I represented in *porteño* male/female relationships a period of great change and male gender uncertainty. Men were confused and bewildered by what was viewed as "deviant behavior" in *porteño* women that became apparent in the 1920s. They became assertive and demanding and therefore less "feminine." As in the United States and Europe, the 1920s were the crazy years (*los años locos*). In the popular fox-trot "Pero hay una melena" ("But there is a curly head") by José Bohr, the most startling changes are well described:

> Before women were feminine,
> now fashion has thrown all that out.
> Before only the face and foot showed,
> but now they show all there is to be seen.
> Today all the women seem to be men,
> they smoke, drink whiskey, and wear pants.

Women now cut their hair, smoked in public, and even drove automobiles. While many tango authors noted changes in fashion with humor, female assertiveness was seen in less charitable terms. For example, in the famous 1924 tango of Pascual Contursi, "La mina del Ford" ("The 'skirt' with a Ford"), the modern woman is described as one who wants all the material benefits of the good life—an apartment with balconies, gas heat, waxed floors, carpets, beds with mattresses, and a maid who announces, "Madam, the Ford is here!" Women expected men to provide these things, and when the man could not, he was left out in the cold, such as in the 1930 tango "En la palmera" ("Down and out"). The song's protagonist claims he wants to get married but all that the girls want is a man with "an account with the National Bank," so therefore he must go out on the streets where he can at least find a girl who will go out with him.[4] The changing roles of modern women and their newfound assertiveness seemed to disorient and even anger men, who sought solace in the arms of the understanding prostitute. A significant change in urban nightlife occurred also in the 1920s. By city ordinance of March 23, 1919, houses of prostitution were outlawed. The bordello was the home of the tango, which in turn was closely associated with the folk types of the bordello, especially the *compadrito* (ladies' man), the *malevo* (criminal), and their women—*mujeres de la vida, minas, chinas, prendas, hembras* (streetwalkers, skirts, bitches, et al.). Now the tango moved into the environment of the cabaret and the popular theater: *sainete porteño* and the *teatro de revistas* (somewhat similar to the vaudeville theater of the same period in the United States). The cabaret in the 1920s, with its quasi-French environment, attempted to meet the needs of many young men of the upward-striving middle class, who sought to emulate the errant life of the upper-class swells who had spent time in Paris in the Belle Epoque of pre-World War I. It was in the cabaret that the tango put on a smoking jacket, and the *copetinas* (women, usually prostitutes, who worked the bars to get men to buy drinks) "spoke" French (*franchutas papusas*).[5]

The women from the now-closed bordellos moved into these two new areas of "entertainment." If they did not have the prerequisites for success in either the cabaret or the theater, they took to the streets. Because women of *la vida* were closely associated with *porteño* nightlife, "decent" women of all classes stayed at home, thereby creating a male-dominated atmosphere in the entertainment centers. In view of this reality, prostitution remained an important theme in tango lyrics throughout the 1920s, especially in the story of the understanding prostitute who eased the loneliness of single men in search of affection. This situation was threatened by the political coup of 1930.

One of the effects of the September 6, 1930, revolution of General José F. Uriburu was further restrictions on prostitution. After the disclosure in the same year of the scandal of Zwi Migdal (a purported Jewish benevolent society which in fact was a white slavery ring), even protectors of prostitution such as Alberto Barceló, a close friend and political patron of the tango star Carlos Gardel, had to check their activities. Taking advantage of these circumstances, the Catholic church and conservatives sought to cleanse Buenos Aires of its image of the world's center for prostitution. This new morality, added to the effects of the Great Depression, no doubt cut deeply into cabaret and popular-theater attendance even by those who could afford it. It did not, however, seem to affect basic tango themes because the *papusa* was still a popular topic. Even with the new morality, the streetwalkers continued to have clients. *Porteño* nightlife was still male dominated and so was the tango. It had, however, lost its gaiety of the 1920s. A tango written in the early 1930s clearly shows this change in attitude and its effect on one *mujer de la vida*, Madame Ivonne. It tells the story of a beauty brought to Buenos Aires from the Latin Quarter of Paris in the 1920s by a young Argentine who later abandoned her. Now she has only her memories, and with "sad eyes drinks her champagne" ("Madame Ivonne," Enrique Cadícano, 1933).

The 1920s proved to be the entry point for the female tango vocalist, especially in the new medium—radio. While Rosita Rodríguez Quiroga was the first to make it in 1923 in what had been a male-dominated field, other female vocalists soon followed, such as Azucena Maizani ("La ñata gaucha," also in 1923), Libertad Lamarque (1926), Sofía Bozán (1926), and Manolita Poli and Ada Falcón in the late 1920s. The importance of women to radio is twofold: they served as stars as well as listeners and consumers. The radio brought the tango into the home and drew women into its audience. If the tango was male dominated in terms of *porteño* nightlife, it was not so on the radio. Nevertheless, the entry of women into the world of the tango in roles that were not easily equatable with prostitution and criminal behavior (that is, women as evil) did not substantially change their negative image in the lyrics.

Respectable women could listen to the tango on the radio, enjoy it, admire male vocalists, and perhaps identify, through the female vocalists, with the forbidden (that is, naughty) tango world. The merchandisers of radio used the tango to sell products and, above all, wanted women to buy the products associated with radio programs.[6] Even so, respectable women identified with the tango in the privacy of their homes and not in public. Perhaps this explains why little attention was given in the tangos of the period to themes that could be viewed as female oriented, even though women were now part of the audience. Further, a review of publicity photographs of the period shows that many female tango artists dressed as men and wore their hair short, especially the singer Azucena Maizani and the only female tango musician, Paquita Bernardo (1900–1925), a famous *bandoneónista* of the 1920s. A 1928 silent film showed that, although tolerated by most social classes, the tango was still not accepted. *La Borrachera del Tango* (The drunken frenzy of the tango) made clear that "home, the sacred sanctuary, was threatened by the implacable virus of the tango." Therefore, because of the old association of the tango with prostitution, women who participated openly could be considered "loose."

Recognizing this reality, women disguised themselves as men to protect their femininity and their reputation. The fact that they had to use male dress or assumed names reflected their tenuous status in the tango world, where they were still defined as a "necessary evil." Men dominated as lyricists, as tango interpreters, and as the merchandisers of the dance. If women were to participate in this milieu, therefore, they did so according to the parameters set by men.

The supreme irony of this gender relationship is that, in the tango lyrics, the dominant male is insecure and dependent on women for his protection (the mother figure) and, in a sense, for his definition as a male: either as a victim (woman as the betrayer) or as a macho aggressor (woman as the victim). An analysis of the respective tango repertoires of male and female artists after 1920 shows a continuing unequal relationship between the sexes and disjointed views of one sex toward the other.

Rosita Quiroga (d. 1984) was an almost perfect stereotype of the tango singer. Raised by a single mother who worked as a seamstress, she has been called "the sweetheart of Buenos Aires . . . the expression of its essence. She is the tango in the form of a person." Quiroga distinguished herself from other female vocalists by composing a number of tangos, including "Oíme me Negro," "Carta brava," and "De estirpe porteña." One of her most famous renditions, "En la via," by Eduardo Escarís Méndez, introduced in 1926, was really written for a male vocalist because it is about a man jilted by a woman. The negative image of the woman is not untypical in Quiroga's repertoire, because most of her tangos were "pure Gardel." It seems ironic that in order to have tangos of Gardelian caliber, Quiroga had to sing lyrics that debased women. In doing so she may have further reinforced the negative images—if a woman could sing with feeling of the evils of her sex, then the lyrics must represent truth.

Even when tangos were written by women, as in the case of María Luisa Carnelli (b. 1898), more often than not the lyrics are not gender specific and can be sung by either a man or a woman. Typically, they depict women negatively and in a subservient role. For example, in 1929, Carnelli wrote the Gardel standard, "P'al cambalache" ("To the pawnshop"), which is about a man jilted by a woman. He sits alone and looks around his room seeing things that remind him of his lost love. These he will take to the pawnshop and thus symbolically end the relationship.

Male/female relationships as described in the tangos of the Golden Age are depicted in vivid psychological terms. In the lyrics, love is passive, with the man with a "victim of love." In the dance, however, the man is aggressive, with the woman forced to follow his lead passively in a tight embrace.

Alcohol is an important element in the tango. In lyrics such as those of "La última copa" ("The last drink") by Juan Andres Caruso (1925),

and "Esta noche me emborracho" ("Tonight I am going to get drunk") by
Enrique Santos Discépolo (1930), what is significant are the sorrows that
lead to drink. Love is unrequited and often ends in betrayal. For example,
in "Barajando" ("Warding off the blows of life") by Eduardo Escarís
Méndez (1923), love is compared to a game of cards and success is a
matter of luck. Woman again is a "necessary evil" in the post-1920s tango:
the lonely man repeatedly rejected still needs female companionship, even
if it is illusory.

The "love" that Carlos Gardel (d. 1935), the most famous of the male
vocalists, sang about is not of the simple boy-meets-girl variety. In most
cases, Gardel's protagonist suffers failed love affairs because of the
female's betrayal (*traición*). The tangos "Nunca más" and "La cumparista"
are good examples. Gardel's love affairs are irregular (not marital), nor is
there any mention of husbands, wives, home, and family. In some cases,
when the affair ends through the woman's *traición*, the man experiences
relief at his restored liberty—perhaps a cover for his wounded ego. The
lyrics to "¿Te fuiste? ¡Ja, Ja!", a tango written by Juan Bautista Abad
Reyes, confirm this freedom:

> My room [*bulín*] is so much nicer now,
> airier, better ventilated and friendly
> with the dust devils on the floor
> a complete mess.
> Now I have no one to yell at me
> nor a little dog to bite back at me.
> I thank the foolish girl
> for having left me.

The word *bulín* used by Abad Reyes implies a place of assignation. *Porteño*
males secured lodgings for affairs on a class basis, with only upper-middle-
class men able to rent rooms for a long term. Most *porteño* men rented
hotel rooms by the hour (*hotel alojamiento*). Also, the use of the term
*bulín* implies both a certain status and suggests that the love affair in
question was not with a wife or girlfriend but rather was casual and irregular. This sort of male role is so omnipresent in tangos that it may be
seen as representing the ideal male gender role, although the relationship
was clearly hurtful to both parties.

As the greatest interpreter, Gardel personified the tango and was the
epitome of *porteño* masculinity. He was also a great innovator and, in
"La gayola," by Armando José Tagini (1906–1967), made substantive
changes to the lyrics. Unlike most tangos of male defeat, "La gayola" is
predicated on actual rather than symbolic violence. A man kills his rival,
the one with whom his lover has betrayed him. In the original lyrics the
knife kills the man. Gardel's verse reads, "You played me dirty . . . and,

thirsting for revenge, one night *I* raised *my* knife and carried it to the heart" (emphasis added). This story line is unusual for tangos, in which the man is usually a passive agent carried along by uncontrollable love. Gardel makes it clear that the murder is an act of passion and therefore pardonable. The woman, as in other tangos, is the cause of all this grief, and the man is freed after a long prison term.

In another famous Gardel tango, "Madre hay una sola" ("There is only one mother"), the theme is that in this life of betrayal and adversity there is one good that transcends all—one's mother![7] In fact, this was appropriate for Gardel, given that his only long-term relationship was with his mother: he never married. The only love affair that came into public view was with an American socialite, Mrs. Sadie Baran Wakefield, "The Baroness," and even that affair was shrouded in mystery; Gardel, as a "man of honor," refused to discuss it. His friends, however, suggested that he indeed had had affairs.[8] What is noteworthy is that Gardel, as the symbol of the ideal *porteño* male, was himself unmarried, the son of an adoring unmarried mother, and a man purported to have many lovers. Such men do not anchor a stable society.

The right-wing military coup of 1943 ushered in a new era for the tango. Influenced by a citizens' commission led by Monsignor Gustavo Franceschi, who has been described as a man of "inquisitional" zeal, the government in 1944 adopted a *ley seca*. This law, "dry" in the sense of austerity, sought to purify Argentine Spanish of slang. It also attempted to protect young people from the corrupting influence of the tango. Radio stations were required to change tango titles and lyrics to present Argentine women in a better light. Under the new law the 1926 tango "El ciruja" ("The ragpicker"), by Francisco Alfredo Marino (d. 1973), was banned. Considered the classic example of the *lunfardo* tango, it was banned not only because its subject was a prostitute but also because she was the product of a refuse dump, not someone whom the promoters of the "new" Argentina wished to call attention to:[9]

> She was a showy piece of work
> raised in a refuse dump,
> daughter of a faith healer,
> petty thief by profession;
> she worked for a flashy pimp
> to whom she passed all her money
> after she fleeced her mark.

In addition, the classic Discépolo tango "Yira . . . Yira" ("Aimless wandering") was changed to "Dad vueltas . . . dad vueltas" because *yira* came from the *lunfardo* verb *yirar*, which pertained to the aimless short turns a streetwalker makes while waiting for a client to appear. Ricardo

Luis Brignolo's 1929 Gardel tango "Chiqué" ("Simulation") was changed to "El elegante" ("The elegant man"), which appeared less offensive than the *lunfardo* term *chiquer* (equal to *simular* in Spanish, which is to pretend to be something that one is not). Tangos such as "Shusita" (or *soplón* in Spanish—one who squeals but on the sly) became the far less descriptive "La aristocrata" ("The aristocrat"), and "La mavela" ("The gangster's moll," evil in a criminal sense) became "La mala" (bad but not necessarily evil).

Moreover, the tangos that portrayed women as prostitutes, deceivers, connivers, and betrayers were no longer valid. The conditions that made such women no longer existed in the "new" Argentina. As of 1947, women had the vote and full rights. Evita Perón had clearly stated what this new role was to be in a speech given on July 26, 1949, at the first national conference of Peronist women—"not only to give sons to the Fatherland but as well men to humanity." How could a woman of Argentina now be described as *papusa* or *franchuta*? The woman of the "new" Argentina was to be the sacrificing mother.

The example of women in Perón-era tangos can be seen in "Domani" ("Tomorrow" [1951]) and "Anoche" ("Last night" [1954]) by Cátulo Castillo, and in "Recién puedo llorar" ("It is only now that I can cry" [1951]) by Homero Manzi. Both of the Castillo tangos contain the theme of betrayal, but it is either clouded in the past, as in "Domani," or, while presented with sadness, done without rancor, as in "Anoche." In the "new" Argentina, separation and suffering are shared equally, as witnessed in "Domani":

> In the fogginess of the years,
> and soon in the death
> that will greet him,
> there is a song like a wail
> that comes in from the sea . . .
> that cries for his little girl to return.

Neither man nor woman was truly the betrayer or the betrayed. An end to love happens, but not in the way that it did in the Abad Reyes tango "¿Te fuiste? ¡Ja, Ja!" in which the man sighs in relief that the bitch has gone. In the Manzi tango "Recién puedo llorar," separation is not due to betrayal or to an end of a love; it is through death "that we are separated by shadows and mystery/that my cry for your return is useless/because you can never return."

Evita Perón's tragic life, beautiful on the outside and cancerous on the inside, easily could have been a theme for a Discépolo tango. Further, even while she was dying, her good works for the poor and the sick were symbols of her sacrifice. When she described herself as the "bridge of love" between her husband and the people, was she not the same as the self-sacrificing mother of the tangos of Celedonio Flores? This image was cultivated while she lived by both Eva and Juan. After her death, Perón encouraged the people to call for her beatification because her sacrifice was comparable to that of the Madonna. Was not this idea tangoesque?

As we know, the general use of the radio in *porteño* households—again cutting across class lines—also served to revolutionize the entertainment industry in Argentina. What had been largely a male-oriented cultural form in terms of audience—because of its traditional dissemination in the bordello, the tango bar, and the cabaret—now became sanitized as the tango entered the home of the "decent" woman. The popularity of radio and movie magazines with their largely female readership demonstrates the incorporation of women as active relaters to the tango and to its stars, particularly to its male stars such as Carlos Gardel and Ignacio Corsini. These gallant or virile men served as important images projected via a radio speaker, or as photographs in a radio or movie magazine, or as the heroes in a romantic movie.

It is clear that the tango environment was male dominated and that the tango reflected the masculine *porteño* society (even though men were depicted as weak and insecure). Female tango singers in the 1920s and 1930s essentially had to assume male roles, altering their dress and manners and perhaps further reinforcing their image as beguiler. Women, if they wanted to succeed, had to sing what the male public wanted—lyrics with negative images of women.

Yet, women represented a large potential market for the tango, particularly as the radio began to be common in Argentine homes. Merchandisers of this era attempted to maintain tango traditions while reaching out to a new audience, which included women. They did so by fusing the risqué with the moral and by blurring gender lines. Although the tango world evolved to include women, it continued to manipulate them. Even during the *ley seca* era and a period of self-censorship under Perón, the tango never glorified the status of women or the institution of marriage. Love in tangos was never fulfilled through marriage but rather was marred by seduction, infidelity, and betrayal, all perpetrated by women.

The coming of woman's suffrage under Perón did not substantially change the subservient role of Argentine women. In the official literature of the period, they were depicted as helpmates, faithful wives, and sacrificing mothers—but not as men's equals. They never became three dimensional, and they never were able to break out of parameters long ago established in the tango.

**Notes**

1. For an interesting contrast, see Octavio Paz, *Labyrinth of Solitude* (New York: Grove Press, 1962). In this work originally written in the 1950s, Paz developed the concept of the first contact between Europeans and Native Americans as situations of rape, where the by-products were *hijos de la chingada*.

2. While compiled from various sources, one of the primary dictionaries for Argentine slang is José Gobello, *Diccionario Lunfardo* (Buenos Aires: A. Peña, 1982).

3. Many Jews were reportedly involved in the "trade" as both madams and as prostitutes. The major scandal of the Zwi Migdal, a Jewish benevolent society which in fact was a cover for a white slave ring, rocked the *porteño* Jewish community in the early 1930s. Based on anecdotal information from my own grandfather (who emigrated from the Tsarist Empire in 1904) and from friends who emigrated from Poland in the 1920s, the role of Jews in the trade was well known and significant.

4. Tango written by Francisco Lomuto and recorded by Ada Falcón in December 1930. Reissued from the original recording as EMI-Odeon #14198 in 1982.

5. For an excellent description of the cabaret and the folk types associated with it, see Manuel Galvez, *Nacha Regules* (1919). The publication of this novel scandalized polite Buenos Aires society and may have led in part to the March 23, 1919, ordinance. *Franchuta* in *porteño* Spanish was equivalent to a whore from France or at least a "frenchified" whore. *Papusa* is a slang term for a pretty girl (often a "working girl").

6. This is very clear in a review of the radio and tango magazines that became popular in the 1920s. Cf. *La Canción Moderna* (1925) and its evolution into *Radiolandia* (1936).

7. José Gobello and Juan Bossio, eds., *Tangos, letras y letristas*, 2 vols. (Buenos Aires: Editorial Plus Ultra, 1979–1990), pp. 1–85.

8. This issue is of such importance that Francisco García Jimenez devoted a chapter to the subject in *Carlos Gardel y su época*, "El amor en la vida de Carlos Gardel," pp. 308–311. See also *Revista Gente,* special edition "Carlos Gardel," June 2, 1977, pp. 36–37. The television homage to Gardel, on the Spanish International Network's "Homenaje a Gardel," also devoted time to an interview with Isabel del Valle, reputed lover of Gardel. She was very circumspect. Another tango star on the program and a contemporary of Gardel, Mona Mares, stated that he was "muy tímido con las mujeres" (very shy with women). Simon Collier discusses this issue as well in his study *Carlos Gardel* (Pittsburgh: University of Pittsburgh Press, 1986), p. 176.

# II  Reconstructing the Past

Primary and secondary sources and scholarly studies are arranged in chronological order here to demonstrate how the historical experience of Latin American women in the nineteenth and twentieth centuries can be and has been recovered using the traditional historian's tools. A brief consultation of the bibliography of Latin American women's history reveals that the nineteenth century is to date the least studied period, not because of a lack of written documents but because of the difficulty associated with recovering the history of inarticulate or marginalized individuals. Nineteenth-century Latin American women did not perform great or dramatic deeds; they were homebound, and, because few of them were literate and their lives were so ordinary, they did not write about themselves. That task was left to others, such as Isaac Holton, a nineteenth-century naturalist who wrote straightforward descriptions of what he saw during a five-year visit to Colombia in the 1850s (Selection 8). The travel book is an important source for the social historian because it is useful in reconstructing the patterns of daily life. It also demonstrates that some documents pertinent to Latin American women's history are available in English and can be found in most university libraries. Other similar sources are newspapers, journals, and U.S. and British consular reports.

Sometimes writing women's history requires using a traditional source, such as the law, in new ways. Family law in particular yields rich information concerning the status of women, as Silvia Arrom aptly demonstrates in "Changes in Mexican Family Law" (Selection 9). To write "Women, Peonage, and Industrialization" (Selection 10), Donna Guy combed the national and regional archives of Argentina for labor laws, census data, travelers' accounts, and the writings of experts to reconstruct the employment patterns of poor women during the transition to modern labor systems. In "The Catholic Church, Work, and Womanhood in Argentina" (Selection 11), Sandra McGee Deutsch combined data from ecclesiastical, labor, and party archives to examine the significant political action of women and the gendered thinking of the Catholic hierarchy in that country.

Travel to Latin America was considered dangerous and rough and kept all but a few of the most determined and rugged individuals away.

Nevertheless, a few women undertook the challenge. In the nineteenth century, Helen Sanborn was one of them. After completing her studies at Wellesley College, she accompanied her father, a partner in the Chase and Sanborn Coffee Company, on a horse- and mule-back tour of coffee *fincas* (plantations) throughout Central America and Mexico. She wrote *A Winter in Central America* in 1886 and listed herself in the 1887 edition of *Who's Who in America*. Another nineteenth-century traveler was Mrs. Alex Tweedie, an English gentlewoman who, in *Mexico as I Saw It* (New York, 1911), paid much attention to how women lived, presenting her findings in a comparative framework that reveals as much about the author as about her subjects. Her observations about elite Mexican women did not differ very much from those by contemporary social scientists, who also analyzed the condition of women in a comparative framework. Alice Peck visited Bolivia in the early 1900s to pursue her hobby, mountain climbing; many more North American women traveled to Latin America as missionaries and as wives of businessmen. The North American woman traveler was usually well educated, observant, and from the middle class. Some, like Josephine Hoeppner Woods, whose *High Spots in the Andes* is excerpted in Selection 12, shared their adventures with the reading public back home.

During the 1920s and 1930s, interest in Latin America in this country was encouraged by international agencies such as the Pan American Union and by the expansion of U.S. business into the region after World War I. Of particular interest was the development of the women's suffrage movement. While the United States was a source of inspiration to Latin American women, Francesca Miller explains in "The Suffrage Movement in Latin America" (Selection 13) how variance in the region's local political cultures led women to different conclusions about the importance of suffrage and to adopt distinct strategies for achieving it.

Research focuses on women from the popular classes because they comprise the majority. Although Latin America has many middle-class women who are working in professional careers in medicine, law, city planning, and engineering, little is known about them. Elite women have been dismissed outright because they are viewed as unproductive, except for those who write and have established themselves as intellectuals— Victoria Ocampo, for example. One exception to the stereotypical portrayals of elite women is offered by Larissa Lomnitz and Marisol Pérez-Lizaur in Selection 14. Their essay is a good example of how social scientists must reconceptualize women's activities.

One of the goals of the Castro revolution in Cuba, the first in a series of people's liberation movements to improve the lives of women and children, was to emphasize human rights over political franchise. To that end, in 1974 the state offered new family legislation, a sample of which is included in "The Revolution Protects Motherhood" (Selection 15). Recently, in *Healing the Masses: Cuban Health Politics at Home and Abroad*, Julie Feinsilver confirmed the continued Cuban commitment to healthy women and children. She noted that "priority is given to maternal and infant-care programs. . . . Of the thirteen stated objectives of the program for women, nine deal with pregnancy and . . . four . . . with contraception, the early detection of uterine or cervical cancer, venereal disease, and other gynecological pathologies."[*]

Just as the Pan American Union provided an international forum for advocating political rights for women in the 1920s, 1930s, and 1940s, in our time the United Nations, through its various agencies, such as the Economic Commission for Latin America, is intent on improving the conditions in which the vast majority of women in the region currently live. Reports such as the one excerpted in Selection 16 provide data that is used to create development programs. Two stages can be distinguished in the process of women's integration in development. In the first, the effort focused on improving their status as beneficiaries of the process. In the second, the emphasis changed to designing policies that would incorporate women as participants.

The Nicaraguan Revolution followed in the footsteps of the Cuban Revolution and increased its commitment to women's liberation. Deliberately, the Frente Sandinista de Liberación Nacional (FSLN) developed a strategy that would appeal to the country's large population of working women. In Selection 17, Barbara Seitz combines personal observations with material gathered from interviews with Nicaraguan women to assess their status today. While many women were directly mobilized by the FSLN, there were other factors at work in Nicaraguan society in the early 1970s that prepared women for a public role. A sizeable portion of the bibliography dealing with contemporary Latin American women consists of testimonial literature that allows women—especially humble ones like Indiana Acevedo (Selection 18), who would have been the victims of the laws of documentary elitism in past times—to record the details of their lives.

Participation in guerrilla armies has been a part of the experience of Latin American women since colonial times, and there is no country in the region that has not produced several revolutionary-era heroines. The Mexican Revolution (1910) produced the *soldadera*, who has become a folk heroine for contemporary Mexican and Chicana women. Unlike her

---

[*]Julie M. Feinsilver, *Healing the Masses: Cuban Health Politics at Home and Abroad* (Berkeley: University of California Press, 1993), 48.

Mexican *compañera*, female participants in Peru's Sendero Luminoso are more likely to be found fighting than cleaning up the campground. Daniel Castro explores, in Selection 19, why ordinary women choose to enlist in armed struggle. Although they have participated in revolutionary activities in Latin America for over a century, the rate of change in their lives has been slow. Nicaragua's FSLN, for example, extended women's privileges because they had earned respect through combat—in other words, they were paid what was due them, not because they had intrinsic rights. Some believe that how Latin American women think and act—as mothers—is an obstacle to change: they go to war to feed their families, they protest on behalf of their "disappeared" children and spouses. At the Casa Sofía in Santiago, as described in Selection 20, North American and Australian feminists try to take *pobladoras* beyond grass-roots organizing to the next level—awareness of themselves as women.

# 8  Isaac F. Holton ◆ Daily Life in Nineteenth-Century Colombia

*In 1853, Isaac Holton, a professor of chemistry and natural science at Middlebury College in Vermont, began a five-year tour of Venezuela and Colombia as a member of a botanical expedition. Fortunately, he kept a diary, which formed the basis of* New Granada: Twenty Months in the Andes *(1857), one of the best travel books ever produced about nineteenth-century Latin America.*

*Holton was a keen observer of everyday life and filled the pages of his journal with rich descriptions of ordinary people's lives. As a trained scientist, he was as impartial in his judgment as a human being could be, but he could not completely overcome his New England upbringing. Remember, too, that* New Granada *was written for the general reading public in the United States, for whom travel books provided verbal snapshots of foreign cultures. Notice the language Holton uses to paint his sketches— his use of "kennel," for instance, to indicate a rural dwelling house. These types of descriptions of rural and urban scenes add flesh to people in history.*

### from "Rural Life"

As I was going up a steep pitch, I met a sight which I shall not soon forget. It was a young girl, apparently fifteen. . . . She had on her back a large load of wood, but was descending the steep road with a quick, elastic step . . . and on her left arm her babe unconsciously drawing its nourishment from the living fountain. . . . She, living possibly in a mud hut, seven feet long, six feet wide, and five feet from the eaves to the ground, contrives to eke out a subsistence for herself and babe by picking up a load of sticks near her kennel, carrying them and her babe from seven to twelve miles, and selling her load for three half dimes.

### from "The Rustic Ball"

There were no seats, or not enough for the women, so they sat on the ground at the sides of the room. Men stood in two groups just within the doors, and some also were permitted farther in. Cakes and *aguardiente* were for sale in the corridor. . . . The staple of the dances was waltzes and

From *New Granada: Twenty Months in the Andes* (New York: Harper and Brothers, 1857), 162, 173–75, 225–26, 400–402, 439–42, 445–46, 450–51, 463–69.

the *bambuco*. . . . One couple I saw that were not over eight years of age, managed to skip about so that none of their seniors should tread on them.

One couple needs the whole floor in the *bambuco* . . . thus they advance, recede, turn side to side, or even entirely round; so they dance without ever touching each other, till she becomes tired, drops a curtsy, and sits down. . . . For music, we must content ourselves with a *bandola* (banjo) and *pandereta* (tambourine), the noisy *alfandoque* [hollow cane shaken as a musical instrument] held over the performer's head in the extreme left, and a noisier drum.

### from "The Angelito"

I was called to see a sick child, three years old. . . . It had worms and was quite sick. The mother wrung her hands and cried, "Oh dear! What can Mother do for her poor little nigger girl?" *Negrita* is a favorite term of endearment here, even for white children. . . . They gave [her] wormseed herb . . . in *aguardiente*. I directed the dose to be increased in size and frequency. . . . Hearing nothing from them, I went, two days after, and they had not complied with any of my directions, as they thought the child "too weak to bear medicine"! One morning, soon after, I said, "There was a ball last night?" "No, Señor." "But I heard a drum—was there no dancing?" "Yes, Señor, there was dancing, but not at a ball. That little girl died last night, and they were rejoicing over the little angel (*angelito*). . . . "

I never saw this strange ceremony, for they preferred I should not. The little thing was tied into a chair, and put on a kind of shelf, like an image of worship, high enough up to leave the whole room for dancing; and there, parents and friends had danced most or all the night. The anticipation of this merrymaking tends, I think, to mitigate the dread of losing a child.

### from "A Wedding"

On Tuesday a couple went to Libraida to be married. Their return on Wednesday noon was celebrated and announced by a sufficient number of . . . rocket-crackers. . . . This was also the signal for the commencement of a day ball. . . .

The [bride's] hair was short all over the head, but, being as crisp as wool, retained without difficulty a side-comb of gold and some artificial flowers on each side, and a complete garland behind. The ear-rings were of gold. . . . On the neck was, first, a chain of gold going twice around;

second, a string of pearl beads; third, another gold chain. The *camisa* was of fine white muslin; sleeves of another muslin, shot with red, reaching below the elbow. . . . A belt of material resembling that of gentlemen's braces passes twice round the waist and tucks in. Below this, the skirt sags in front three inches. In the mouth, a cigar; on the hands, four gold rings with emeralds; on the feet, nothing, with pantalettes of the same.

The ball [lasted] some sixteen hours without intermission.

### from "The First Families of Cauca"

It will be recollected that when I introduced Señora Eladio Várgas . . . I mentioned that, in the times of slavery, they were wealthy. Besides this estate of La Ribera, and their mines in Chocó, that now yield not a dollar, they have two haciendas in this valley, though there is a lawsuit with an adverse claimant to one of them. La Ribera alone could support them handsomely were it well managed, but their chief desire seems to be to keep things [going] there, and spend in Cartago all they can scrape from this estate. . . .

The house is 115 feet by 19, and divided into eight rooms. . . . Number 1 was bachelor's hall. It was 15 feet by 19, matted, had a door and a window, and three bedsteads. Gentlemen travelers sometimes slept here, and more or less of the males of the family. Number 2, 21 feet by 19, was the female room. Don Eladio, his wife, and their sisters, occupy it when they are here. . . . It had a window down to the floor, and a door opening into Number 3, a narrow room 7 feet by 19, occupied by either sex according to convenience. This has a window, and is a thoroughfare from the women's room to the *sala* [living room], Number 4. . . .

If we pass out the back door of the *sala* into the corridor, we at once enter on the domain of a small army of female servants. A brick bench (*poyo*) runs along the wall, about 20 inches high and 24 broad. East of the door this serves for a forge for minor cookery, as chocolate-making, etc. Next the door, on both sides, it is used for seats. The next portion is used for a dresser for dishes, etc., by day, all of which must be carried in at night for fear of the goats. The west end is built into a *tinajera*, pierced for three *tinajas* [earthen jars], with a space under them where pans may be placed to catch what water exudes through the unglazed earthen vessels. Near this, too, is the grinding-stone, with a place under it to put fire to heat the stone when chocolate is to be ground. . . . Again, in the extreme south end . . . there are two large kettles of cast brass (*pailas*). . . . They are used for making sweetmeats on a large scale and for other extraordinary operations, as soap-making.

Over all this space Pilar reigns supreme. She is a mulatto woman of about twenty or twenty-five. Her mother is the negress who rules the Várgas kitchen in Cartago. As to her father, it is a matter that defies my conjecture. She directs affairs, sets the table, waits on it, sews, teaches three little black girls to read, using the corridor as a schoolroom, and is, in fact, the most efficient person of either sex on the whole place, and does more work than any two of them.

Pilar, the little girls, and one or two of the adults, sleep in Number 10, separated from my room only by a partition so thin that I can hear them at their prayers occasionally of an evening after the family have all gone to bed. . . .

As rises the sun rises also Pilar. The "mistress of keys" crosses herself. She sets herself to sweeping the back corridor. . . . Now there passes out of the front door a procession of five women and girls, carrying on their heads an earthen jar, a round calabash, a long calabash, a *tarro* [pot] of *guadua* [bamboo cane] of two joints, and a green jar in the form of a double cone. Those who can not carry their vessels mouth upward have served themselves with an orange for a cork. They go to the river for water.

## from "The Rich and Comfortless of the Cane-Mill La Vega"

There was the owner, Don Ramón González, his wife, Rita Pinto de González, her sister, Reyes Pinto, and too many little ones to count. . . . This house is the residence of his wife's father, Señor Pinto, [and] her sister Reyes. . . . Reyes is unmarried, and these children are all accidental.

The house consists of two cottages, with a space between them for a patio. It is dusk. . . . Nothing is said about dinner. . . . It is all a notion that two good meals a day at least are essential to health and happiness. . . .

La Vega [was] two cabins standing in a sheepfold. . . . Within was an absence of comfort that was very striking in a man of so much . . . wealth as Don Ramón. . . .

Yet, besides his kitchen, his whole house is three small rooms with earth floors. The *sala* is twelve feet square. It has a *poyo* running all round, two heavy, coarse arm-chairs . . . and an immovable table made by fastening a board thirty inches long and eighteen inches wide on the tops of four stakes driven into the ground. . . . His bedroom is twelve feet by seven. Two shelves, seven feet by four, and two feet from the ground, are the beds. In the remaining four feet hangs a frame in which the babe sleeps. She can thus be swung by the occupants of either bed.

**from "The Poor of Bogotá"**

On the next block . . . is an old convent . . . converted into a poor-house. . . . To fit it for a foundling hospital, it was necessary to cut a small door in the wall next the street. Open the door wide, and you will pull a chain and ring a bell within. You see a wheel thirty inches in diameter, with an opening in it. If a babe is put in, a turn of the wheel will bring it into the presence of a porteress within. She can not see out, and the depositor may walk off. She will never know her child, nor her child her. . . .

Among [the poor] are a large proportion of females. . . . The *guarichas* [unwed mothers] furnish an ample supply of wet-nurses at a very reasonable price, only that when they have gained the affections of their charge they abuse their advantage, as the heartless of that class are apt to do. Their own children are no obstacle, for, if they live, they can put them into the foundling wheel as soon as a good offer for their services occurs. . . .

I called on my washerwoman one day. She lives in a tenement on the ground floor [basement] of a *casa alta*. Cold as is the weather in Bogotá, the door is open to admit light, for she has no glass. To prevent the intrusion of prying eyes, a screen—*mampara*—is placed before the door. It is too high for a five-foot Indian to look over, and placed just so that we can run round it. The little room looks like a prison cell, only it has no grated window, nor loophole, nor breathing hole, except the open door. Within is an inner cell, smaller than the outer, with no door, and all its light and air comes from the outer door. A table, as large and as high as an ottoman, a low stool, the seat of which is made of two equal surfaces descending to the center like a trough, two or three little earthen dishes, the *poyo* or immovable seat built around the walls, pieces of rawhide or mat for beds, and the *mampara*, are all her furniture. The washtub? It is the river. The ironing apparatus? Another woman does the ironing.

Where is her door leading into the patio? She has none, and can have none. A fine house would it be if any *guaricha* that chose to rent this miserable tenement could come into the patio. But what can she do? Where can she go? For modern improvements are not dreamed of, and sewerage there is none. She has no rights outside these two little holes, except in the streets, vacant lots, and by the river side. Blame not, then, the poor peasant women by the river side: they keep the laws of decorum as far as is in their power; and when you are sickened at the sight of filth in the street in a city 314 years old, washed by two rivers, and placed on a side hill to make drainage as easy as possible, let it be a motive to urge upon the *gobierno* [governor] of the province some such radical measures as health and decency demand.

The number of families living in this way exceeds, perhaps, the number of well-living families in Bogotá. The ground floor is often regarded as not so healthy as the first floor, so each house has but one respectable family that has access to the patios. The front room of these lairs, excavated, so to speak, in the foundations of the best houses . . . are often used as shops by shoemakers, tailors, saddlers, etc., some of whose implements even occupy part of the street, to the inconvenience of every passer-by.

# 9  Silvia M. Arrom ◆ Changes in
# Mexican Family Law in the Nineteenth Century

*Silvia M. Arrom, professor of Latin American history at Brandeis Univer-*
*sity, received her Ph.D. from Stanford University. She has written exten-*
*sively on the urban experience of Mexican women and has explored the*
*attitudes and policies of Mexican elites toward the urban poor during the*
*nineteenth century. Here she examines the Civil Codes of 1870 and 1884.*
*She analyzes them in the context of the changes taking place in the family*
*due to the growth of the state, the expansion of the economy, and the*
*spread of liberalism. She finds that while the reforms embodied in the*
*new civil codes expanded individual freedoms, both of the personal and*
*the economic variety, they weakened the structure of the family, in the*
*process undermining the importance of lineage and marriage.*

The Mexican Revolution is often credited with initiating the modernization of Mexican family law, beginning with the landmark 1917
Law of Family Relations, which diminished the control of husbands over
wives and introduced absolute divorce. The few studies of nineteenth-
century family law minimize the changes in this area, instead emphasizing the persistence of colonial private law despite the achievement of
independence in 1821 (Carreras Maldonado and Montero Duhalt, 1975:71;
Morineau, 1975). But that was not how nineteenth-century Mexicans saw
it. On the contrary, they praised the "notable innovations" in republican
private law that corresponded to the "new necessities of society"
("Exposición," 1872:2, 22–23). They portrayed their times as "our century of advancement" and their laws as "resplendent with liberalism"
(García, 1891:46, 72). They saw the "darkness of the past" (Zarco,
1852:184) dispelled by statutes that reduced patriarchal dominance of the
family, expanded the rights of women and children, facilitated legal separations, and released family members from the traditional restrictions of
inheritance law.

  At first glance these claims appear much inflated. For example, the
1859 Law on Civil Matrimony, which, according to its preamble, "raised
women from the degradation" to which colonial law subjected them (Minister of Justice, 1859:690), merely removed marriage from ecclesiastical
jurisdiction, while reaffirming the church's centuries-old definitions of

  From "Changes in Mexican Family Law in the Nineteenth Century: The Civil
Codes of 1870 and 1884," *Journal of Family History* (Fall 1985): 305–17. Reprinted by permission of JAI Press Inc.

proper gender roles and admissible grounds for legal separations. The 1870 Civil Code, which, according to its author, amounted to a "rehabilitation of women" ("Exposición," 1872:23), actually incorporated most of the colonial laws that excluded women from politics, protected and punished them according to a double standard, and subjected wives and children to the paterfamilias's control. In fact, the new codes often repeated ancient patriarchal provisions almost verbatim.[1] Although these discriminatory measures brought sharp criticism from the jurist Genaro García in his brilliant feminist tract, *Notes on the Condition of Women* (1891), they were widely accepted in late nineteenth-century Mexico and were reiterated in the 1884 revision of the 1870 Code.

The 1870 and 1884 Civil Codes did, however, depart from colonial family law in a few instances. These innovations merit close attention, for they were far more than minor modifications of the colonial legal system. The authors of the civil codes considered them important enough to single out for detailed comment in the preambles to the codes. And, on further inspection, the changes reveal significant shifts in nineteenth-century Mexican society. For, small as each change appears in isolation, together they embody what historian Lawrence Stone calls the "critical changes" of the modern period: namely, the gradual questioning of relations of dominance and subordination that had characterized every aspect of colonial society, and the rise of the individual who believes in "the right to personal freedom in the pursuit of happiness" (Stone, 1979:22). It is this broad pattern, this liberal and individualistic trend, that the new statutes represent.

To be sure, laws do not always reflect current social norms, especially when the statutes are centuries old. Yet late nineteenth-century Mexico is one of those rare times when the law illuminates the values of educated elites. After Independence, Mexicans scrutinized the colonial legal system, discussed it openly, and proposed new constitutions and civil, criminal, and commercial codes to replace the body of law inherited from Spain. Because of the turbulence that followed Independence, this process of legal revision was not completed until the end of the nineteenth century. It was only in 1870, three years after the end of the Wars of Reform, that the first national civil code was adopted.[2] Fourteen years later, when peace had been firmly consolidated, the civil code was revised to eliminate a few imperfections of the earlier document.

Although most colonial private law continued in force until 1870, a consensus had been building since 1821 about the changes required to bring it into line with "modern society" ("Exposición," 1872:22). By the middle of the nineteenth century, Mexican legal commentators agreed on the major parameters of the new legislation (Arrom, 1985:chap.2). Moreover, it was a consensus that transcended partisan bounds. In matters of family law the liberal Justo Sierra's draft of a national civil code, written from 1858 to 1860 in the midst of civil war, was nearly identical to the Imperial Civil Code, written by a committee of conservative lawyers under the Emperor Maximilian's direction and promulgated during the French intervention in 1866. Indeed, the drafting commission worked directly from Sierra's document. The 1870 Civil Code, written by liberal jurists after the expulsion of the French and the restoration of the Republic, followed the two earlier codes closely, since its aim was to adapt Mexican law to existing social realities, and therefore "to innovate as little as possible" ("Exposición," 1872:5; Arrom, 1981:494–95). The 1884 Civil Code, drafted by positivists at the behest of a new president, introduced only one major change, otherwise copying with minor modifications the articles regulating family relations in the 1870 Code. The similarities between the earlier legal proposals and the late nineteenth-century codes suggest that their few departures from colonial family law reflect attitudes that were widespread, at least among the dominant classes.[3]

The first set of changes in the 1870 and 1884 Civil Codes modified the relationship of fathers and children: the age of majority was lowered from twenty-five to twenty-one years, and single children were freed from the *patria potestad* on reaching that age (1870, Arts. 415, 694; 1884, Arts. 388, 596). These measures increased the autonomy of children by releasing them from their father's authority earlier than was usual under colonial law, which granted them independence only when they married or their father died. The new statutes affected unmarried children the most, for they alone had been subject to the *patria potestad* after attaining the age of majority (unless the father or a judge chose to "emancipate" them, a term used for the liberation of the child as well as the slave). After 1870, children gained the right to control their personal acts and property at the of twenty-one, where they might never have before, had their father lived to be very old.[4] These statutes had less impact on those children who married, since marriage released them from the *patria potestad* even if they were minors, and they did not reenter it if they were widowed. Still, those who married after the age of twenty-one now gained their full juridical sovereignty younger than they would have under colonial law.

These changes, which augmented individual freedom at the expense of paternal authority, reflect the ongoing weakening of patriarchy over the last few centuries. As the state grew stronger, the patriarch surrendered power to such government agencies as the courts and the schools. As institutional structures undermined the cohesiveness of the extended family, his authority was restricted to his spouse and unmarried children.

In Hispanic law, for example, he had gradually lost the Roman patriarch's *patria potestad* over grandchildren as well as children, which once had included the right to sell his offspring if [he were] impoverished and to judge and punish—even kill—adulterous daughters. The Mexican civil codes further restricted his authority, not merely to the nuclear family, but to his wife and minor children only.

The expansion of adult children's freedom also reflects the spread of ideals of liberty and the enshrinement of the individual rather than the family as a unit of concern. It is noteworthy, however, that Mexican legislators were reluctant to extend full independence to single daughters. The civil codes therefore introduced a distinction between adult sons and daughters by requiring the single daughter to obtain parental permission to move out of the family home until the age of thirty—in order to guard her reputation, "the most precious jewel of the Fair and Delicate Sex" (José María Lacunza in Verdugo, 1897, II:59–60; 1870, Art. 695; 1884, Art. 597).[5] Even though the new codes restricted the single daughter for nine more years than the son, they nonetheless gave her more autonomy than did colonial law, which kept her under the father's *potestad* so long as he was still alive. At twenty-one she now gained the right to manage her own property, take a job, enter into contracts, and marry without paternal permission; at thirty she gained the right to choose her own residence as well. Despite the qualification of their new rights, then, women shared in the trend reducing the duration of the father's authority.

The second change in the 1870 and 1884 Civil Codes modified the relationship between mothers and children by granting new authority over her offspring to the widow, the legally separated mother whose husband's misbehavior gave grounds to the separation, and the single mother who legally recognized her children.[6] Under colonial law only the father had the *patria potestad*, which gave him the right to control the child and its property, and to use any income from that property for his own benefit. If the father died, the mother was never given the *patria potestad* over her children; she was given the more limited responsibility of guardianship over minor children, but even that only if the father had not named another guardian in his will and only for as long as she lived "honestly" and did not remarry.[7] Widowed fathers, however, automatically retained both forms of authority regardless of their behavior and regardless of any stipulation the mother made in her will. These distinctions show that colonial law did not consider mothers, like fathers, to be the natural "rulers" of the child. In contrast, the 1870 and 1884 Civil Codes automatically granted widowed mothers (and most separated and single mothers as well) both the guardianship and the *patria potestad*; the widowed grandmother could also exercise both forms of authority over her orphaned grandchildren, though mothers and grandmothers still lost their new rights if they remarried or lived scandalously (1870, Arts. 268–71, 391–92; 1884, Arts. 245–49, 365–66).

The conferral of the *patria potestad* on women was a radical departure from colonial law for two reasons. As Justo Sierra explained when he proposed this change in his draft code of 1859, the natural rights of maternity were finally "recognized as they should be" (Sierra, 1861:iii; José María Lacunza in Verdugo, 1897, I:306). Furthermore, the *patria potestad* represented the power of governing another human being. Colonial law had given widows and adult emancipated single women complete authority to control their own acts, but, unless they owned slaves, no class of women had the authority to control others until the 1870 Civil Code gave mothers the *patria potestad*. This new empowerment of women implicitly challenged the basic principle of patriarchal society: that only men rule.

It is possible to see the conferral of the *patria potestad* on women as an attempt to lessen the differences between men and women; indeed, that was the view of the jurist who declared this measure an important part of the "rehabilitation of woman" in modern society ("Exposición," 1872:22–23). Certainly the extension to mothers of a right previously restricted to fathers responded to the growing recognition of women's competence, for the authors of the 1870 Civil Code conceded that most women had enough intelligence, education, and experience to manage their children's affairs ("Exposición," 1872:23). It also responded to the growing specialization in childrearing, which increasingly became a female domain. As childhood was recognized as a separate and critical stage in human development, motherhood gained in importance, making it unreasonable to deny women the power they needed to perform their duties effectively.[8]

Yet the limitations Mexican legislators placed on a mother's authority again show their ambivalence about granting women equal rights with men. The widowed mother's authority over her children and grandchildren was not exactly like that of the widowed father or grandfather. She alone lost the guardianship and *patria potestad* if she lived dishonorably or remarried. She could also be forced to consult with advisers if her husband, lacking faith in her judgment, had so stipulated in his will.[9] Furthermore, the new statutes did not aim to increase the rights of mothers across the board: they only empowered the mother in default of the father (and, in their absence, the grandmother in default of the grandfather, with the paternal grandparents favored over the maternal line).

Thus the expansion of women's rights did not apply equally to women of all marital statuses. The single adult woman, already accorded considerable independence under colonial law, was released from the father's *potestad* and granted the *patria potestad* over her legally recognized children. The widow, already able to govern herself with complete liberty under colonial law, was likewise given the authority to govern her children. In contrast, the married woman, the most restricted of any woman under colonial law, retained approximately the same status as before, being under the control of her husband and needing his permission for most of her legal acts. As Genaro García noted wryly, "The light of our legislation has unfortunately been unable to penetrate the institution of matrimony" (1891:47).

The exclusion of married women from these legal changes might at first appear paradoxical. The recognition of women's aptitude to handle their own affairs, used to justify changes in single and widowed women's status, could also have applied to wives. So, too, the growing prestige of motherhood could logically have led to an extension of married as well as widowed, separated, and single mothers' authority over their children. It did not because the equality of husbands and wives was incompatible with corporate notions of social control.

In colonial society, people had been controlled through hierarchically organized corporations, such as the nobility, clergy, military, and Indians. Far from being based on the concept of natural equality, this system was composed of groups with different functions and rights, whose members accepted their differences and lived in harmony. The nuclear family played a crucial role in preserving the system, for it was the basic social unit on which the entire structure rested, with men governing their wives and children just as they were in turn governed by the state. Since effective government was believed to result from the imposition of decisions through a hierarchical chain of command—and not from consensus or negotiation among equals, as in a pluralist system—the subordination of wives and children was essential to maintaining social cohesion. Legislators thus admonished wives to "recognize the authority of their consorts as heads of the family" so as to "maintain the order and tranquility of families, on which the State's in large part depend" (Clarification of the 1776 Pragmatic Sanction on Marriage, May 26, 1883, in Pérez y López, 1798:243–46 [*sic*]). In the nineteenth century, though most vestiges of corporatism were abolished, corporative concepts continued to shape notions of the nuclear family as the pillar of the social order. Thus legal commentators still warned that husbands and wives could not be equal because that would risk the "continual mutiny of the subjects against the established authority," and undermine the stability of the Mexican state (*Nuevo Febrero*, 1850:1, 64–66).[10]

The difference was that the Civil Codes of 1870 and 1884 no longer vested the control of the nuclear family solely in the male. Recognizing the existence of female-headed households, the new statutes gave female household heads the same authority as male [ones] (although the *patria potestad* for both was now more circumscribed than the father's had been in colonial times). By strengthening the rights of female household heads, the civil codes therefore strengthened the control of individuals through nuclear families. The effect for children was to regularize the status of minors in female-headed households, who had previously been subject only to the guardianship of the mother or perhaps of someone outside the household. The new authority of the widowed, single, and separated mother did not affect children after they turned age twenty-one, however. Neither did it conflict with the man's rule of the household, since it applied only to the female-headed households, which had previously been outside the patriarchal structure of control. Certainly patriarchal authority was reduced in families where adult children remained at home and fathers were still alive, but contemporaries viewed this situation as exceptional and justified it as part of a necessary defense of individual rights, which included the right of adults to establish their own households. The line was clearly drawn at wives, though, for their personal autonomy was perceived as a threat to the stability of the basic social unit.

Like the conferral of the *patria potestad* on women, the third major set of changes in family law, which altered the grounds for legal separation, left the relationship of the spouses untouched. What the civil codes did was to weaken some of the restraints that Canon law (and, after 1859, Mexican law) had placed on married couples. Yet they did so without permitting absolute divorce, which was only legalized in 1917. There has been some confusion on this point, since the 1870 and 1884 Civil Codes referred to legal separations as "divorce"; but only *divortium quoad thorum et mutuam cohabitationem*, or separation of bed and board, was permitted.[11]

The grounds for such separations were expanded when the 1870 Civil Code allowed couples to "divorce" on the basis of mutual consent. This innovation represented an important philosophical shift, for colonial law had envisioned divorce merely as a protective mechanism to separate an innocent spouse from a delinquent partner—for example, one who seriously violated the marital vows by committing adultery or treating the other cruelly. Divorces, therefore, had been granted only when the misbehavior of one spouse could be amply proven (Arrom, 1985:chap. 5). In contrast, the civil codes allowed couples to separate simply because they desired to. This measure made the recourse of legal separation accessible to couples who could not pin charges on each other—or who did not want to air dirty laundry in public.

By making incompatibility grounds for separation, the civil codes manifested a growing belief in the importance of happiness in marriage. Whereas colonial law had subordinated the happiness of the individual to the duty of maintaining family unity, the civil codes now recognized that incompatible couples should be allowed to go their separate ways in view of "the sad truth that nothing is worse than matrimonial discord" ("Exposición," 1872:18–19). By facilitating separations, the codes also expanded personal freedom. In fact, the link between individualism and divorce on the grounds of mutual consent is demonstrated by the Spanish term for it: "voluntary divorce." It thus represented an expansion of the sphere of individual will.

Still, Mexican legislators felt considerable ambivalence about releasing people from the bonds of marriage. The committee drafting the 1870 Civil Code only accepted the grounds of mutual consent after a heated debate, and both the 1870 and 1884 drafting committees rejected absolute divorce even though this reform had some vocal supporters in Mexico at the time (Arrom, 1981:508–11). Furthermore, the 1870 and 1884 Civil Codes placed a series of limitations on the use of this recourse. For example, they prohibited couples from seeking divorce by mutual consent unless they had been married more than two years; they required the judge to attempt to reunite the couple; and they stipulated that the separation was only temporary, decreed for a specific period of time (1870, Arts. 240–59; 1884, Arts. 227–36). These restrictions attempted to reconcile social obligations with personal liberty and the right to happiness, a conflict from which the individual had not yet emerged unfettered.[12]

Another change in the grounds for legal separation extended the personal liberty of husbands by reducing the circumstances in which their adultery could give rise to a divorce. Both Canon law, in force until matrimony was removed from ecclesiastical jurisdiction in 1859, and the Law of Civil Matrimony that replaced it had defined the infidelity of either spouse as equal cause for separation. The 1870 and 1884 Civil Codes introduced a distinction: whereas the wife's adultery was always grounds for divorce, a man's was grounds only if he committed it in the conjugal home, if he took his lover as a concubine or caused a public scandal, or if his lover insulted or mistreated the legitimate wife (1870, Arts. 241–42; 1884, Arts. 227–28).

This strengthening of the double standard in the late nineteenth-century codes reflects the secularization of society and the circumscription of the church, defender of equal matrimonial duties for husbands and wives, by the liberal Reform. The new law also reflects the expansion of

individual freedom, for it released men from one of the confining pre-
cepts of Catholicism. This freedom was not likewise extended to women
because it would undermine the principle of obedience of wives to husbands. Moreover, because of women's reproductive role, it would undermine the inheritance system based on legitimate heirs. Thus the redefinition
of adultery as grounds for separation again demonstrates how tentatively
the liberal ideal of equality was applied to married women.

The final innovations in family law, which embodied liberalism in
the economic realm, offer further proof that the legal changes of the late
nineteenth century did not always favor women. One provision of the
1870 and 1884 Civil Codes created a new option in marital regimes, allowing couples to choose whether to marry under the system of separate
or community property (1870, Art. 2099; 1884, Art. 1965). Colonial law
had only recognized the community property system where a couple's
earnings were pooled together and managed by the husband, and where
he administered (but did not own) any property his wife brought to the
marriage in the form of a dowry or property she inherited afterward
(Arrom, 1985:chap. 2).

The commission that drafted the 1870 Civil Code considered the new
option in marital regimes an advance for the married woman, since she
could administer her own properties and retain any interest they earned,
so long as she renounced her half share of the community property
("Exposición," 1872:74). The separation-of-property system may have
favored the lower-class working woman who earned an income and could
now control it as she wished. But the benefits for the propertied woman
are dubious, since she had previously retained the ownership (if not the
control) of her dowry and inheritances, and had in addition enjoyed half
the husband's earnings in the event of widowhood or separation. Certainly, her property was safer as separate property than as dowry, which
might conceivably be lost if she committed adultery or if her husband
squandered it (though he was legally prohibited from alienating it). Still,
the absolute security of her property was gained only by foregoing a share
of her husband's future earnings. And for the woman of modest means
who neither earned a salary nor owned property (or whose property was
less than her husband might earn), the separation-of-property system represented a loss of protection, for she could be left penniless if separated
or widowed.[13]

Still, as the drafting commission explained, "the spouses are at full
liberty to arrange their personal situation in marriage" according to their
wishes ("Exposición," 1872:74). The option of marrying under the regime of separate property fit the more flexible, diversified economy and
society of the nineteenth century. It also reflected the changing purpose

of marriage, which was becoming less a family business strategy than a way to find personal fulfillment. The new option recognized that a growing number of individuals did not want to subsume their personal property in a jointly owned marital regime. Thus it weakened the legal restraints imposed on those who married, at the same time expanding the realm in which they could exercise personal choices.

A related set of changes in the civil codes abolished restrictions on the right of individuals to dispose of their property. This is the only area where there was an important difference between the 1870 and 1884 Civil Codes, and it would be of great consequence to children in the propertied classes, who under colonial law automatically inherited a share of their father's and mother's property. The 1870 Civil Code dropped the requirement that parents with the means to do so endow their daughters, and the 1884 Code, amid a furor of controversy, abolished the *legítima*, or the equal share of the parents' property guaranteed to each child, female and male (1870, Art. 228; 1884, Art. 217).[14] The end of the mandatory dowry was not as significant as might first appear, since the dowry was a form of advance inheritance deducted from the daughter's eventual share of her parents' estate. This provision therefore merely ended the daughter's right to inherit before her brothers. In contrast, the abolition of the *legítima* was a radical change, for it ended the guaranteed inheritance of daughters and sons altogether.

From the parents' perspective, these provisions enlarged their freedom, allowing them to do as they wished with their property during their lifetimes without having to provide a dowry for the daughter who married, and at their deaths without having to bequeath an equal share to each legitimate offspring. It also prevented the dispersal of capital when parents could no longer control the marriages or occupational choices of their children. Testamentary freedom was consequently a logical accompaniment to the decline in the authority of parents over their children.

From the children's perspective, the effect was very different, since it decreased the protection afforded them under colonial law. This protection was especially important for women in the propertied classes, because they were more economically vulnerable than their brothers, who had careers. The dowry had given the married woman a power base in marriage and a source of support if she was separated or widowed. Yet the end of mandatory dowries in 1870 did not increase the woman's vulnerability so long as she continued to inherit automatically from both parents; it simply meant that she had to wait longer to obtain her share of her parents' estate. Given the short life expectancies in the nineteenth century, many daughters probably did not wait long for their inheritances. However, when testamentary freedom was introduced in 1884, ending the system of equal partition, women's legal protection was significantly reduced, for now they might receive neither dowry nor inheritance depending on their parents' wishes. Although the 1884 Civil Code recognized women's vulnerability by requiring parents to provide a pension for unmarried daughters—as well as for minor or incapacitated sons (Arts. 3393–3401)—this provision did nothing for married daughters who lost their guaranteed right to an inheritance. Even spinsters, though assured of their economic survival, were not assured the kind of position that comes from property ownership. The proponents of the measure were well aware of its effect: as the minister of justice argued in a preface to the new code, parents have no "obligation to make their children rich and opulent," only to educate them and provide for their subsistence until they can take care of themselves (Macedo, 1884:5–6).

The abolition of the *legítima* was accompanied by a heated controversy precisely because the expansion of individual freedom here came at so high a price: it reduced the protection not only of children, but of marriage itself, since legitimate children might now lose out to illegitimate ones; it reduced the protection of lineage, since some descendants might fare far better than others. In short, it threatened the very institution of the family, which had been protected by protecting each of its members. Thus legislators of the time recognized it as the most "radical reform" of the 1884 Civil Code (Macedo, 1884:5). Indeed, Justino Fernández, one of the members of the commission that drafted the code, refused to approve the measure and instead wrote a dissenting opinion in which he argued that testamentary freedom would undermine the harmony and love so essential among family members ("Voto particular del C. Diputado Justino Fernández," in Macedo, 1884:26–36).

The abolition of the *legítima* also aroused opposition because it was out of step with the nineteenth-century practice of dividing inheritances equally among all legitimate offspring.[15] In introducing the reform, the commission drafting the 1884 Civil Code acknowledged that the measure was inspired by the laws of England, "that great nation . . . that is today the most free and perhaps the most civilized in the world," where testamentary freedom "stimulates the citizenry to devote themselves to their work, . . . the source of public and private virtues" (Macedo, 1884:23–24). Yet, as Fernández cautioned in his dissenting opinion, this measure broke with the legal systems of most European as well as Latin American countries. It had been explicitly rejected by the commission that drafted the 1870 Civil Code, which considered testamentary freedom inappropriate for Mexican society ("Exposición," 1872:128–30). Further, Fernández viewed its adoption as premature because it had not been adequately discussed by the Mexican public (Macedo, 1884:24, 27–31).

Fernández had a point here, since the other changes in the civil codes brought Mexican law into line with contemporary customs. In fact, my research on the first half of the nineteenth century reveals the new attitudes and practices a decade before they were embodied in the civil codes (Arrom, 1985:chaps. 2, 5). Thus, for example, social commentaries and didactic pieces show that Mexicans already gave mothers the major responsibility in childrearing before the 1870 Civil Code expanded their authority over their children. The liberalization of the grounds for legal separation in the civil codes was foreshadowed in the demands of litigants who came before the ecclesiastical divorce court, in the arguments of their lawyers, and, by midcentury, in the response of the judges as well. The strengthening of the double standard was likewise visible in ecclesiastical divorce records before it was incorporated in the late nineteenth-century codes.

Similarly, the dowry had been declining long before the 1870 Civil Code dropped the colonial requirement that parents with means provide a dowry for their daughters. Despite the presence of that requirement in the law books, few well-to-do brides in Mexico City brought dowries to their marriages by the middle of the century (Lavrin and Couturier, 1979; Arrom, 1985:chap. 3). The decline of the dowry reflects the new economic situation of Mexican elites in the nineteenth century. With the expansion of investment opportunities, parents were loath to finance their children's new families, instead preferring to control large sums of capital on their own. With the expansion of higher education and professional jobs, new families did not need this financing as much as before, since they could support themselves on a husband's earnings alone. And as families no longer viewed marriage as a strategy for a woman's father to obtain a business partner or a young man to acquire an investment base, the children's personal decisions could be made apart from the extended family's business considerations (Nazzari, 1984; Chowning, 1984; Kuznesof, 1984).

Unlike the other changes in family law, which reflected contemporary practices, the abolition of the *legítima* was introduced to bring about social change: it was meant to foster economic development by lifting restrictions on capital accumulation and the free flow of property. Proponents of the new measure also hoped it would discourage sloth, since parents who could now invest their capital in the most advantageous way would be stimulated to greater exertions, and children who were no longer guaranteed an inheritance would apply themselves to study and work (Macedo, 1884:5–9, 21–26). Thus the commission drafting the 1884 Civil Code explained that "the right to property requires this liberty as a complement to individual guarantees and as a necessity for the enhancement of public wealth" (Macedo, 1884:26).

Taken together, the innovations in the 1870 and 1884 Civil Codes show a consistent trend. They were "resplendent with liberalism" because they expanded individual freedom in both the personal and economic realms. And, though gender equality was not one of their goals, they reduced some of the distinctions between men and women. Other legal manifestations of this trend are familiar to historians: the end of racial distinctions, noble titles, and slavery reduced the differences among individuals; [and] the abolition of entail, church property, and the communal holdings of Indian villages ended restrictions that prevented the free movement of capital and property. It is easy to overlook the same trend in family law because it was so tentative and manifested itself so sparingly. But the changing social and economic relations, and the spread of liberal ideas that accompanied them, also touched the Mexican family. These legal changes did not, however, have a uniform impact on all family members. Greater freedom for some, such as propertied parents, meant a loss of protection for others, such as children. Furthermore, as liberty replaced duty, the legal ties among family members were loosened. As the individual was released from the legal demands of family relations, marriage and lineage themselves emerged in a weakened condition, witnesses to the circumscription of the family by an expanding state and economy and by an ideology that favored individuals over kin.

## Notes

1. For a detailed discussion of colonial family law, see Arrom (1985:chap. 2); also Bernal de Bugeda (1975). On the Law of Civil Matrimony, see Arrom (1981:496)

2. The first two books of a national civil code were enacted during the French occupation (1866), but it was abrogated soon afterward when Maximilian was executed. Previous codification attempts, which began as early as 1822, included the promulgation of short-lived state codes in Oaxaca, Zacatecas, and Jalisco. On the codification process, see González (1978:95–136).

3. This essay focuses on the major innovations of the 1870 and 1884 Civil Codes; other changes are catalogued in Arrom (1981), which also gives additional detail on the laws discussed here.

4. One exception was the right of the minor to choose a spouse freely, so long as the girl had reached the female legal age of marriage of twelve and the boy fourteen. Although the parents' consent was required for the marriage of minors, a marriage dictated by the father against the child's will was not legally binding (Arrom, 1985:chap. 2; 1870 Civil Code, Art. 289).

5. Adult single daughters under age thirty, however, were allowed to leave the parental home without permission either if they married or if a widowed parent

remarried, thereby introducing a stepparent into the household (1870 Civil Code, Art. 695; 1884 Civil Code, Art. 597).

6. The right to exercise the *patria potestad* only applied to the single mother of natural children, that is, children born to a man and woman who had no legal impediment to marrying. Children fathered during an adulterous affair with a married man, for example, would not theoretically be eligible. On the recognition of natural children, see Book 1, title 6, chap. 4 of the 1870 and 1884 Civil Codes.

7. Although in practice the guardian's power over a child might resemble the father's, the law distinguished between the two by denying the guardian the right to retain any income from the child's property and subjecting him or her to the direct supervision of the court. Furthermore, the law did not explicitly grant a guardian the right to punish the child. See discussion in Book 1, title 6, chap. 4 of the 1870 and 1884 Civil Codes.

8. For an elaboration of these points, see Arrom (1985:esp. chaps. 1, 2, 5).

9. Mexican legislators did not, however, require a widow to accept the opinions of the advisers. In this respect they followed García Goyena's 1851 draft for the Spanish Civil Code rather than the more restrictive Code Napoléon (Arrom, 1981:501–2).

10. For an elaboration of this point, see Arrom (1985:chap. 3).

11. Annulment was also possible, although rarely granted, since it required the marriage to have been invalid in the first place because of some prior impediment or violation of the law in contracting the union (Book 1, title 5, chap. 6 of the 1870 and 1884 Civil Codes).

12. The progress of the ideal of individual freedom in the fourteen years between the two civil codes can be seen in a few minor modifications of the articles on divorce. By omitting several restrictions on spouses' eligibility to seek separations, the 1884 Civil Code made separations more accessible than in 1870, and one new grounds was added: the violation of *capitulaciones matrimoniales*, or prenuptial agreements. Cf. 1870 Civil Code, Arts. 240–59; 1884 Civil Code, Arts. 227–36; discussed in Arrom (1981:508–9).

13. The benefits of the separation-of-property system for wealthy women also seem doubtful since colonial law had allowed a woman to circumvent the husband's management of her property through a *capitulación matrimonial*, or prenuptial agreement, in which she could retain the control of her property while still married under the community property system. (This practice was, however, rare in nineteenth-century Mexico.) Furthermore, the wife's right to administer her separate property was restricted in the 1870 and 1884 Civil Codes by the requirement that she obtain her husband's consent to sell or donate her property (1870 Civil Code, Arts. 2208–20; 1884 Civil Code, Arts. 2075–77; Arrom, 1981:514–15).

14. Until 1884, the law dictated that a parent with legitimate children should divide four fifths of the estate equally among them. The testator was free to bequeath the remaining fifth (the *quinto*) as he or she wished. Some children could therefore inherit more than others by receiving part of the unrestricted fifth. The proportion of the estate distributed by law was smaller when there were no surviving legitimate descendants. For the complicated regulations of inheritance see Book 4, title 2 of the 1870 Civil Code.

15. It is noteworthy that in the absence of a will, the probate court followed the old formulas guaranteeing each legitimate child an equal share of the parents'

estate (Book 4, title 4 of the 1870 and 1884 Civil Codes). The principle of equal partition thus continued to be the norm in the absence of a specific directive from the testator. Indeed, Margaret Chowning's research on elite families in Michoacán (1984:3) shows the egalitarian principle was so strong that before 1884 they rarely availed themselves of the *quinto*, or unrestricted fifth of the estate, to favor one child over another, and after 1884 even those who made wills continued to divide their estates equally among their children.

## References

Arrom, Silvia M. "Cambios en la condición juridica de la mujer mexicana en el siglo XIX." In José Luis Soberanis Fernández, ed., *Memoria del II Congreso de Historia del Derecho Mexicano*, pp. 493–513. Mexico City: Universidad National Autónoma de México (UNAM), 1981.

———. *The Women of Mexico City, 1790–1857*. Stanford: Stanford University Press, 1985.

Bernal de Bugeda, Beatriz. "Situación jurídica de la mujer en Indias." In Facultad de Derecho, ed., *Condición jurídica de la mujer en México*, pp. 71–126. Mexico City: UNAM, 1975.

Carreras Maldonado, María, and Sara Montero Duhalt. "Condición de la mujer en el derecho civil Mexicano." In Facultad de Derecho, ed., *Condición jurídica de la mujer en México*, pp. 71–126. Mexico City: UNAM, 1975.

Chowning, Margaret. "Combining Business and Kinship: Patterns of Inheritance and Formation of Family Empires in Nineteenth-Century Michoacán." Paper presented at the American Historical Association, Chicago, 1984.

"Exposición de los cuatro libros del Código Civil del Distrito Federal y Territorio de la Baja California que hizo la comisión al presentar el proyecto al estado de S. Luis Potosí," pp. 1–85. In *Código Civil del Distrito Federal y Territorio de la Baja-California adoptado para el estado de S. Luis Potosí*. Mexico City, 1872.

García, Genaro. *Apuntes sobre la condición de la mujer*. Mexico City: Compañía Limit. de Tipógrafos, 1891.

González, María del Refugio. "Notas para el estudio del proceso de la codificación civil en México (1821–1928)." In *Libro del cincuentenario del Código Civil*, pp. 95–136. Mexico City: UNAM, 1978.

Kuznesof, Elizabeth. "Property Law and Family Strategies: Inheritance and Corporations in Brazil, 1800–1960." Paper presented at the American Historical Association, Chicago, 1984.

Lavrin, Asunción, and Edith Couturier. "Dowries and Wills: A View of Women's Socio-economic Role in Colonial Guadalajara and Puebla,

1640–1790." *Hispanic American Historical Review* 59, 2:280–304, 1979.

Macedo, Miguel. *Datos para el estudio del nuevo Código Civil del Distrito Federal y Territorio de la Baja California.* Mexico City: Imprenta de Francisco Diaz de León, 1884.

Minister of Justice. "Preamble to the Law of Civil Matrimony, July 23, 1859." In Manuel Dublán and José Maria Lozano, eds., *Legislación mexicana o colección completa de las disposiciones legislativas expedidas desde la independencia de la República*, vol. 8, 690, 1859.

Morineau Iduarte, Marta. "Condición jurídica de la mujer en el México del siglo XIX." In Facultad de Derecho, ed., *Condición jurídica de la mujer en México*, pp. 41–54. Mexico City: UNAM, 1975.

Nazzari, Muriel. "Women and Property in the Transition to Capitalism: Decline of the Dowry in São Paulo, Brazil (1640–1870)." Paper presented at the American Historical Association, Chicago, 1984.

*Nuevo Febrero Mexicano: Obra completa de jurisprudencia teórico-práctica.* . . . Mexico City, 1850.

Pérez y López, Antonio. *Teatro de la legislación universal de España e Indias* . . ., vol. 19. Madrid: En la impr. de M. González, 1783 [*sic*].

Sierra, Justo. *Proyecto de un código civil mexicano formado de orden del supremo gobierno.* . . . Mexico City: V. G. Torres, 1861.

Stone, Lawrence. *The Family, Sex, and Marriage in England, 1500–1800.* London: Harper and Row. Abr. ed., 1979.

Verdugo, Agustín, ed. *Revisión del proyecto de código civil mexicano del doctor don Justo Sierra* . . ., 2 vols. Mexico City, 1897.

Zarco, Francisco. "La mujer." In *Presente Amistoso Dedicado a las Señoritas Mexicanas*, vol. 3:181–84, 1852.

## 10  Donna J. Guy ◆ Women, Peonage, and Industrialization: Argentina, 1810–1914

*Since the time of Independence, Latin American nations have experimented with dozens of schemes to bring about economic modernization and thereby cure existing social and political ills. The scholarly community has re-acted in kind, and publications dealing with the successes and, more of-ten, the failures of modernization policy must number in the thousands. Until the appearance of this essay, reprinted here from the* Latin Ameri-can Research Review, *the effect of modernization on the lives of Latin American women had been neglected, however, because it had rarely occurred to anyone that the workplace was gendered and that labor legis-lation carried a gender bias. Donna Guy conducted extensive archival research to recreate the employment opportunities available to poor women in a rapidly expanding Argentine economy. She examines how the change from a cottage to a factory system of production affected working women and how the state responded to women in the work force.*

In recent years, a body of literature analyzing development and mod-ernization since the world wars has emphasized the diverse tasks women perform in premodern agrarian societies as compared to incipient indus-trial economies. The greater input of women in many nonmechanized societies, compared to their role thereafter, has been seen as the key to understanding why the introduction of machine technology has often re-sulted in the subsequent general unemployment or underemployment of working-class women.[1]

Much of the data related to the history of working women are based upon historical studies of the industrial, commercial, or bureaucratic de-velopment of Europe and the United States, or upon anthropological and sociological studies of contemporary Africa and Asia. Similar works per-taining to contemporary Latin America have pointed to changing demo-graphic and fertility rates and to the nature of tasks defined as women's work as additional factors to be considered. Further, the coexistence of modern and premodern forms of female employment, so characteristic of developing areas, has been grouped into four main categories: household production, simple production of merchandise, capitalist organization, and state public administration.[2]

These studies help explain how poor Latin American women often find it difficult to secure employment in the modernizing sector now, but

From *Latin American Research Review* 16, no. 3 (1981): 65–89. Reprinted by permission.

few studies exist that confirm this problem historically. Features such as international trade, regional work attitudes, the transition from slave labor to peonage in rural areas, and the formulation of industrial labor legislation in urban areas are analyzed rarely from the perspective of female work opportunities, yet they both affected directly the sexual composition of the labor force.[3] Equally important is the combined effect of both types of labor systems.

The evolution of women's work in Argentina provides an ideal historical example of the effects of modernization on females. On the eve of independence in 1810, women's cottage industries formed a mainstay of the provincial economies in the north, west, and center of the country and became even more important after the outbreak of war. Traders in the interior, especially from Tucumán, sold cotton, woolen and fur garments, and foodstuffs, prepared in slave workshops and at home by women of all classes, to workers in the mines of Potosí, Bolivia.[4] These products, in addition to livestock and finished leather goods, constituted the basic items of trade. In contrast, the eastern riverine provinces, less populated and more exclusively dependent upon pastoral activities, had minimal levels of female artisan activities. Proportionately few women, the availability of cheap imported European textiles, and the unsuitability of cotton cultivation there had discouraged strong female work traditions in the littoral.[5]

In less than a century the coastal area eclipsed the interior in economic, demographic, and political importance. Populated by European immigrants and stimulated by the export of cash agricultural and pastoral products, the littoral, particularly the capital city of Buenos Aires, also became the principal urban industrial site. Thus, the transition from colony to nation, from slave owning to wage labor and peonage after 1813, and from rural to dominantly urban social patterns after 1914 fundamentally transformed the regional fabric of Argentine society. Buenos Aires, an outpost until the late eighteenth century, became the hub of the new nation. Changing market conditions due to wars and competition, first with European and then with coastal manufactures, caused the interior provinces to stagnate. They ultimately became economic and political tributaries of the capital.

The decline of cottage industry in the interior as well as the spectacular economic development of the coastal region resulted in a drastic reduction in the percentage of adult women who either claimed a profession or received remuneration for their labor. Although it is impossible to determine the exact proportion of female artisans or salaried women workers in early nineteenth-century Argentina, evidence suggests that a greater proportion participated in artisan tasks in 1810 than that 58.8 percent of all women over the age of ten who reported in 1869 that they claimed a trade. By 1914, when the third national census was taken, the percentage of identified female workers had dropped to 27.4, even though their actual numbers had increased throughout the period.[6] Furthermore, the geographical location and type of work had changed, and the nationality of the woman worker had become a factor as well.

Many difficulties involved in tracing the general impact of modernization on women in Argentina become less formidable when viewed regionally. Since the coastal pastoral sector had few traditions that perpetuated defined economic roles for females, it can be presumed that there would be little justification for urging the employment of women there. Similarly, while the interior, with its female work tradition, might concern itself with the plight of unemployed women, economic conditions would ultimately limit attempts to find them work. In both regions, distinct patterns of labor legislation related to peonage, added to the advent of modern protective industrial legislation influenced by European conditions, all created precedents that led to the channeling of women into domestic service or unemployment. In this way, the changing reality of work and the demand for labor enable us to place Argentine women in the world created by modern economic development.

## The Expansion of Female Cottage Industry, 1810–1869

The reliance upon women's work that distinguished the interior from the coastal area in 1810 continued to characterize the inland provinces until the 1870s. Partial census data, as well as travelers' accounts of those years, point to the availability and need for female laborers in the interior. For example, local censuses for the interior provinces of La Rioja (1855), Catamarca (1812), and Tucumán (1845), along with those for the riverine provinces of Corrientes (1820, 1833), Entre Ríos (1849), and Santa Fe (1816), all showed those provinces to have more female inhabitants than male. This imbalance can be accounted for by military conscription, the tendency of male immigrants to remain in the littoral, and by the migration of native-born men from the interior to the coast or to other interior provinces in search of work.[7] These factors, added to the casualties of the civil wars, reinforced those economic patterns that could be maintained by women, and thus females remained a dominant force in the economic life of the interior.

Provinces in the northwest had been hard hit by the wars of independence due to requests for provisions and military recruits, both of which seriously hampered a once-thriving trade in mules, textiles, and food.[8] When the English Captain Andrews, a mining specialist, made a tour of the northwest in 1825, he noted the sharp reduction of male economic activities occasioned by the wars. According to him, Santiago del Estero province's livelihood consisted mainly of the trade in "ponchos, *pilliones* [*pellones*, or fur saddle blankets], and woolen fabrics for men and women's dresses." All these goods were the output of traditional female handicrafts. In Salta he noted similarly that the provincial economy had deteriorated seriously and that its earlier mainstay, cattle and mule raising, still languished because of a paucity of male ranchers. Nevertheless, he had hopes that the nascent sugar industry would thrive and that it would replace livestock as the dominant male economic activity. Upon reaching the northernmost province of Jujuy, Andrews observed that a renaissance in international trade had already begun there and that a major component was the production of woolen articles that were traded locally and in Peru.[9]

Andrews's analysis of the nature and extent of women's productive activities was confirmed by the visit of another British traveler, Woodbine Parish, in 1837. Working-class women, he reported, continued to produce the main items of regional and international trade in the interior, and even middle-class women supplemented, or often provided the bulk of, family income through embroidery and weaving. Further, Parish noted that cottage textiles, along with other regional economic pursuits, were becoming linked to the peonage-based sugar industry, because Indian laborers (principally male) could be induced to work the harvest season with payments in coarse cloth, often handwoven. This relationship between dominantly female and male pursuits persisted into the 1850s in some areas, and probably later in others not yet affected by the introduction of British textiles, which was facilitated by railroad construction.[10]

One other northwestern province, Catamarca, also became known for its female artisans, a reputation that has endured into the twentieth century. Although the textile fame of Catamarca was eclipsed at first by more extensive production in Tucumán, Santiago, Jujuy, and Córdoba, eventually the lack of alternative economic pursuits, isolation from competitors, and the uncertainty of the principal male activity, mining, enabled a number of towns in Catamarca to sustain production of traditional ponchos and shawls of wool and llama. Originally a center of cotton cultivation and spinning, this province adapted to market demands and soon entire families of daughters and other female relatives replaced a slave labor textile-production system and specialized in woolen production.[11]

Other interior provinces outside the northwest depended upon female labor to varying degrees. The western provinces of San Luis and San Juan, for example, also benefited from women's work, although on a much more modest scale. Perhaps the most vivid picture comes from a former Argentine president, Domingo Sarmiento, in his account of San Juan in the 1820s and 1830s. A man of modest middle-class origins, Sarmiento credited his mother's and sisters' needlework, weaving, and jam production for the survival of his family during the civil wars and economic insecurity of those years. He also recounted poignantly how his female relatives, aided by domestic servants, tried other activities such as candle making in an attempt to make more money.[12] Their experiences differed markedly from middle-class women in the coastal area, who, unless widowed, were not prepared to work.[13]

The central province of Córdoba, commercial gateway to the interior provinces of the northwest and west, was often caught up in both civil turmoil and attacks by Indian marauders. Consequently, as in the north-west, the military needs of the province tended to discourage male-oriented pursuits for many years. In the interim, local products of female handicrafts, ranging from textiles to food and sweets, helped maintain trade.

## Peonage and Women Workers

The shortage of male labor in Córdoba was so great in the 1830s that women known to be poor or convicted of crimes such as vagrancy were put to work on public projects. Their assignments ranged from road build-ing to working in a candle factory run by the police, who sold the product of female convicts' labor to the local military garrison.[14] Women were also forced to work for employers chosen by the local police and were rearrested if they abandoned their jobs.[15]

The fact that female convicts were put to work in Córdoba as re-placements for a scarce male labor force, or forcibly dispatched there and elsewhere in the interior to work as domestic servants, demonstrated the main function of peonage in Argentina: the regulation of a scarce labor supply to secure sufficient numbers of workers for critical areas of the economy. This was accomplished by the enactment of antivagrancy laws, labor contracts, and involuntary servitude caused by indebtedness. For the interior this meant the control of laborers of both sexes so long as there was need for their labor. Women comprised the domestic servants desired by the merchant and rancher class, while men were either put to work in the countryside as cowboys or agricultural laborers or conscripted into the militia. Only the lower class—the slaves, ex-slaves, and poor of humble birth—were affected by these laws. Middle- and upper-class men and women who became impoverished or who worked as artisans were neither arrested nor forced to register.

Peonage in this region also signified the application of work and vagrancy laws as prescriptive measures to regulate female morality. The supervision of female conduct, or at least the desire to codify such supervision, created another main distinction between the application of labor laws to working men and women. The result was that men were much more frequently assigned to work by the police than women, but women were more frequently arrested for activities deemed immoral. Although antivagrancy and worker-registration laws had existed in the Argentine interior since 1772, such legislation did not include provisions specifically related to women or to female morality. The wars of independence and the presence of a large number of female ex-slaves in interior cities after 1813 prompted officials to enact special female antivagrancy laws. In Tucumán province, where a general antivagrancy decree had already been issued in 1823, Governor Heredia supplemented it with the first *ley de conchabo*, or forced-labor law, in 1832, one that specified that women be steered away from prostitution by giving them honest work. In fact, it ordered all women "who cannot live honestly" to seek proper employment in eight days or be considered vagrant and idle (*ociosa*). The police were instructed to find them employment if necessary but to work with "discretion" and not interfere in the "private domain of families."[16]

In Jujuy, similar antiprostitution legislation was enacted in 1836. In the explanation that accompanied the decree it was observed that the government had "gradually tried to extinguish slavery . . . but in its place another type of servitude, much graver and more repugnant, has been substituted." Consequently, all women reputed to behave in an "abandoned and scandalous fashion" would be sent back to their families. If parents or other relatives were too poor to care for them, the police and local judges would find the women suitable employment and determine the salary. The decree was also designed to restrict child labor by encouraging more women to work. As in the case of Tucumán, police in Jujuy were to refrain from forcing women to work against the wishes of male relatives.[17] This decree preceded the enactment of male-focused work laws in 1843, 1849, and 1851.[18] All the earlier laws were based upon the belief that there existed an acceptable economic alternative to prostitution and that the police would be able to find work for those women who needed employment.

The relationship between peonage legislation and women's work in Argentina has been overlooked because much of what has been written about antivagrancy, forced labor, rural codes, and passport legislation deals with the coastal area. There, antivagrancy laws deriving from a pastoral society forced rural native-born workers to choose between an autocratic rural employer or military service.[19] According to Gastón Gori, such laws "before the end of the nineteenth century reflected an extremely particularistic social environment which was intimately linked to a pastoral economic system, to the misery of the rural workers, and to military necessities, all of which needed male labor and led to the abandonment of women and children."[20] Those needs, he believes, diminished after 1870 when immigration and the cessation of civil disorder made antivagrancy laws less crucial. His study also includes the admonishment that such legislation proved to be arbitrarily enforced and dependent upon the whims of rural judges. Nevertheless, these laws helped shape the social environment of the pastoral region of eastern Argentina while they dealt with females in an indirect fashion.[21]

Examination of the legal codes regarding nonslave labor in the littoral from 1804 on confirms Gori's thesis. Originating in legislation that helped regulate the labor of transients and cowboys in the province of Buenos Aires, the codes were later adopted almost word for word by neighboring provinces with similar pastoral pursuits. According to the laws, workers, especially those accused of vagrancy, were threatened with terms of forced labor or conscription in the army. Poor people were required to have papers identifying their employers and passports in order to proceed from one province to another. By 1865 most of these laws had been incorporated into a comprehensive rural code under the control of justices of the peace, and by 1870 immigrants were excused from the most onerous provisions. Few regulations referred specifically to women, and it appears that few women were forced to comply with the many provisions. . . .[22]

By the time the first national census was taken in 1869, the Argentine interior had already passed its most extreme stage of dependence upon female cottage industries. Still buttressed by these now-declining industries, interior provinces were gradually becoming characterized by subsistence agriculture and stock raising and by pockets of prosperity from wine and sugar industries. According to the census takers, "of 61,424 widows, 247,602 single women and more than 25,000 orphans in the republic, nearly 140,000 are seamstresses, laundresses, weavers, ironers, cigarmakers. . . . The result is that half the female adult population waits with uncertainty for daily sustenance."[23] If compilers had noted regional trends, they would have still found women far better off in the interior at that time than in the littoral. At least in the interior many still eked out a meager existence in crafts and food production in comparison to their counterparts in the littoral whose washing, sewing, breadmaking, and domestic service earned them less. In the province of Buenos Aires, for example, there were only 556 weavers, 1,815 cigarmakers, and 2,208 bakers included in the census, compared to more precarious professions such as laundresses (9,322), domestic servants (15,793), seamstresses (15,219), and ironers (3,598). In Santa Fe province a similar situation prevailed and the majority of women there also labored as seamstresses, maids, and laundresses when they could secure employment.[24]

In sharp contrast to the occupational breakdown in the littoral was the artisan nature of female workers in the interior. In Córdoba province there were 13,694 weavers; Tucumán had 7,635 weavers, 1,429 saddle-blanket makers, 1,552 cigarmakers, and 592 wool spinners. Over one half of Santiago del Estero women listed their occupation as weavers (32,181), and in the poor province of Catamarca, 6,898 were recorded as weavers and 5,533 as seamstresses, and only 2,562 people labeled themselves as domestic servants.[25]

By 1914 the opportunities for women within these two regions had diminished for all, but the decline of artisan activities was especially notable in the interior. Faced with increased competition from imported factory-made goods and unable or unwilling to migrate to incipient industrial areas in Buenos Aires and Rosario (Santa Fe), women retreated from artisan activities or found work as their coastal counterparts had done earlier—in low-status and poorly paid jobs as laundresses, ironers, and maids. In contrast, the rise of factories in the littoral, along with increased need for maid service, enabled women in that region, especially immigrant women, to find jobs.

### Peonage and the Decline of Women's Work in the Interior, 1870–1914

Since Córdoba province was apparently the only one that enacted further female antivagrancy and forced-work laws after 1860, the causes and effects of such legislation merit consideration. In July 1869, Cordobese officials ordered that all women, "who according to current Laws and Regulations are condemned to prison or public works for a period of not less than six months, can be sent for an equal time to the frontier." A little more than a year later a new female antivagrancy act again authorized public officials to force vagrant women to relocate to rural areas for a period not to exceed four years.[26]

Why were Cordobese officials so concerned about unemployed women? The need to populate the frontier areas to ward off Indian invasions was usually accomplished through the construction and defense of military forts, not communities of female vagrants. Perhaps the best answer is that Córdoba, as the closest of the interior provinces to the coastal area, was consequently among the first to feel the impact of national economic and political unification. As a result, the provincial wool industry was hard hit by an international wool market crisis, and by the subsequent inability of that province to sell its wool to exporters in Buenos

Aires. Wool washing, as well as spinning and weaving, had been an integral part of female economic activities in Córdoba, and the disappearance of export markets had thus led to widespread female unemployment.

As Ezequiel Paz wrote in May 1869:

> An industry here has completely disappeared and the work force of thousands of women who earned their livelihood washing wool and the large investments in ranches and equipment for this operation are today left unutilized. This has been the greatest consequence [of the wool crisis] that Cordobese people have suffered. Working women, unable to continue their traditional work, have no other employment possibilities so suited to their conditions. . . . These unfortunate facts would not be so important if Córdoba had some other industrial activity whose productive needs were suited to female labor, but in our interior provinces it is impossible to diversify suddenly the use of this type of labor as it is in the coastal provinces where the cities need women workers.[27]

Paz concluded that women in Santiago del Estero province were also being adversely affected by increased female unemployment due to the international situation. Thus, as testimony to the decline in traditional female work and the lack of new work opportunities, added to the fear of increased immoral behavior due to such conditions, new antivagrancy laws were enacted to remove women physically from established towns and rural communities. Thus, thousands of women who might have been included in the 1869 census as laborers were among those listed as unemployed.

These new Cordobese antivagrancy laws and others, despite the haphazard administration that typified all police enforcement at that time, were applied to women as late as the 1890s. The number of arrests and the registration of female servants, however, compared to corresponding figures for other provinces such as Tucumán, indicate that the laws were rarely applied to find women work, but rather as a warning against turning to prostitution. In 1880 only 146 women were arrested; in 1882 this number increased to 247, and to 313 in 1887. Most of these arrests were for drunkenness and yet, during this same time period, women fearing the application of new antivagrancy laws were reported to have run at the sight of a policeman.[28] Fears of enforcement became a reality two years later when the police, in the process of seeking pay raises, presented recent arrest statistics to demonstrate the need for their services. At that time the number of women arrested for crimes other than inebriation totaled 175, of whom 148 were charged with vagrancy; no adult men faced similar charges. Since no sex distinctions were made among the 9,140 people arrested for drinking, the principal charge against women in earlier years, it may also be assumed that the total number of women arrested was much higher. Equally important, only 434 women were listed in the Servants' Register.[29]

Córdoba responded in a unique fashion by enacting special legislation, but it was not the only province affected by the weakened demand for female handicrafts and production. The reaction of other interior provinces to high female unemployment depended upon the dominant economic activity in the area as well as on the demand for household servants. Tucumán province, due to its increased need for male field hands to harvest sugar and household servants to meet the demands of a relatively affluent urban group, periodically revised forced-work laws through its Police Codes of 1856 and 1877, and *ley de conchabo* of 1888. Tucumán [was] one of the few provinces with a relatively efficient police force, [and its] archives contain extensive evidence of female worker registration.

In the early years of the sugar industry, when there was no tariff protection for local production, female registration was sporadic. For the most part, women were arrested for having run away from their employers. In 1870, before enactment of the 1888 law that technically prohibited debt peonage, women were jailed for leaving their employers while still in debt to them and for similar offenses.[30] The publication of provincial statistics in 1882 offers a more complete view of female crime that year: of the 452 women arrested, 249 (or 55 percent) were charged with vagrancy and scandal (men charged with the equivalent offense represented .5 percent of total male arrests). However, only 87 women (19.2 percent) were arrested for drunkenness and scandal (their male counterparts represented 46 percent of the total) and 38 women (or 8.4 percent) were charged with running away from employers (18.1 percent of all males arrested were accused of similar offenses). In other words, antivagrancy measures in Tucumán were applied with greater frequency to women than to men. . . .

If the application of antivagrancy and forced-work laws disappeared in the coastal areas after 1870, as Gastón Gori suggests and evidence indicates, no such diminution appears in the interior until the end of the century. In the case of Tucumán, poor sugar harvests led to the abrogation of forced-labor laws in 1896 so that plantation owners would not have to hire all the unemployed peons sent to them by the police. Yet, in other places with more stable economic activities—such as lumbering and maté gathering in the northeastern provinces after 1900, sugar plantations in Salta and Jujuy, and sheep ranches in the far south—contract labor and debt peonage continued well into the twentieth century.[31] The universal military conscription law of 1901 eliminated the threat of arbitrary conscription, but other statutes remained in effect, especially for the native born.

As long as antivagrancy and worker-registration laws were enforced at all in most interior provinces, poor women continued to be victimized in a sporadic fashion, depending upon the province, its willingness to enforce moral codes, the labor needs, and [the] alternatives to female employment. When poor women were forced to carry work papers, they were uniformly described as *sirvientas*, regardless of the tasks at which they might have worked. When women were arrested, they were accused of vagrancy, failing to carry work papers, or exhibiting scandalous behavior. Yet, despite the way the peonage system was applied to women caught in its provisions, the fate of the majority of women in need of work, who were ignored by provincial authorities in both the littoral and the inland provinces, was far worse. Not deemed exploitable by the most important sectors of economic activity, they became invisible.

Just as the opportunities for women declined in Córdoba, they soon began to disappear elsewhere in the interior. Perhaps the easiest way to demonstrate the decline of skilled female employment in the interior, as well as its alternatives, is to compare the 1895 national census with that of 1869. Traditional occupations such as weaving still appeared in 1895, but in Tucumán province the numbers decreased from 7,635 to 4,944. Saddle-blanket makers no longer appeared as a category. Catamarca province experienced a real decline of almost 2,000 weavers. In Salta and Jujuy local women beer brewers also disappeared from the list. In the northwest, domestic service and the sewing trades declined, as well as weaving. Only Tucumán and Santiago recorded increases in the number of seamstresses (*costureras*), but not nearly enough to compensate for the loss of over 5,600 weavers there. Furthermore, only Santiago del Estero showed an increase of household servants compared to the first census. In general, only laundresses and ironers increased their numbers in a significant fashion.[32]

In total, the number of weavers in Argentina declined 54,653 in twenty-six years while the general population doubled. At the same time, the number of washerwomen in the nation increased by 44,363, dressmakers (*modistas*) by 8,091, and ironers by 18,088. Equally significant was the doubling of the number of part-time male and female *jornaleros*. These working-class people, added to those who claimed no employment, led census takers in 1895 to comment that "masculine employment percentages have increased to 866 per thousand, but in contrast, female employment has diminished to half that amount, as it equals only 445 per thousand. This demonstrates that we still have not learned how to give a useful and remunerative direction to women's work and that, destitute of a means of subsistence, women have to depend upon men's protection."[33]

## Women and Argentine Industrialization, 1875–1914

The decreased demand for female labor in the interior was in part compensated for by the development of industry in the coastal area, principally in the city of Buenos Aires. Among the first enterprises was a wool spinning and weaving factory, which began operations in 1873. President Sarmiento, the man whose mother had supported his family through cottage weaving, gave the inaugural speech. Still concerned with the nature and availability of women's work, he welcomed the attempt to initiate the textile sector in Argentina, since he believed it would enable women to "live honestly from their work."[34] Sarmiento's aspiration for mechanized jobs for women, especially in the textile industry, was filled only partially.

Besides the prospects of new urban industries, the coastal area also witnessed a vast expansion of farmland under cultivation. The introduction of machinery, particularly threshing and plowing machines, converted the former importer of grains into one of the world's principal cereal producers. With men running the machines and performing the bulk of the harvest labor, the locus of grain production shifted from the interior to the coastal pampas area, and from male and female to dominantly male harvest labor. Further mechanization and the reliance on seasonal harvest labor consisting of migrant male Europeans enabled the population of rural areas to increase rapidly Argentine cereal production.[35] Fencing and the introduction of pedigreed cattle and sheep had similar repercussions in the cattle industry. Consequently, the need for female labor in agroindustry was also circumscribed.

The main demand for female labor came from the bustling cities of the littoral where a variety of new businesses offered significant opportunities for working-class women. Industries associated with the production of locally consumed food, cigars, shoes, and clothing tended to hire females. Initially, they also served as the main labor force in the production of *alpargatas*, or jute-soled canvas shoes, burlap bag assembling, shirt and hat factories, tailors' shops, and commercial laundries. Of all the women employed in the aforementioned businesses, many had no contact with machinery other than sewing machines, and even those were often operated by men. Furthermore, many never saw the inside of the factory, as they worked at home and were paid by the piece. Typically, they were engaged in the production of garments, although a similar situation existed in the shoe industry, where women hand-finished leather uppers at home until new machines and male technicians in the factories displaced them.[36]

According to Adrian Patroni, who conducted a survey of the Argentine labor force, in the late 1890s the demand for unskilled male laborers in Argentina decreased as women and children were hired to perform nonmechanical tasks. In the case of hats, jobs for everyone declined with mechanization. As for the cigar factory employees, only women and children were hired to wrap the packets.[37] Thus, at least in the beginning, women were an important component in coastal industries. By 1895, the city of Buenos Aires far outstripped traditional artisan centers of the interior in the numbers of women employed in specialized tasks such as cigarwrapping and shoemaking. Equally significant was the number of women employed as household servants. In the city and province of Buenos Aires the number of domestic servants had more than doubled, while the number of washerwomen and laundresses almost equalled that of household help in terms of percentage increase. This meant that women could benefit both directly and indirectly from the increased economic well-being experienced by that city.[38]

*Immigrant versus Native-Born Women*

Of the women who could find jobs within the artisan and household service sectors in the city of Buenos Aires, initially immigrant women had more work opportunities than the native born; this advantage was evident in the commercial sector as well. In 1898, immigrant women equalled only 19 percent of all women in Argentina above ten years old; in the city of Buenos Aires, however, immigrant women outnumbered the native born by a two-to-one margin, and there they had already begun to displace Argentine women in a number of professions. For example, there were proportionately more foreign-born *modistas* and shoemakers than natives. Similarly, aliens outnumbered, proportionately, their Argentine counterparts as *alpargata* makers, ironers, washerwomen, cigarmakers, dressmakers, hatters, tailors, and merchants. . . .

By 1914, the percentage of all foreign-born women over the age of ten had increased from 19 to 24 percent of all Argentine residents, and the percentage of those employed increased from 21 to 28 percent. Thus, as women in general were being forced in greater numbers out of the paid labor pool, immigrant women managed to increase their participation nationwide.[39] Although this was a temporary phenomenon, a comparison of the same two areas, Buenos Aires city and Córdoba province, indicates which sectors then employed the most women, especially immigrants. Once again, in contrast to the capital, the small numbers of female craft workers in Córdoba were related not only to the lack of work for women but also to the general decline of all industrial and artisan pursuits in that area. Further, by 1914 . . . immigrant women in Córdoba only outnumbered Creole women as merchants. In Buenos Aires, on the other hand, although immigrant women were employed more frequently than in Córdoba, they were losing their predominance in a number of jobs. . . .

The migration of European females to Argentina and their ability to locate employment in newly formed industry and commerce in the capital city and in Córdoba province reveals why few native-born women from the interior migrated eastward at that time to find work. Even though second-generation Argentine women had begun to displace aliens in some trades, many immigrant-owned factories and shops, which comprised 81 and 74 percent, respectively, of all establishments in Argentina, often agglomerated immigrants of the same nationality;[40] in contrast, few native-born Argentines owned such firms. Creole workers, both male and female, untrained in most factory tasks, were also considered less efficient workers. Thus, when jobs for females appeared, those women affected by changing economic conditions in the interior could not take advantage of the immigrant-directed and nontextile-related industrial boom in the littoral.

*Women and Industrial Legislation*

The large numbers of women engaged in sewing trades in Argentina superficially resembles a comparative stage in other nations undergoing industrial transformation. Yet, besides the fact that nations with strong textile industries also utilized piecework wages and sweatshop conditions in the garment trade, the Argentine experience provides a strong and significant contrast. In Europe and the United States the textile industry provided one of the first sites of applied technological innovation through the cotton gins, the mechanization of looms and sewing, new dyes, and the reorganization of garment production.[41] In the Argentine case, none of these transformations occurred prior to the 1930s. Even the garment industry rarely used large-scale factory procedures for most production, since their market was restricted to local consumption. Thus, even the industrialization of the most traditional area of female employment failed to integrate women into the technologically advanced part of the modernization process.

Although weaving wool and cotton had served as an economic buttress in the interior during the early nineteenth century, cotton cultivation practically disappeared by the turn of the century, as fewer women chose to spin thread and weave cloth when they could purchase factory-made

British and U.S. products. A similar situation existed among the wool weavers. Even the company praised by Sarmiento found it difficult to produce woolen cloth at a profit in Argentina, and closed down. Consequently, by 1914, wool and cotton spinning and weaving were either absent or poorly represented in the Argentine industrial sector. According to a report of 1909, only one cotton thread mill with nine thousand spindles and five cotton weaving mills with twelve hundred looms operated in Argentina. Those six firms employed 1,575 workers.[42] These factories, added to wool mills and the production of thousands of seamstresses and rustic weavers working at home, provided only 22.6 percent of all textiles sold in Argentina by 1914, mostly in the form of rugs, blankets, knitted stockings, and underwear.[43]

The backwardness of the Argentine textile industry can be attributed to three interrelated factors. First, the politics of free trade, accepted by most Argentines, emphasized the international division of labor that relegated Argentina to a producer of raw materials unless such products could be obtained at a lower cost elsewhere. Thus, even though Argentina had always had small amounts of land devoted to cotton cultivation in the interior, the prospects of entering the world cotton market did not exist for Argentina until the 1920s, and the few attempts made to expand cotton production prior to that date had failed.

Second, traditional objections to a large-scale textile industry, added to a paucity of locally produced cotton, further bolstered the free-trade philosophy. Importers of textiles, particularly from Great Britain, deplored efforts to restrict such importations, particularly if tariffs were the only means by which the local textile industry could expand. Even the representatives of organized labor in Argentina objected to a domestic textile industry because it would add to the cost of living for immigrant workers. Consequently, manufacturers could count on no labor support for the tariff protection that they deemed crucial for further expansion.

Finally, and perhaps most importantly, Argentine political reformers as well as free traders adopted the ideology of protective legislation for women long before female labor exploitation by industry became a major feature of Argentine industrial patterns. Influenced by European socialist thought, which was a response to the heavy dependence upon women and children for many industries in Europe, Argentine legislators, particularly those from the coastal area, pioneered industrial labor legislation designed to prevent such exploitation before it became a significant problem in their country. Intended to benefit working women by protecting them from abuse, such industrial labor legislation, although poorly enforced, often resulted in discouraging the expansion of industries that relied on female labor. These legislators saw no conflict between their desire to protect women and the prospects that women might be prevented from working, because they basically believed that women should not work in an industrial setting.

A perfect example of how reformers rejected women's participation in industry, even though they recognized that the alternatives for poor women were even more exploitative, comes from the career of Juan Bialet Massé. A Spanish physician and the first professor of labor law at the National University of Córdoba, Bialet Massé was commissioned by Minister of the Interior Joaquín V. González in 1904 to study the conditions of workers in the Argentine interior. He returned three months later with a three-volume work filled with statistics, interviews, and photos. From those pages the situation of poor Argentine men and women becomes evident. In a special section on women and children he informed the reader that initially he believed that industrial societies, such as the ones developing in Buenos Aires and Rosario, exploited women more than agrarian ones, but, after returning from his trip, he had changed his mind.[44]

In his tour through the interior he had seen situations that made industrial exploitation seem insignificant. When he stopped in San Juan province, for example, he noted that domestic service was not common for women. Those employed this way were subject to extreme exploitation because "the women from the countryside *give* their little girls away as if they were puppies. The ladies of the recipient family care for the children more or less affectionately, and sometimes the wards are considered part of the family. But what usually happens is that . . . the *chinita* is considered artless and incapable of reason . . . and the result of all this is a detestable form of slavery. . . . Consequently female servants who work for wages are scarce, earn little, and are not given steady employment."[45] Alternatives to domestic service were laundering and ironing, both of which were even less remunerative and more insecure forms of work. Such women worked in their own homes for a variety of employers, all of whom had an enormous choice of which poor women might do their laundry. Yet other jobs related to agroindustry were closed to women. The major industries, such as preserved fruits, would not employ females even though they often made better employees. In the case of the sugar industry in the northwest, wives might accompany their husbands in harvesting, but they received no salary of their own unless they worked as cooks for bachelors.[46]

In Tucumán, Córdoba, and La Rioja, among other provinces visited, the physician continued to find both the conditions of women's work, as well as the remuneration, deplorable. Clandestine prostitution and tuberculosis were widespread phenomena and direct results, according to him, of the underemployment of women as laundresses and poorly paid maids.

Only in the western province of Mendoza was domestic labor relatively well paid, and it was in that province that upper-class women had established a school to train servants. This contrasted sharply with the *gente decente*, or upper class, of Tucumán who, according to Bialet Massé, had so many impoverished women that 25 percent of the seamstresses in the capital city came from that class.[47]

Yet, despite the bleak picture painted of conditions in the interior, and even though he documented the desperate conditions for men there as well, the physician still objected to the employment of women in industry in all areas of Argentina. As he put it:

> The mission of women, since each sex has its role in the perpetuation of the species, is maternity, nurturing and educating children. . . . For married women, factory life is incompatible with these functions, as it is in general for the single woman, a minor, as [work] can affect her reproductive organs. . . . Work for women is unacceptable except for the misfortune of destiny: for the widow without means of support, and for the unmarried woman who has no family to care for her, or for those called the *third sex* . . . women who for one reason or another remain unmarried.[48]

When forced to earn a living, women should receive equal pay, but Bialet Massé basically rejected the idea that women needed to work. Thus, even though he demonstrated that the male-dominated agroindustry existing along with a subsistence economy in the agrarian and pastoral areas of the interior combined to abuse working-class women even more than in urban industrial areas, he concluded that even "honest" work was unsuited for women of childbearing age. And, rather than improve working conditions for all, the physician remained content to suggest more reliance on cheap imported products and the exclusion of women and children from night labor and unsafe industries that remained.[49] In this way he paralleled the view of the Argentine Socialist party as well as of many Argentine legislators at the beginning of the twentieth century.[50]

By the time modern industries were seen in the interior, reformist legislation had started to constrict the view of appropriate work for women. In August 1905, the Argentine Congress enacted a Sunday rest law for industry and commerce in the capital city. Women were protected by this law only if they worked in factories and shops, although in practice few businesses complied with the loosely enforced provisions. Two years later, however, national law number 5291 further delineated the special conditions necessary for factory-employed women and children, which included limited work hours, prohibition from working in "dangerous or unhealthy" industries, special rest privileges, and the right of mothers to nurse children.

During discussions of the 1907 law, national legislators admitted the law was premature but urged its passage as a sign of progressivism. They also attempted to extend the authority of the provision not only to Buenos Aires but also to national employees and federal territories. The end result of these laws was detrimental to women as seen in industrial census figures for the capital city as early as 1914. At that time as many women worked at industrial tasks at home as in the factory. Similar conditions also existed in many commercial establishments. Out of reach of factory inspectors and protective legislation, these women, along with all domestic servants, had no legal protection from dangerous or unhealthy working conditions.[51]

Gradually, other provinces followed the lead of the national capital and enacted their own Sunday rest laws and protective legislation that resulted in further directing working-class women away from factories and into household work not protected by law. The province of Salta was one of the first to grant Sunday rest to industrial and retail employees but exempted domestic servants from the provisions. Buenos Aires and Córdoba provinces had similar loopholes for household workers and agricultural and pastoral employees.[52] Mendoza province was even more explicit about how women could be exempted from Sunday rest if needed. It insisted that not only domestic servants be exempted but also women working in hospitals, hotels, boardinghouses, and bathhouses. Although work in the factory for women appeared to be the major source of exploitation, the same government that passed progressive factory laws in 1918 enacted a national home-work law that excluded from inspection conditions of household service, as well as any place where family members constituted the work force supervised by another relative.[53] As for specific industrial legislation related to women, Santa Fe followed the lead of the national capital by passing law number 11.317, which delineated the regulations for industrial establishments and listed thirty-six industries in which women were forbidden to work; these included the production of chemicals, liquors, and certain aspects of textile processing.[54] As in the past, although these laws were often left unimplemented or arbitrarily enforced, they still expressed the attitudes of the interior and coastal provinces regarding women's work in the industrializing society.

## Conclusions

From a regional perspective, the linkages can be seen between the decline of skilled work for women in the Argentine interior and such diverse phenomena as peonage and industrial protection laws. These were both expressions of value systems attached to the modernization of the labor force in rural and urban areas. Both tried to direct female labor away from economic activity unless they were deemed essential as a source of labor. Such forms of labor management operated at different times because the transformation of the countryside preceded that of the city, and their application depended upon the region. Yet, ultimately, urban-focused labor legislation replaced that of the rural areas, and in a similar fashion the ideology of enforcing morality and preventing prostitution or that of ignoring women was replaced by the paternalistic desire to segregate women from factories in order to preserve them for childbearing.

The ultimate results of such policies depend upon the region one considers, whether the workplace was urban or rural, as well as the type of employment sought by women. The countryside in Argentina, traditionally active with female artisans prior to industrialization, becomes the area with the highest rate of female unemployment. This is true even outside the capital city of Buenos Aires.[55] Within the urban industrial sector, women performed nonmechanized and low-paid tasks.

Immigration and internal migration over time also affected the prospects for employment for women during modernization. From 1869 to 1914, the immigration of females limited the patterns of mobility for Argentine women. Thereafter, in response to reduced numbers of immigrants and expanding industries in the capital city and elsewhere, women from the interior began to migrate to the coastal area in search of work.[56] That fact, added to the expansion of cotton cultivation there after the war, as well as increased production of textiles, further improved the opportunities of women within the industrial sector.

Throughout this investigation of distinct regions, another variable related to industrialization that has not been assessed is the increased opportunity for employment as maids and domestic servants caused by the expansion of commerce and industry. In areas with weak urban industries, such as those in the Argentine northwest, the demand for maids was restricted. The alternatives, washing and ironing, were even less satisfactory for both employer and employee. In contrast, the coastal area, with its active cities and prosperous hinterland, was better able to integrate female labor in the service trades as well as in industry. Thus, one more conclusion that can be drawn is that measurement of the type and demand for domestic labor present in an industrializing society can be another index of how successfully women have been able to participate in and benefit from modernization.

The final confirmation of these tendencies of modernization in Argentina will be possible when additional studies of coastal and interior provinces are undertaken, particularly in the western mountain area as well as in the humid as compared to the dry-pampas section of the littoral. Equally important, similar studies should be undertaken for other Latin American countries to test the ideology and timing of legislation and changing economic patterns that affect women's work. In that way modernization in dependent industrializing societies of Latin America can be integrated with the history of working women.

**Notes**

1. The number of theoretical and case studies of women and work has increased significantly in the past ten years. Among the pioneering works are Ester Boserup, *Women's Role in Economic Development* (New York, 1970); Michelle Zimbalist Rosaldo and Louise Lamphere, eds., *Women, Culture and Society* (Stanford, 1974); Nadia H. Youseff, *Women and Work in Developing Societies* (Berkeley, 1974); and June Nash and Helen Icken Safa, eds., *Sex and Class in Latin America* (New York, 1976). Marysa Navarro, "Research on Latin American Women," *Signs* 5:1 (Autumn 1979): 117–19 discusses the most recent literature on women's work in rural areas of Latin America.

2. Elizabeth Jelin, "The Bahiana in the Labor Force of Salvador, Brazil," in *Sex and Class in Latin America,* p. 129. See also Emily M. Nett, "The Servant Class in a Developing Country: Ecuador," *Journal of Interamerican Studies and World Affairs* 8 (July 1966): 437–52; Margo Lane Smith, "Domestic Service as a Channel of Upward Mobility for Lower-Class Women: The Lima Case," in *Female and Male in Latin America: Essays,* ed. Ann Pescatello (Pittsburgh, 1973), pp. 191–207; and the essays on women and development in *Latin American Perspectives* 4:1–2 (Winter and Spring 1977) and *Signs* 3:1 (Autumn 1977). For general and bibliographic discussions of women and work in Latin America, see Asunción Lavrin, ed., *Latin American Women: Historical Perspectives* (Westport, 1978), pp. 302–20; Navarro, "Research on Latin American Women," pp. 111–20; and Zulma R. de Lattes and Catalina Wainerman, "Empleo femenino y desarrollo económico," *Desarrollo Económico* 17:66 (July-Sept. 1977): 301–17.

3. For a review essay of recent literature on peonage, which fails to question what happened to women during the transition from slave to free labor or during the process of modernization in general, see Arnold J. Bauer, "Rural Workers in Spanish America: Problems of Peonage and Oppression," *Hispanic American Historical Review* 59:1 (Feb. 1979): 34–63.

4. Tulio Halperin Donghi, *Politics, Economics and Society in Argentina in the Revolutionary Period,* Cambridge Latin American Studies, vol. 18 (Cambridge, 1975), pp. 57–58, 12.

5. Ibid., pp. 57–58; Pedro Santos Martínez, *Las industrias durante el virreinato (1776–1810)* (Buenos Aires, 1969), p. 48.

6. These are adjusted figures based upon Zulma Recchini de Lattes's study in Zulma Recchini de Lattes and Alfredo E. Lattes, comps., *La población de Argentina* (Buenos Aires, 1975), pp. 149–67. See also R. de Lattes and Wainerman, "Empleo femenino," pp. 301–17; Nancy Caro Hollander, "Women in the Political Economy of Argentina," Ph.D. dissertation, University of California at Los Angeles, 1974, p. 55.

7. Ernesto J. A. Meader, *Evolución demográfica argentina desde 1810 a 1869* (Buenos Aires, 1969), passim; Alfredo E. Lattes, *La migración como factor de cambio de la población en la Argentina* (Buenos Aires, 1972).

8. Letter from Manuel Lanfranco, Síndico Procurador, to Cabildo, Jujuy, 25 June 1812, Jujuy Province, *Archivo Capitular de Jujuy*, 4 vols. (Buenos Aires, 1974), 4:564–67 graphically describes the initial impact of the independence struggle on the commerce and industry of Jujuy; Halperin Donghi, *Politics*, pp. 239–69.

9. Captain Andrews, *Journey from Buenos Ayres through the Provinces of Cordova, Tucumán, and Salta, to Potosi, Thence by the Deserts of Caranja to Arica, and Subsequently, to Santiago de Chili and Coquimbo* . . . , 2 vols., reprint of 1827 ed. (New York, 1971), 1:159, 302–3; 2:14–16.

10. Sir Woodbine Parish, *Buenos Ayres and the Provinces of the Rio de la Plata* (London, 1838), pp. 256, 265, 269, 288; A. Belmar, *Les provinces de la Fédération Argentine et Buenos Ayres, description générale de ces pays sous le rapport géographique, historique, commercial, industriel et sous celui de la colonisation* (Paris, 1856), p. 77; Victor Martin de Moussy, *Description Géographique de la Confédération Argentine*, 3 vols. (Paris, 1864), 3:110. Inventories of cloth for Indians still formed part of the bookkeeping process in the Tucumán sugar factory and plantation of San Pablo in 1888, although the origin of the weaver is unknown; San Pablo Factory, Inventario I, 1876–1890, pp. 201, 218.

11. Esther Hermitte and Herbert Klein, *Crecimiento y estructura de una comunidad provinciana de tejedores de ponchos: Belén 1678–1869* (Buenos Aires, 1972), pp. 37–38; Martin de Moussy, *Description Géographique*, 3:370–71; Federico Espeche, *La provincia de Catamarca* (Buenos Aires, 1875), pp. 192–93; Esther Hermitte, "Ponchos, Weaving and Patron-Client Relations in Northwest Argentina," in *Structure and Process in Latin America: Patronage, Clientage and Power Systems*, ed. Arnold Stricken and Sidney M. Greenfield (Albuquerque, 1972), pp. 159–77.

12. Domingo F. Sarmiento, *Recuerdos de provincia* (Navarre, 1970), pp. 99, 102–4.

13. Susan Socolow, *The Merchants of Buenos Aires 1778–1810: Family and Commerce,* Cambridge Latin American Studies, vol. 30 (Cambridge, 1978), p. 34. Middle-class women in the interior were allowed to work throughout the nineteenth century, although they soon shifted from needlework to teaching. Other early examples are found in Hermann Burmeister, *Descripción de Tucumán* (Tucumán, 1916), p. 51.

14. List of poor people to be put to work on public projects, Archivo Histórico de la Provincia de Córdoba [hereinafter referred to as AHC], Gobierno, 1835, T. 139, ff. 310–11; expense account for Córdoba police, Anexo B, 15 February and March 1838, AHC, Gobierno, 1838, T. 555, ff. 323, 325.

15. Scattered evidence of women's arrests abounds in the Córdoba archives and needs a more comprehensive analysis. Having picked several years at random, I found accounts of women's arrests for all years. An example of this was the year 1859 . . . for February, May, June, and November. During those months women were sent to jail . . . for running away from their employers; for their employers' dissatisfaction with employees; for helping other women, especially minors, [to] flee employers; and for refusing to serve employers assigned to them by the police. AHC, Gobierno, 1859, T. 3, ff. 297, 285, 302, 396, 398, 400, 428, 392, 394, and 581.

16. Marcela B. González, "Sobremonte y la papeleta de conchabo," in Academia Nacional de Historia, *Primer congreso de historia argentina y regional* (Buenos

Aires, 1973), pp. 526–32; Manuel Lizondo Borda, *Historia de Tucumán* (*siglo XIX*) (Tucumán, 1948), p. 78; Julio López Mañan, *Tucumán antiguo* (Tucumán, 1972), p. 51; Tucumán province, *Actas del Cabildo, Prólogo y notas de Manuel Lizondo Borda*, 2 vols. (Tucumán, 1940), 2:398–400.

17. Jujuy Province, *Registro Oficial: Compilación de leyes y decretos de la provincia de Jujuy desde el año 1835 hasta el de 1884*, 3 vols. (Jujuy, 1885), 1:41, 43–44.

18. Ibid., decree of 1 October 1843, pp. 167–68; ibid., 7 October 1849, p. 248; ibid., 12 April 1851, p. 323.

19. The classic literary treatment of this theme is José Hernández, *El gaucho Martín Fierro y la vuelta de Martín Fierro* (Buenos Aires, 1960). See also Gastón Gori, *Vagos y malentretenidos*, 3d. ed. (Buenos Aires, 1974); and Ricardo E. Rodríguez Molas, *Historia social del gaucho* (Buenos Aires, 1968). There are also studies of labor legislation for interior provinces that are less widely known. . . . Donna J. Guy, "The Rural Working Class in Nineteenth Century Argentina: Forced Plantation Labor in Tucumán," *Latin American Research Review*, 13:1 (1978): 135–45; and Marcela B. González, "Sobremonte y la papeleta de conchabo."

20. Gori, *Vagos y malentretenidos*, p. 11.

21. Ibid., pp. 8, 63.

22. These comments are based upon an examination of compilations of laws for the provinces of Buenos Aires, Entre Ríos, and Santa Fe. . . . George Reid Andrews claims that even though the need for female domestic labor existed in Buenos Aires between 1830 and 1853, no special laws were passed. George Reid Andrews, *The Afro-Argentines of Buenos Aires, 1800–1900* (Madison, 1980), pp. 60–61.

23. Argentine Republic, Superintendente de Censo, *Primer Censo de la República Argentina* (Buenos Aires, 1872), p. xlv.

24. Ibid., pp. 69–73, 118–25. Since the 1869 census does not reveal sex in occupations, these figures include some male workers. However, the 1895 census does separate male from female workers, and at that time these professions were practiced by men who rarely comprised more than ten percent of the total work force for each category.

25. Ibid., pp. 642–48.

26. Córdoba Province, *Compilación de leyes, decretos, acuerdos de la exma. Cámara de Justicia y demás disposiciones de carácter público dictadas en la provincia de Córdoba desde 1810 hasta 1900*, 2 vols. (Córdoba, 1870), 2:675, 827–28.

27. Ezequiel N. Paz, *Derecho de exportación. Mercado americano y nuestros productos. Serie de artículos publicados en la prensa del Rosario*, 2d. ed. (Rosario, 1869), pp. 33–34.

28. Aníbal Arcondo, "Notas para el estudio compulsivo," p. 143; report on police statistics from Oficina de Estadística, 20 June 1882, AHC, Gobierno, 1882, T. 5, f. 169; Córdoba Province, Oficina de Estadística, *Memoria de la Oficina de Estadística General: 1887* (Buenos Aires, 1888), p. 85.

29. Chart indicating statistical composition of arrests made between 1 April 1888 and 31 March 1889, with indications of the nature of the crime, AHC, Gobierno, 1889, T. 19, ff. 101–09. Foja 110 lists 434 women in the Servants' Register during the same period of time.

30. Donna J. Guy, "The Rural Working Class," especially footnotes 25 and 26 and figures 1 and 2; Archivo Histórico de Tucumán, Comprobantes de Cortaduría, 1870, T. 176, ff. 130, 311, 628.

31. Alfredo L. Palacios, *Pueblos desamparados: Solución de los problemas del noroeste argentino* (Buenos Aires, 1942); Ian Rutledge, "Plantations and Peasants in Northern Argentina: The Sugar Cane Industry of Salta and Jujuy, 1930–1943," in *Argentina in the Twentieth Century*, ed. David Rock (Pittsburgh, 1975), pp. 88–113; Donna J. Guy, *Argentine Sugar Politics: Tucumán and the Generation of Eighty* (Tempe, 1980), p. 132.

32. Argentine Republic, Comisión Directiva del Censo, *Segundo Censo de la República Argentina*, 3 vols. (Buenos Aires, 1898), 2:513–16, 552–55, 365–66.

33. Ibid., pp. cxliv, cxciii, cxlii.

34. Sociedad Industrial de Río de la Plata, *Lista de accionistas. Discursos pronunciados en la inauguración de la fábrica de paños* (Buenos Aires, 1874), p. 13.

35. James R. Scobie, *Revolution on the Pampas: A Social History of Argentine Wheat, 1860–1910* (Austin, 1964).

36. U.S. Department of Commerce, Bureau of Foreign and Domestic Commerce, Special Agents Series No. 37, "Shoe and Leather Trade in Argentina, Chile, Peru and Uruguay," by Arthur B. Butman (Washington, 1910), p. 11; No. 177, "Boots and Shoes, Leather and Supplies in Argentina, Uruguay and Paraguay," by Herman G. Brock (Washington, 1919), pp. 52, 54–55. As late as 1910, 90 percent of all shoe uppers were finished at home by women, although eight years later most work was done in the factory.

37. Adrian Patroni, *Los trabajadores en la Argentina* (Buenos Aires, 1897), pp. 94–95, 99–100.

38. Argentine Republic, Comisión Directiva del Censo, *Segundo Censo*, 2: cxcl, 48–50, 139–42, 297–300.

39. R. de Lattes and Lattes, *La población de Argentina*, p. 154.

40. Oscar Cornblit, "European Immigrants in Argentine Industry and Politics," in *The Politics of Conformity in Latin America*, ed. Claudio Veliz (Oxford, 1967), p. 227. See also James R. Scobie's fine study of urbanization patterns in Buenos Aires and how it affected immigrant women and their work. James R. Scobie, *Buenos Aires: Plaza to Suburb, 1870–1910* (New York, 1974), pp. 152–53, 226. He also stresses the agglomeration of European immigrants by nationality into tenement housing; see table 8, p. 267.

41. Edward Chase Kirkland, *Industry Comes of Age: Business, Labor and Public Policy, 1860–1897* (Chicago, 1967), pp. 1, 325–32, observes that the U.S. textile industry was the first to create a foreign market and that its main workers were women and children. In fact, "the movement of industry toward pools of labor was usually a movement toward women and child laborers" (p. 328). Tom Kemp, *Historical Patterns of Industrialization* (New York, 1978), chapter 4, reviews the historical viewpoints regarding the relationship of the textile industry to the industrial revolution. . . . Samuel Lilley, "Technological Progress and the Industrial Revolution 1700–1914," in *The Fontana Economic History of Europe: The Industrial Revolution, 1700–1914*, ed. Carlo M. Cipolla (Lanham, MD, 1976), pp. 187–226, integrates the history of the modernization of textile manufacture with other trends in European economic history.

42. U.S. Department of Commerce and Labor, Bureau of Manufactures, Special Agents Series No. 40, "Cotton Goods in Latin America, Part III, Argentina, Uruguay, and Paraguay," by W. A. Graham Clark (Washington, 1910), p. 24.

43. Argentine Republic, *Tercer Censo Nacional*, 10 vols. (Buenos Aires, 1917–1919), 4:384–89; Emilio J. Schleh, *La industria algodonera en la Argentina, consideraciones sobre su estado actual y su desarrollo futuro* (Buenos Aires, 1923), summarizes efforts made after the war to stimulate the cotton and textile industries.

44. Juan Bialet Massé, *El estado de las clases obreras argentinas a comienzos del siglo,* 2d. ed. (Córdoba, 1904, 1968), p. 423.

45. Ibid., p. 596.

46. Ibid., p. 611; Mark Jefferson, *Peopling the Argentine Pampa*, Research Series No. 16 (New York, 1926), p. 33.

47. Bialet Massé, *El estado*, pp. 424, 553–54, 151, 566. Among the interior provinces, Mendoza provides the exception to the general status of women in that region during the nineteenth century.

48. Ibid., p. 426.

49. Ibid., p. 429.

50. Richard Walter, *The Socialist Party of Argentina, 1890–1930* (Austin, 1977), chapters 4 and 5.

51. Law No. 4.661, Congreso Nacional, Cámara de Diputados, *Diario de Sesiones,* 1905, 3:811–12; 1907, 2:192–93. It was up to the Argentine president to determine which industries were dangerous or unhealthy. Ministerio de Agricultura, Dirección General de Comercio e Industria, *Censo Comercial e Industrial de la República, Boletín No. 20, Capital Federal* (Buenos Aires, 1914), pp. 22–23, 60–61; Nancy Caro Hollander, "Women and the Political Economy of Argentina," pp. 109–111; Carolina Muzzilli, "El trabajo femenino," *Boletín Mensual de Museo Social Argentino,* 15–16 (1913): 65–90.

52. La Vanguardia, *Leyes del trabajo nacionales y provinciales con sus decretos reglamentarios hasta el año 1943,* 8th ed. (Buenos Aires, 1943), pp. 495, 542. These laws were passed between 1905 and 1908.

53. Ibid., 1906 law, pp. 636–37; ibid., 481–82.

54. Santa Fe Province, *Ley 11.317, trabajo de mujeres y menores. Decreto reglamentario* (Santa Fe, 1927), p. 408.

55. Argentine Republic, *Segundo Censo,* 2:139–42.

56. Elizabeth Jelin, "Migration and Labor Force Participation of Latin American Women: The Domestic Servants in the Cities," *Signs* 3:1 (Aug. 1977): 131.

## 11  Sandra McGee Deutsch ◆ The Catholic Church, Work, and Womanhood in Argentina, 1890–1930

*Although the Roman Catholic church believed and taught women that their place was in the home, by the mid-nineteenth century the church began to rely on the public and political action of women to support it against what it considered to be the spread of rampant secularism and other ideologies that threatened to diminish further its role in society. By the end of the century the church had involved the laity completely in its strategies to slow, if not defeat, the spread of socialism and other philosophies based on materialism. This essay also makes a contribution to the important but slowly expanding body of literature dealing with popular religion and the history of the laity. Although the church has been extensively studied in colonial history and has received much attention in recent years because of the Liberation Theology and Christian base community movements as well as rapidly spreading evangelical and pentecostal Christianity, the topic of religion in society has been neglected for much of the National period. In the future, scholars may also turn to a particularly rich, and as yet untapped, source of information, namely, the correspondence of Protestant missionaries to Latin America.*

The strength and perseverance of its rightist traditions distinguish Argentina from its Latin American neighbors, even in a region known for the conservative character of national governments. The Catholic church has long been identified with the Argentine right, [with] both clerics and lay activists contributing to rightist doctrine, joining rightist organizations, and lashing out against leftist unions and political movements.[1] Little is known, however, about the viewpoint of the right and the church on gender issues. Scholars have commonly assumed that the church helped frame popular perceptions of women's roles in the home and workplace, yet few studies have documented church-sponsored attitudes or actions pertaining to women in the years since independence.[2] One can only understand the Argentine right by inserting analyses of women into its history; similarly, the study of women in Latin America will be incomplete without examinations of their relations with right-wing movements.

An important entry point for such analyses are Catholic opinions on women's work in Argentina. The full-scale incorporation of Argentina

From *Gender and History* 3, no. 3 (Autumn 1991): 304–25. Reprinted by permission.

into the world market after 1870 transformed many aspects of the society and polity. The changes of the period, including the formation of a working class and alterations in female roles, appeared to threaten the church's position as well as the social order it upheld. At the same time, the government limited the church's role in society by creating a secular public education system, civil marriage, and a civil register in the 1880s. Church leaders decried their loss of influence in what they saw as an increasingly godless and materialistic nation. Thus, the varied responses of church officials, confessional organizations, and prominent laypersons to the shifting pattern of women's work between 1890 and 1930 reflected a range of political and institutional concerns fostered by economic upheaval and anticlericalism.

This, then, is a study of these responses.[3] Diverse and modern in certain respects, Catholic leaders nonetheless favored female subordination to hierarchical relations in the home, workplace, and society. Resolutely opposed to leftism and the autonomy of women and laborers, suspicious of electoral democracy and desirous of order, Catholic spokespersons helped to consolidate the right as a political force at the turn of the twentieth century.

**The Argentine Context**

In the late nineteenth century, the Argentine government was dominated by a landowning elite, or "oligarchy," which promoted mass European immigration and encouraged the development of the beef and grain export sectors. While liberal in the classical sense, the oligarchy was hardly democratic. In the 1890s, opposition to its rule coalesced through such groups as the Socialist party, representing the emerging urban working class, and the Radical Civic Union, including disaffected members of the elite and of the growing middle sectors. After much struggle, the Radicals achieved their primary goal of creating an electoral democracy, and from 1916 to 1930 voters elevated their candidates to the presidency. Disturbed by their loss of power and a growing militancy among workers, members of the former oligarchy criticized the democratic government and attacked all forms of egalitarianism. In the coup of 1930 they allied with the military to overthrow the Radical government, ending Argentina's short-lived experiment in democracy and ushering in decades of alternating authoritarian rule and instability. While the church did not play an official role in these events, during the 1890s its leaders sympathized with the opposition to the anticlerical oligarchy. By the twentieth century, however, its spokespersons professed antileftist and antidemocratic ideas that contributed to the rightist climate.

The economic and political upheavals of the late nineteenth and early twentieth centuries redefined not only the role of the church but also the status of women. From the late colonial period on, the importation of cheap European goods destroyed domestic and small-scale industries in the interior, forcing female artisans into service occupations or destitution. By the turn of the century such women migrated to the littoral cities, where they competed for available jobs with immigrant women. By 1914 women occupied 84 percent of the personal service positions, which included seamstresses, laundresses, ironers, and maids. Forming 30 percent of industrial and manual workers in that year, women in this sector performed mostly nonmechanized tasks, often in sweatshops. Female laborers were especially common in dairies, the textile industry, chemical and tobacco processing, and match factories. They were a small but growing presence in meat-packing plants. Nevertheless, adult female participation in the labor force declined from approximately 60 percent in 1867 to 22 percent in 1914.[4] Although national figures are not available for 1914 to 1930, one scholar estimated that women made up about one fifth of the labor force in the capital city during those years.[5]

The problems of unemployment and the loss of skilled work demonstrate that economic development did not necessarily benefit women. Contemporary observers catalogued the plight of homeless, jobless women in the cities and the spread of prostitution. Women who were fortunate enough to find employment earned wages significantly lower than those of men: as much as 60 percent less for skilled and semiskilled workers and at least 10 percent less for the unskilled. Women also tended to work longer hours in more unpleasant environments than did men, who hardly enjoyed excellent working conditions themselves.[6]

Women protested these conditions in various ways. Some joined unions, the Socialist party, or a variety of anarchist and feminist groups. Women were active in several strikes, particularly the Tenant Strike of 1907 in which over one hundred thousand tenement residents of Buenos Aires and other major cities protested high rents. Housewives rather than union members dominated among female participants.[7] Middle-class professionals, including Socialists, joined feminist organizations which attracted several thousand followers by 1920.[8] Feminists envisioned a secular and humane society in which the government, rather than Catholic charities dominated by upper-class women, would provide welfare services for the masses. Tied to the left or the democratic center, they supported an egalitarian and reformist vision of society. This set them apart from Catholic advocates of women's programs, who stressed piety, submissiveness, hierarchy, and maintenance of the socioeconomic status quo. Yet, affluent Catholic laywomen did not necessarily disagree with the

middle-class feminist aim of legal equality with men and the expansion
of women's role beyond the domestic sphere.

To complicate matters further, not all feminists shared a common attitude toward women's labor outside the home. Like other sectors of Argentine society, many feminists placed a high value on women's roles as
mothers and housewives, sometimes justifying female extradomestic labor by arguing that skilled and active women made better mothers. By
working, women improved themselves as well as society.[9] Yet some feminists advocated women's economic independence from men as the basis
of all forms of female independence and demanded higher wages and
better working environments for women. These left-wing feminists, including some anarchists, still urged working-class women to concentrate
their efforts on raising strong, healthy class-conscious children and supporting their spouses and male comrades in the struggle against capitalism. Female radicals agreed that conditions in the future socialist society
would permit mothers to remain all day with their families.[10] From this
standpoint female extradomestic work seemed, at best, a short-term and
necessary evil.

Male statesmen, whom feminists fought with and against, also held
diverse views on women's place, although their opinions ranged from
ambivalent to traditional. Some members of the Radical Civic Union and
of the former oligarchy declared their support for additional female rights,
such as the vote.[11] While parties were by no means united on these issues,
Congress revised the civil code in 1926 so as to grant legal equality to
married women, including the right to enter the professions and dispose
of their earnings. Despite these concessions, most male politicians and
intellectuals viewed women's labor outside the home as an attack on the
family. Even male Socialists feared the effect of extradomestic work
on motherhood, though they seemed to regard it as inevitable, given
working-class poverty.[12]

### The View from Rome

The opinions that Argentine Catholics expressed on women's work were
influenced by directives from Rome as well as by local circumstances.
Facing many challenges, the church entered a period of change in the late
nineteenth century. Liberal anticlericalism had weakened its secular powers and diluted its appeal. Industrialization and urbanization had diminished its rural, small-town, and lower middle-class constituencies, creating
in their stead a proletariat and bourgeoisie which shared little, in the
church's view, save adherence to material goals and disdain for religion.
A financially powerful institution which traditionally had preached order

and obedience, the church was identified with the upper echelons of society. Nevertheless, it had no sympathy for free-market economics, a precept of the despised liberal doctrine which had so damaged the church over the past half century. Yet, it also opposed left-wing ideologies which threatened to convert workers from spiritual apathy to active anticlericalism. With these concerns in mind, church leaders decided to go on the offensive in seeking additional souls for their flock, particularly among the growing proletariat. Antiliberal and antileftist, Social Catholicism offered an alternative response to socioeconomic and political change.[13]

Today, it is common to associate Social Catholic texts with Liberation Theology, but in their original context papal encyclicals such as Leo XIII's *Rerum Novarum* (1891) were hardly progressive. It decried the abuses of capitalism and blamed them on upper-class avarice, yet at the same time lamented that no *legitimate* worker organizations had taken the place of guilds. Pope Leo XIII argued against the notion that capital and labor inevitably opposed each other, insisting that each needed the other and that social order required harmony between them. He also viewed private property as part of the natural order, disagreeing with Aquinas and other medieval theologians, who regarded it as an imperfect human institution. Men worked precisely to acquire property, and, according to Leo, it was their natural right and even their duty to do so. As head of the family, the father's obligation was to provide for his children, and he accomplished this task by increasing his wealth and handing it down to them. By seeking to confiscate private property, socialists would deny workers' aspirations for mobility and weaken the family unit.[14]

Leo XIII regarded socialism as utopian and anti-Christian. Believing that natural inequalities of ability accounted for inequalities of wealth, he viewed the socialist advocacy of leveling as a threat to the proper functioning of the family and the society. Hierarchy and inequality were inevitable and not necessarily evil; only unbridled greed and striving were sins. Since its fall from grace, humanity's lot had been to suffer. Thus, life and work must be painful, but those who patiently endured this suffering would redeem themselves from sin and receive their reward in heaven. By promising relief from these burdens on earth, socialist utopianists contradicted Christian teachings and pushed their followers out of salvation's reach.[15]

Leo XIII wanted the church to mediate between capital and labor. It should exhort employers to treat workers fairly and participate in church social works, and the proletariat to labor obediently and faithfully. Thus, the church would increase the virtue of both groups. It would also encourage the state to regulate business and would sponsor some associations consisting solely of workers and others embracing both capitalists and workers.[16]

Despite his approval of workers' organizations, Leo XIII was ambivalent about union activities. He thought that conflicts between capital and labor should be resolved through arbitration, and he opposed strikes, whether they were peaceful or violent. The pope did not say what workers should do if arbitration failed, or why employers would compromise with laborers who wielded no strike weapon, but he urged workers to stay away from socialists and militant unionists, whom he called "firebrands" and "men of evil principles." Moreover, he thought that the state had the right to dissolve associations whose purposes were unlawful or subversive. The rightful goals of workers' groups were to increase their members' material and spiritual well-being, not to assert themselves or challenge the social hierarchy.[17]

Leo XIII also briefly addressed the issue of women's roles in *Rerum Novarum* and *Arcanum Divinae Sapientiae* (1880). In the earlier encyclical, he noted that the husband represented Christ and the wife represented the church. Just as Christ headed the church, the husband was the "chief of the family and the head of the wife." Women should obey their spouses, to whom they were subject, yet their obedience should be "honorable and dignified," as that of a companion rather than that of a servant. "A heaven-born love" should guide both he who commanded and she who obeyed in their respective duties.[18] Leo XIII's comparison between women and what often has been called the "mother church," with its nurturing roles of dispensing spiritual and moral guidance, love, comfort, and alms to its flock, reflected his conception of women's proper tasks.

As Leo went on to explain in *Rerum Novarum*, the husband's duty was to rule over the family and support it financially; subservient to her spouse, the woman was to remain in the home. "By nature," the woman was best suited for household work, which was the occupation most likely to "preserve her modesty" and maintain the well-being of her children and spouse. If females had to labor outside the home, employers should not assign them tasks unsuitable to their sex. Furthermore, the mixing of the sexes in the workplace should be avoided because it could lead to moral dangers.[19]

In these and other statements, Leo XIII proclaimed a set of principles that shaped Catholic programs for female workers throughout the world and certainly in Argentina. Women's status as dependents within the family symbolized and expressed workers' subservient status within society. Whenever possible, women should remain within the domestic sphere, but whether employed within the home or outside it, the church's primary task was to keep them submissive, pious, and morally pure.

**Argentine Catholics**

Influential clergymen and laypersons refined and adapted these ideas to fit Argentine conditions.[20] Father Gustavo J. Franceschi was active in Social Catholic endeavors until the late 1910s, when he turned increasingly to intellectual pursuits. He was best known for his editorship of *Criterio*, the most influential Catholic journal in the country in the 1930s and early 1940s. Even before he became editor of this right-wing journal in 1932, Franceschi criticized economic individualism which, he claimed, condemned laborers to "choose" between starvation or working under the frequently brutal conditions established by owners. These conditions, in turn, alienated employees from employers, thus engendering discord. Social justice and harmony could only be achieved by organizing all active individuals within their appropriate economic sectors. As society restructured itself along these corporatist lines, class differences per se would not disappear, but the best minds of all the classes would gradually assume control over each productive sector. "Vertical stratification" eventually would replace "horizontal stratification" in the new society.[21]

Franceschi did not describe in detail his conception of women's roles in this future corporatist state. Nevertheless, one can piece together his ideas from his statements on family life. Ideally, families rather than individuals would constitute the basic unit of society under corporatism as they had during the Middle Ages. Franceschi debated which form of family would best achieve the "material and moral prolongation of one's line." He rejected what he called "family parliamentarianism," in which each member tried to accomplish a variety of tasks, because he thought it resulted in the same chaos that, in his opinion, characterized parliamentary political systems. Instead, like all collectivities, families required a degree of organization. This presupposed a division of labor and an authority structure. There had to be a family head, and that head must be the husband. Franceschi noted that Christian men could not exercise this power arbitrarily, but only through love. Citing Leo XIII, the priest deemed husband and wife "equal in dignity but subordinated one to the other by virtue of the diversity of their personal functions." In fact, he preferred not to use the terms equal, superior, or inferior; men and women were simply different.[22]

Franceschi denied that the church sentenced women to domestic slavery. During the Middle Ages, women had founded religious orders and convents, administered landed estates, studied in schools and universities, and voted in communal elections when their husbands were absent. The church's approval of these activities, Franceschi claimed, indicated its broad conception of women's roles and abilities. Nevertheless, the cleric

regarded women who performed such tasks as exceptions to the general
rule, believing that because of their physical strength, men were better fit
than women for outside occupations. Moreover, manual labor for women
would impede or complicate the bearing and upbringing of children. At
least one parent needed to remain at home to care for and educate the
young, and logically, he believed, this task fell to the mother. Ideally,
male workers' salaries should be sufficient to allow their wives to devote
themselves to the domestic labors to which they were suited.[23] Ironically,
Franceschi expected this to happen in the future corporatist society, while
some leftist feminists predicted it would occur under socialism.

In the corporatist state, the father would represent his family in the
public sphere. But Argentines still lived in an individualistic society, and
under these circumstances Franceschi saw no reason to deny women political participation.[24] His tepid endorsement of female suffrage, and other
women's programs, suggests that he reluctantly accepted female employment outside the home, at least during the transitional stage from individualism to corporatism.

The prominent Monsignor Miguel de Andrea more fully addressed
the interrelated questions of work in general and female employment in
particular. The archbishop of Buenos Aires promoted Andrea's career,
and when the former died in 1923, Andrea, now bishop of Temnos, was
the government's choice to succeed his patron. His ambition, his personalism, and, perhaps, his strong ties to the elite made him a divisive candidate, however, and the Vatican spurned him. After this controversy, Andrea
devoted himself for the next thirty years to organizing female laborers.
His ties to the church hierarchy in the early stages of his career and his
later interest in women laborers make his views a particularly useful index of the role of the religious right. Agreeing with Leo XIII, he did not
see hard work or even poverty as evils in themselves, since those who
accepted their lot learned to appreciate and share the burdens first assumed by Jesus and thus benefited spiritually. Andrea accused leftists of
viewing work as a yoke which enslaved and humiliated workers and reinforced their inferior status. By challenging employers, they hoped to lift
workers' status and make labor pleasurable. This egoistic aim, according
to Andrea, threatened to strip work of its higher, religious meaning and
thus "de-Christianize" the masses.[25]

Andrea did not deny workers' need for higher wages or healthier
working conditions, nor did he fail to indict capitalist abuses. Nevertheless, he believed that laborers should humbly accept their position and
uplift themselves spiritually as well as economically. Workers' lack of
morality and education, not their lack of wealth, was primarily responsible for the "social problem"; self-indulgent, materialistic, yet unskilled

and impoverished, laborers were easy prey for revolutionaries.[26] Andrea seemed unaware of the great competition for jobs even among the literate, and he failed to recognize the dependent structure of the economy as a major barrier to social mobility.[27] Rather, according to Andrea, Argentines were excessively concerned with increasing the nation's material wealth at the expense of its "moral equivalent." The penchant for luxury that he observed in all classes gave the appearance of an equality that did not exist—and that he did not favor. Only "moral wealth" could firmly establish social order, he concluded, making it "indispensable to cultivate virtue in the popular soul."[28]

Andrea claimed that under ideal conditions women defend virtue and tradition through their base in the home, instead of seeking "inappropriate" employment in factories, workshops, and offices. He understood, however, that many women were forced to work outside the home because they lived alone or their families required additional income. Given these economic imperatives, Andrea concluded that women should be able to improve their skills and self-confidence through vocational training. This training must include a moral component, however, so that female students—and through them, the entire female proletariat—would accept the existing social order. These educated working women could also exercise a positive influence on feminists, a group Andrea did not clearly define but whose existence he found inevitable. He embraced female suffrage without Franceschi's reluctance; like his fellow priest, however, he did not think that an expanded electoral system would necessarily solve Argentine problems. Andrea's belief in male rule in the household and in a hierarchy of authority in society[29] indicated his ambivalence about feminism and democracy. He supported education for female workers but did not expect it to increase their autonomy from men, the family, or employers.

Church-sponsored organizations such as the Catholic Workers' Circles manifested antileftist and hierarchical ideas that resembled those of Andrea and Franceschi. Father Federico Grote, a German priest, introduced this European institution to Argentina in 1892. In 1912, Andrea succeeded Grote as the Circles' spiritual director. The Circles included persons of different ranks within a particular industry or profession, promoting the class conciliation advocated by Leo XIII and Franceschi. They aimed to defend and promote the material and spiritual welfare of the laboring classes against sacrilegious leftist propaganda, using such means as mutual aid, education, lobbying for legislation, and supplying employers with strikebreakers. By 1920 there were eighty-five Circles with thirty-six thousand members. Only one of these groups was female, yet all the Circles directed some attention to issues related to women's work. For instance, among other legislative proposals, they urged the passage of a law regulating conditions faced by female laborers in sweatshops and those doing piecework at home.[30]

Other Catholic labor groups voiced similar views on female roles in the work force. Founded in 1902, the Christian Democratic League set out to create confessional unions. Under Grote's leadership, it organized at least six such unions, including the female Society of Weavers. Although these associations rejected noneconomic, political motives for action, one of them, the port workers, initiated a strike with Grote's approval. This militancy alienated the Argentine church hierarchy as well as prominent Catholic employers. As a result, the League and some of the unions dissolved in 1908, although the weavers' union survived at least until 1919.

Despite this controversy, the League's views on female workers followed the church's line. Like Leo XIII, the League declared itself in favor of defending the family unit by protecting young working women against unhealthy conditions and by separating the sexes in workplaces. Similar to Franceschi, the League supported the eventual phasing out of all women's labor in factories.[31] A congress of Catholic workers in Rosario in 1922 also echoed the League's broader aim of keeping women as close to the home as possible.[32]

These opinions resembled those expressed by an anonymous author in *Criterio* in 1928. That women in combatant nations during World War I had carried out men's tasks did not justify the continuation of that situation, according to the writer. Although they performed well, they did so at the expense of their families, which may have suffered irreparable harm in their absence. While the author seemed to understand the pressures forcing women to work outside the home, he could not approve of such labors, which took women too far from their "essential, eminent function." If women carried out two different roles, they would compete with their husbands and thus divide the family. The author was careful to note that he favored improving women's situation in the household as well as truly emancipating them, but these goals rested upon a "fundamental dignification of the home," which should remain "strong, united, and respected."[33] Women's liberation, in other words, meant enhancing their capacity as wives and mothers.

Alejandro E. Bunge's conception of women's roles contrasted with that of the previous author, yet he, too, advocated a separate female sphere. A member of a prestigious and devout family, Bunge was president of the central junta of the Circles from 1912 to 1916. His relationship to the church hierarchy is not clear; evidently he had close relations with Franceschi but cool ones with Andrea. Bunge was also an eminent economist and economic nationalist, the lifelong editor of the influential *Revista de Economía Argentina*, and an official in the federal labor department, and, as such, his professional interests may have affected his views on women and labor more than his Social Catholicism. Significantly, as the Circles' president he advocated greater participation by labor in the leadership of the organization. Nevertheless, he opposed socialism, distrusted mass politics, and supported the overthrow of democracy in 1930.[34] Given his political conservatism, his views on women were surprisingly progressive. He found no fault with the "moderate participation" of women in the labor force. "Coarse, absorbent, unconditional work" equivalent to that of a man, for which the women had received no preparation, was a "very grave danger," yet "ordered, adequate work" for which one had been trained could benefit most women and the society as well. He did not criticize women for assuming inappropriate duties but instead pointed out that they were poorly prepared to function in the modern world. Like Andrea, he thought that women (and men) needed moral, technical, and economic training. The two sexes should not receive the same kind of instruction, however; education of women should be "feminine, not manly," and much broader and deeper than that offered in the past.[35] Behind these thoughts was an unstated assumption shared by Social Catholics (and most Argentines): that female and male "natures" were distinct.

Whereas Andrea stressed the moral and technical dimensions of education, Bunge focused on the economic aspects. He observed that Argentines lacked thrift, efficiency, forethought, and pride in locally manufactured goods; in other words, they did not possess an "economic sense." Cultivating this sense in women would help them become better workers, housewives, and consumers, thus facilitating economic development.

Another Social Catholic and an honorary factory inspector for the federal labor department, Celia LaPalma de Emery had more in common with the antileftist Andrea than with the pragmatic Bunge. An upper-class woman, her primary concern was to evangelize the laboring classes through their female members. She noted that the left had already won over male workers; the hearts of their female counterparts, however, were not yet totally shut to the Christian message. By extending love and charity to those in need, perhaps laywomen could win the hearts of working women and, through them, the entire family. She advised Catholic women to visit factories and organize female laborers into Workers' Circles, which would protect the Christian family and halt the spread of leftism. As previously noted, however, only one was formed. LaPalma de Emery also valued professional education for women because it would reduce the ignorance which she thought led to the acceptance of leftist ideas.[36]

Although they shared the same assumptions about "woman's nature," LaPalma de Emery accepted female labor outside the home with fewer reservations than did most clergy and laymen. Harking back to the Christian notion of work, LaPalma de Emery declared that manual and other forms of labor dignified women who performed such tasks. She considered female factory workers, store employees, and even young girls forced to support themselves as "meritorious because they have to take positions in order to live honestly, a deed which greatly exalts them."[37]

Their work was also praiseworthy for other reasons. LaPalma de Emery believed that employment outside the home—which she defined broadly to include intellectual and artistic endeavors, liberal professions, upper-class philanthropy, manual and factory labor—benefited women of all social ranks. Deriding the aristocratic notion that it was a "supreme virtue" for women to avoid productive work, she gave examples of prestigious European women who had earned a living on their own despite their families' wealth. Even if they were not impoverished, women should enter the labor force to fulfill themselves, protect themselves in case of future exigency, and preclude frustrations that fed "domestic conflict." In fact, knowledge of a trade was good simply for its own sake. "Valiant at work, learned and independent in society," the model Argentine woman promoted by LaPalma de Emery was also "modest and simple in the home" and always "good and pious."[38] Despite her approval of female labor, she still endorsed the values of female submissiveness, piety, morality, and domesticity stressed by Catholic men.

Moreover, her adherence to the first three values, her upper-class background, and her strident antileftism separated her from Argentine feminists. LaPalma de Emery participated in the Feminine Congress of May 1910, held by the National Council of Women as a counterweight to the feminist First International Feminine Congress, which took place a few days later. Originally broadly based, the Council evolved into an upper-class group that denounced what it regarded as "sectarian and combative feminism."[39] One may assume that LaPalma de Emery shared the views of her cohorts.

A prominent poet, essayist, and member of Catholic intellectual circles, as well as Bunge's sister, Delfina Bunge de Gálvez agreed with LaPalma de Emery that women's employment outside the family was desirable, even when families did not require additional income. God would not have endowed women with ability if he had not wanted them to use it. By employing their diverse capacities inside and outside the home, women could improve society, give their lives a sense of balance, and avoid the boredom which contributed to spiritual torpor and unhappy marriages. In her opinion, women were not destined simply for marriage, nor was any occupation inherently unsuitable for them. Even public tasks were permissible, as long as women performed them with more reserve and modesty than men. She advised women to be humble and open-minded when choosing a profession so as not to reject any job as beneath their station or inappropriate to their sex. Neither men nor other women should oppose women's entry into the labor force.[40]

Although Bunge de Gálvez considered herself a feminist, she did not regard men and women as equal. Men and women inherently possessed different duties, rights, and abilities, and to categorize the sexes as equal or unequal demeaned them both. The desire of some women for "equality with men," for example, demonstrated their contempt for traditional female duties, which she valued more highly than any other tasks a woman might perform. Indeed, here Bunge de Gálvez most clearly distinguished herself from Argentine feminists and allied herself with Franceschi. She implied that true feminists, in contrast to the local variety, were proud of their heritage. The very fact that female professionals necessarily, according to the writer, performed diverse public and domestic chores indicated women's inherent versatility, a quality which set them apart from the other sex. This flexibility gave women an advantage over men, for it helped them maintain equilibrium in their lives and, even if they were intellectuals, kept them in touch with reality and, in this case, the needs of their families.[41]

Although she accepted spinsterhood as an option for women, Bunge de Gálvez viewed the "double day" not only as inevitable but desirable. She did not recognize that the multiplicity of women's tasks inhibited their professional advancement and peace of mind. The many demands on her time affected her own health, which was always precarious, and her career. Her husband noted in his memoirs that her illnesses and her dedication to family and the church dictated Bunge de Gálvez's choice of the essay format rather than a longer, more complex literary genre.[42]

A devout Catholic, Bunge de Gálvez believed in obedience and hierarchy. Unlike most Argentine feminists, she accepted what she viewed as God's decision to grant men authority over the family and the polity. She regarded this "relative and conditional subjugation of woman to man" as a yoke no more severe than the "subjugation of man to other inevitable laws." All beings were subject to obedience in life; why should women's status differ from the norm? Obedience had spiritual merit only when offered voluntarily, however, and not when forced upon women. Increasing their professional independence did not mean freeing women from their submission to men but rather helping them obey another calling, namely, their divinely granted personal vocations.[43]

Permitting women to work freely outside the home did not, in her opinion, justify giving all women the same voting rights. Human beings differed according to ability, virtue, and status, and like other rightists, Bunge de Gálvez therefore thought it illogical to grant each person the same unqualified vote. Agreeing with Franceschi, she saw no reason to deny all women the right to vote as long as universal male suffrage was the rule. She felt strongly that qualified women should help determine policy in those areas related to their "natural" concerns, such as education, social welfare, female and child labor, and family matters even if this entailed women's participation in Congress and appointment to governmental agencies. Although such roles would entail authority over men, they would not necessarily contradict female submissiveness, as long as women abjured personal ambition and labored for the common good. These worthy vocations corresponded with women's customary duty of extending love and charity to those in need.[44] Thus, Bunge de Gálvez ingeniously used her religious and traditional beliefs to justify broader female roles than those envisioned by other right-wing Catholic spokespersons.

María Rosario Ledesma, an upper-class writer and philanthropist, also manipulated a traditional corpus of ideas to rationalize extending female rights and the female sphere of activity beyond the home. Ledesma's interest in such topics was sparked when Franceschi addressed her elite high school on Social Catholicism. After his visit she and other female students founded the Blanche of Castile Studies Center in 1916. The organization's discussion sessions with Franceschi, who served as its spiritual advisor, and the public speeches Ledesma made as its president gave her the opportunity to apply Catholic doctrine to contemporary women's issues.[45]

Ledesma agreed with Catholic leaders that whether one liked it or not, lower-class women had to work outside the home. Many entered the labor force at an early, impressionable age, without adequate moral and professional training or sufficient physical development. For these reasons they were unprepared for the "great dangers and few means of salvation" they faced. Uprooted from their families, women in the workplace experienced brutal conditions, loneliness, and the sad realization that they could not be "true mothers." Ledesma believed that women's salaries could never compensate for sacrificing the "elevated tasks" in the home to which God has assigned them. Yet women, she believed, exercised certain professions as capably as men. For these reasons, one could not justify a wage differential between the sexes; women and men should receive equal pay. Moreover, just like male laborers, females should organize to protect their material and moral interests.[46]

Agreeing with Bunge de Gálvez, Ledesma urged all women to de-velop their God-granted abilities. Nevertheless, she seemed to justify women's use of these capacities outside the home primarily on the basis of need. For middle- and upper-class women, this meant fulfilling the needs of the society by uniting the social classes through the organization of female laborers into Christian syndicates. Women should dedicate them-selves to this task, however, only after completing their household chores. Thus, the female role of "queen of the fatherland" would not interfere with that of "queen of the house."[47]

Similarly, Ledesma thought that expanding women's legal and po-litical rights would not interfere with their traditional role, nor would it conflict with Catholicism. She employed history to prove her point. In her opinion, the ideal woman of the classical and Renaissance eras was mute and unthinking, solely involved with husband, home, and manual labor. The materialism of the contemporary pagan era, inaugurated by the French Revolution, had then enslaved women and robbed them of protec-tion. Since 1789 women had lacked the right to give testimony in court, administer their own goods, or serve as guardians of their children inde-pendently of their husbands. They could not even vote for representatives who deliberated matters relating to the family's welfare. Although Ledesma admitted that Christianity did not establish equality between the sexes, she equivocated by insisting that God had created woman to serve as man's companion—and companions occupied the same level. Echoing Franceschi, she claimed that women had enjoyed more rights and a fuller role in society during the Christian Middle Ages than under a more modern liberal state. Those who demanded improved rights, includ-ing feminists, only sought to recover what they once had possessed. In-deed, "true and just" feminist goals could only be met in a Catholic society. Until the re-creation of such conditions, liberalism could not deny to women what it gave to men—and that included suffrage. Furthermore, voting a few times a year would not diminish femininity, nor would it disrupt female domestic tasks. Nevertheless, Ledesma did not encourage women to lobby for suffrage; she only suggested that after receiving this right, Catholic women should exercise it.[48] In this and other ways, Ledesma and her fellow Center members restricted female initiative even as they pressed for improved economic and political conditions.

## Church Programs for Working Women in Buenos Aires

The Social Catholics' humanitarian projects for female workers in Buenos Aires illustrate the rightist views and motives discussed above. Father

Santiago Barth founded the first such project, the Home and Association of Female Domestics, in 1891. It provided apprenticeships for those who wanted to enter domestic service and shelter for unemployed women. In 1902, Barth created the League of Protection for Young Women, which extended lodging and placement services to young women who had moved to Buenos Aires from the interior or abroad in search of jobs. The League also established the first "respectable" restaurant in the capital serving inexpensive meals to an exclusively female working-class clientele. The Home and the League reflected the church's concern for protecting the virtue of young working women. Barth and Grote, in fact, presented a resolution to this effect at a congress of Argentine Catholics in 1907.[49]

The same preoccupation characterized the League of Argentine Catholic Ladies, founded by the Third National Congress of Social Catholics in 1908. Guided by the Jesuit Father R. P. Segismundo Masferrer, who was esteemed by hierarchy and laity alike, its upper-class members proselytized among female factory workers, urging them to save money for their dowries and to "fulfill their Christian duty" by marrying and having children. For these purposes, the Ladies established a savings bank for working women in 1911 and contributed funds to it. By 1918 the Ladies also had founded five restaurants and a housing project for female workers.[50] Guarding the morals of proletarian women, encouraging them to be pious, and integrating them into the domestic sphere were among the Ladies' main concerns. The fact that the upper-class Ladies worked with proletarian women also manifested the Social Catholic aim of class conciliation.

This goal was evident in the creation of the Cross Society of Match Workers in 1917, an affiliate of the Workers' Circles. The Catholic *El Pueblo* claimed that the Cross was the first all-female union in Argentina; in reality, less successful, non-Catholic ones had appeared as early as 1903. Founded by the prominent Father Bartolomé Ayrolo and 175 female match workers of Avellaneda, an industrial suburb of Buenos Aires, the Cross advocated female education, mutual aid, and economic uplift. Its members organized themselves so as to avoid affiliating with a male anarchist union in the industry. Nevertheless, they did not abjure the use of strikes or joint actions with other unions, providing that their spiritual director, Ayrolo, and the male officials of the Circles ratified these decisions. Women who were "immoral" or who had previously belonged to anti-Catholic groups or radical unions were ineligible for membership. Despite opposition from management and especially from labor militants, the Cross attracted 650 members organized in fifteen locals in Avellaneda and Buenos Aires by 1918, as well as Andrea's support.[51] Separating Catholic women from de-Christianizing influences in the factory was the Cross's main intent. Its theoretical approval of strikes notwithstanding, I found no evidence that it engaged in any, although it did request improvements from management. Subject to male leaders, its female members may have had little opportunity for autonomous decision making.

Young upper-class women established other confessional unions with similar aims under the auspices of the Blanche of Castile Studies Center. That Franceschi named the group for the pious queen who had ruled France and given birth to St. Louis indicated the image he wanted to set for the members: aristocratic, devout, strong, maternal, and socially engaged. At first this engagement consisted of reading works on Catholic social doctrine, discussing their application to modern problems, conducting research on labor issues, and even presenting bills regulating female labor to Congress. As one member recalled, the Center was an excellent place to receive "civic, democratic, and Christian education"; Andrea would have approved of such preparation of women for the modern world. Deciding to put their lessons into practice, the girls visited the workplaces and homes of female laborers and persuaded them to join those unions the Center was organizing, thus fulfilling the mission outlined by Ledesma.[52]

The Center created syndicates for store and bank employees, seamstresses, and workers of Nueva Pompeya, an industrial neighborhood of Buenos Aires. The unions aimed at defending the economic and professional interests of their constituents, who numbered 710 by 1919, through legal and peaceful means. Members enjoyed access to job-placement, medical, legal, religious, and library services, as well as classes in vocational arts, language, arithmetic, home economics, and Catholicism. The curriculum demonstrated the Social Catholics' desire to neutralize possibly harmful effects of female labor by tying women anew to the church and the family.

The Center also emphasized class conciliation and worker submissiveness. The seamstresses' union, for example, emphasized respect for "Religion, Fatherland, Family, and Property" as a qualification for membership. One should also recall Ledesma's desire to counter the appeal of militant unions and Franceschi's corporatist ideas. Employers did not oppose the formation of the syndicates, which never struck or otherwise protested management decisions. Although Ledesma insisted that their role was not "to rule or otherwise impose themselves" but to cooperate fraternally with their working-class sisters, Center members were the organizers, teachers, and speakers, as well as the representatives of the syndicates at Catholic congresses. They even held leadership positions in the unions. As in the Cross, union members seemed to exercise little independent action. One might also question the autonomy of Center leaders, since Franceschi wrote the Center's statutes and oversaw its activities.[53]

Meanwhile, Andrea had also begun to work with female laborers. In 1919 he founded the Feminine Technical Institute, which imparted moral and vocational training to female workers.[54] Two years later he established the Catholic Syndicate of Female Teachers, and in 1922 he organized female employees in five stores and the post office into the Federation of Catholic Associations of Female Employees (FACE). To the disillusionment of some Center members, FACE took over its duties among the working class by absorbing its syndicates. FACE continued the types of programs which the Center's unions had offered, but Andrea interpreted its aims in an even more explicitly religious and political manner than the Center. According to the bishop, FACE's goals were "social pacification" and the "moral elevation of the woman who works" through the inculcation of Christian discipline.[55] By 1931, the seven thousand women of the eighteen FACE locals were, in Andrea's opinion, immune to the appeal of revolutionaries.[56] Thus, he implemented his aim of training women to accept the given order.

### Conclusion

Priests, laypersons, and members of confessional groups, though advocates of rightist political policies, viewed the changing situation of women compassionately and, for the most part, realistically. Except for the anonymous writer in *Criterio*, all of those studied accepted female labor outside the home—and some with few reservations. Perhaps not surprisingly, female leaders and the scholar, Bunge, held the most tolerant views. LaPalma de Emery and Bunge de Gálvez praised all types of female participation in the labor force, while Bunge lauded those he regarded as suitably feminine. Nevertheless, his criteria for deciding which occupations were fit for women probably were broader than those of Catholic traditionalists. Ledesma's conception of female roles was relatively narrow, but she and Bunge de Gálvez, along with Andrea and Franceschi, favored extending political and legal rights to women.

Even some of those who entertained more enlightened ideas, however, such as LaPalma de Emery and Ledesma, combined these attitudes with antileftist and antidemocratic sentiments, and most of the spokespersons, including the women, saw females as inherently pious, maternal, and humble. Center members also viewed the syndicate members in this manner, but, ironically, they were forced to relegate their fledgling organizations to Andrea's control. The Social Catholics' emphasis on female submissiveness, along with their religious and political biases, set even the most progressive of their number apart from feminists. So, too, did their equation of motherhood and the family with the capitalist order.

While the opinions and programs surveyed in this essay were more diverse than one might have anticipated, they all reflected the church's institutional aims and paternalistic notions about women's nature and workers' status. They originated in the concern of church leaders in Rome and Buenos Aires over the poverty of the masses and the greed of the rich in the world economy. These leaders feared that growing disparities of wealth, workers' mobilization, and female participation in the labor force would weaken the family, the social hierarchy, and the church's popular following. Church representatives answered some of these challenges by salvaging as much of the traditional role of women—and the traditional ranks of the masses—as they could. Indeed, the two issues were so intertwined that the Catholic views of female status not only indicated attitudes about women but [also] symbolized and expressed attitudes about the laborers' "rightful" lowly place in society.[57]

How deeply these attitudes permeated the Argentine public is not clear. Nevertheless, the Argentine right and the church continued to hold such opinions, as was apparent during the first presidency of Juan Perón (1946–1954). Neither feminist nor leftist, Juan and Eva Perón's policies nevertheless increased the economic and political status of women and the working class. At the same time, the regime accepted hierarchical relations within the family and society, and it tended to describe both women and the masses as irrational, unthinking beings requiring the control of male leaders. Thus, the extent to which women and workers increased their autonomy under Peronism is debatable.[58] The church and rightist groups divided over Peronism. Fearing the Peróns' mobilization of the masses and his personalism, many former Social Catholics, such as Andrea and Center members, resolutely opposed them. Some, like Delfina Bunge de Gálvez, supported the Peróns' Catholic-style emphasis on social justice.

Significantly, however, the poet praised the Peronist masses for what she regarded as their humility, lack of class hatred, and gratitude to their "protector" Perón.[59] Despite her imaginative advocacy of women and laborers, Bunge de Gálvez, like other rightists and Catholic spokespersons, wanted them to remain submissive.

## Notes

1. On the church's ties to the right, see Marysa Navarro Gerassi, *Los nacionalistas*, trans. Alberto Ciria (Jorge Alvarez, Buenos Aires, 1968); Sandra McGee Deutsch, *Counterrevolution in Argentina, 1900–1932: The Argentine Patriotic*

*League* (University of Nebraska, Lincoln, 1986); David Rock, "Intellectual Pre-cursors of Conservative Nationalism in Argentina, 1900–1927," *Hispanic American Historical Review*, 67:2 (May 1987), pp. 271–300; Comisión de Estudios de la Sociedad Argentina de Defensa de la Tradición, Familia, Propiedad, *El nacionalismo: una incógnita en constante evolución* (Ediciones Tradición, Familia, Propiedad, Buenos Aires, 1970); Enrique Zuleta Alvarez, *El nacionalismo argentino* (2 vols., Ediciones la Bastilla, Buenos Aires, 1975), vol. II: pp. 721–811. Néstor T. Auza, in *Aciertos y fracasos sociales del catolicismo argentino* (3 vols., Editorial Docencia, Ediciones Don Bosco, Editorial Guadalupe, Buenos Aires, 1987–88), described what he viewed as reformist and conservative wings of the church, and he fit some of the persons discussed below, such as Miguel de Andrea and Gustavo J. Franceschi, into the latter.

2. On the need for such studies see Asunción Lavrin, "Recent Studies on Women in Latin America," *Latin American Research Review*, 19:1 (1984), pp. 188–9; Elsa M. Chaney, *Supermadre: Women in Politics in Latin America* (University of Texas, Austin, 1979), pp. 39–40. One work, covering the 1940s and 1950s, is Catalina H. Wainerman, "El mundo de las ideas y los valores: mujer y trabajo," in Catalina Wainerman, Elizabeth Jelin, and María del Carmen Feijóo, *Del deber ser y el hacer de las mujeres: Dos estudios de caso en Argentina* (El Colegio de México-PISPAL, México, 1983), pp. 41–65. Mieke Aerts, "Catholic Construc-tions of Femininity: Three Dutch Women's Organizations in Search of a Politics of the Personal, 1912–1940," pp. 256–68, and Anne-Marie Sohn, "Catholic Women and Political Affairs: The Case of the Patriotic League of French Women," trans. Debra Irving, pp. 237–55, both in Judith Friedlander et al., *Women in Culture and Politics: A Century of Change* (Indiana University, Bloomington, 1986), de-scribe some attitudes and programs similar to those treated below.

3. See also Sandra F. McGee, "Female Right-Wing Activists in Buenos Aires, 1900–1932," in *Women and the Structure of Society*, eds. Barbara J. Harris and Jo Ann K. McNamara (Duke University, Durham, 1984), pp. 85–97. This study begins in 1890, when dissatisfaction with liberal economics surfaced in Argen-tina, and one year before *Rerum Novarum* appeared. The year 1930 marked the end of the golden era of export prosperity and a shift in Catholic thought from the matters discussed here to the conflict between Marxism and fascism.

4. Donna J. Guy, "Women, Peonage, and Industrialization: Argentina, 1810–1914," *Latin American Research Review*, 16:3 (1981), p. 66 [see also Selec-tion 10, this volume]; República Argentina, Comisión Nacional del Censo, *Tercer censo nacional* (Talleres Gráficos de L. J. Rosso, Buenos Aires, 1916), vol. 1: p. 252; Charles Bergquist, *Labor in Latin America: Comparative Essays on Chile, Argentina, Venezuela, and Colombia* (Stanford University, Stanford, 1986), p. 121. The figure for 1867 refers to women over the age of ten (Guy), while the one for 1914 refers to those over fourteen (*Tercer censo*). On women's status and work, see Guy, "Women," pp. 65–90; Carolina Muzzilli, "El trabajo femenino," *Boletín Mensual del Museo Social Argentino*, 2 (1913), pp. 65–90; Katherine S. Dreier, *Five Months in the Argentine from a Woman's Point of View, 1918–1919* (Frederic Fairchild Sherman, New York, 1920); Robert Edward Shipley, "On the Outside Looking In: A Social History of the Porteño Worker during the 'Golden Age' of Argentine Development 1914–1930" (Ph.D. diss., Rutgers Univ., 1977); Nancy Caro Hollander, "Women in the Political Economy of Argentina" (Ph.D. diss., U.C.L.A., 1974); Judith Lynn Sweeney, "Immigrant Women in Argentina:

1890–1914," MS, n.d., pp. 18–30; Mirta Henault, "La incorporación de la mujer al trabajo asalariado," *Todo Es Historia*, no. 183 (Aug. 1982), pp. 42–53.

5. Shipley, "Porteño Worker," p. 51.

6. Ibid., pp. 89, 136.

7. Sweeney, "Immigrant Women," pp. 36–48; James R. Scobie, *Buenos Aires: Plaza to Suburb, 1870–1910* (Oxford, New York, 1974), pp. 156–8; Hobart A. Spalding, Jr., ed., *La clase trabajadora argentina (documentos para su historia— 1890/1912)* (Editorial Galerna, Buenos Aires, 1970), pp. 91–2, 449–96, 482; Asunción Lavrin, "Women, Labor and the Left: Argentina and Chile, 1890–1925," *Journal of Women's History*, 1:2 (Fall 1989), pp. 88–116; Juana Rouco Buela, *Historia de un ideal vivido por una mujer* (Editorial Reconstruir, Buenos Aires, 1964); Maxine Molyneux, "No God, No Boss, No Husband: Anarchist Feminism in Nineteenth-Century Argentina," *Latin American Perspectives*, 13:1 (Winter 1986), pp. 119–45; Marysa Navarro, "Hidden, Silent, and Anonymous: Women Workers in the Argentina Trade Union Movement," in *The World of Woman's Trade Unionism: Comparative Historical Essays*, ed. Norbert C. Soldon (Greenwood, Westport, 1985), pp. 165–98.

8. Hollander, "Political Economy," p. 225. On feminism, see Marifran Carlson, *¡Feminismo! The Woman's Movement in Argentina from Its Beginnings to Eva Perón* (Academy Chicago, Chicago, 1988); Dreier, *Five Months*; Cynthia Jeffress Little, "Education, Philanthropy, and Feminism: Components of Argentine Womanhood, 1860–1926," in *Latin American Women: Historical Perspectives*, ed. Asunción Lavrin (Greenwood, Westport, 1978), pp. 235–53; Cynthia Jeffress Little, "Moral Reform and Feminism," *Journal of Inter-American Studies and World Affairs*, 17 (Nov. 1975), pp. 386–97; María del Carmen Feijóo, "Las luchas feministas," *Todo Es Historia*, no. 128 (Jan. 1978), pp. 7–23; Asunción Lavrin, "The Ideology of Feminism in the Southern Cone, 1900–1940," Washington, D.C., The Wilson Center Working Papers No. 169, 1986.

9. *Primer Congreso Femenino Internacional de la República Argentina* (Alfa y Omega, Buenos Aires, 1911), pp. 35–40. Also see Catalina H. Wainerman and Marysa Navarro, "El trabajo de la mujer en la Argentina: Un análisis preliminar de las ideas dominantes en las primeras décadas del siglo XX," Buenos Aires, Cuadernos de CENEP No. 7, 1979, p. 26; Lavrin, "Women," pp. 93–9.

10. *Primer Congreso*, pp. 210–13, 231–2; Mary Feijóo, "Gabriela Coni: la lucha feminista," *Todo Es Historia*, no. 175 (Dec. 1981), pp. 92–3; Carlson, *¡Feminismo!*, p. 125.

11. Miguel J. Font, *La mujer: Encuesta feminista argentina, Hacia la formación de una Liga Feminista Sudamericana* (n.p., Buenos Aires, 1921), pp. 62–3, 84–7; Asunción Lavrin, "South American Feminists as Social Redeemers and Political Pioneers: Chile, Argentina, and Uruguay, 1900–1940," Paper given at the American Historical Association meeting, San Francisco, Dec. 1983, pp. 11, 20–1.

12. Guy, "Women," p. 83; Font, *La mujer*, pp. 16, 27, 92–3, 99–100, passim; Wainerman and Navarro, "El trabajo," pp. 17–22. In "Politics and Gender: The Socialist Position and Legalized Prostitution in Argentina, 1913–1936," Paper given at the International Congress of Americanists meeting, Bogotá, 1985, Donna J. Guy described the male Socialists' conservatism on gender.

13. On European Social Catholicism, see Richard L. Camp, *The Papal Ideology of Social Reform: A Study in Historical Development, 1878–1967* (E. J. Brill,

Leiden, 1969); Joseph N. Moody, ed., *Church and Society: Catholic Social and Political Thought and Movements, 1789–1950* (Arts, Inc., New York, 1953); Michael P. Fogarty, *Christian Democracy in Western Europe, 1820–1953* (Routledge and Kegan Paul, London, 1957).

14. Pope Leo XIII, *"Rerum Novarum,"* in *The Papal Encyclicals*, ed. Claudia Carlen Ihm (McGrath Publishing Co., Raleigh, 1981), vol. II: pp. 241–57, esp. 241–2, 244–5. Also see Camp, *Papal Ideology*, pp. 52–6.

15. Leo XIII, *"Rerum Novarum,"* pp. 245–6.

16. Ibid., pp. 246, 251; Camp, *Papal Ideology*, pp. 113–14.

17. Leo XIII, *"Rerum Novarum,"* pp. 246, 251, 254.

18. Pope Leo XIII, "On Christian Marriage" (*Arcanum Divinae Sapientiae*), in *The Church Speaks to the Modern World: The Social Teachings of Leo XIII*, ed. Etienne Gilson (Doubleday, Garden City, N.Y., 1954), pp. 93–4. Similar statements are found fifty years later in Pope Pius XI, *"Casti Conubii,"* in *Three Great Encyclicals: Labor—Education—Marriage* (The Paulist Press, New York, 1931), pp. 82, 97.

19. Leo XIII, *"Rerum Novarum,"* pp. 246, 250, 252.

20. On Social Catholicism in Latin America and Argentina, see John Lynch, "The Catholic Church in Latin America, 1830–1930," in *The Cambridge History of Latin America*, ed. Leslie Bethell, vol. IV: *c. 1870–1930* (Cambridge University, Cambridge, 1986), pp. 584–90; Auza, *Aciertos;* José Elías Niklison, "Acción social católica obrera," *Boletín del Departamento Nacional de Trabajo*, 46 (Mar. 1920), pp. 15–28; Spalding, *La clase*, pp. 497–549; Héctor Recalde, *La iglesia y la cuestión social (1874–1910)* (Centro Editor de América Latina, Buenos Aires, 1985).

21. Gustavo J. Franceschi, *La democracia y la iglesia* (L. J. Rosso, Buenos Aires, 1918), pp. 28, 84–6, 100–7. On Franceschi, see Archivo de *La Prensa* (Buenos Aires), File 6375; Auza, *Aciertos*, vol. II: esp. pp. 374–6. Franceschi did not use the term corporatism but his ideas fit this model of class relations.

22. Gustavo J. Franceschi, *Tres estudios sobre la familia: Origen de la familia, su constitución interna, su función social* (Agencia General de Librería y Publicaciones, Buenos Aires, 1923), pp. 116–21, 142, 146–7.

23. Ibid., pp. 146, 151–2; Franceschi, *La democracia*, p. 101. For a more accurate portrayal of women in the Catholic Middle Ages, see Bonnie S. Anderson and Judith P. Zinsser, *A History of Their Own: Women in Europe from Prehistory to the Present* (2 vols., Harper and Row, New York, 1988), vol. 1: pp. 67–84, 181–263.

24. Franceschi, *Tres estudios*, pp. 206–7, and "Sobre feminismo católico," *El Pueblo*, 17 June 1920. Franceschi supported female suffrage less unequivocally in the 1940s; see Wainerman, "El mundo," p. 57.

25. Miguel de Andrea, *Pensamiento cristiano y democrático de Monseñor de Andrea: Homenaje del Congreso Nacional* (Imprenta del Congreso de la Nación, Buenos Aires, 1963), p. 83 (from a speech given in 1912); and *Obras completas* (Editorial Difusión, Buenos Aires, 1944), vol. III, *La perturbación social contemporánea*, pp. 15, 53. The portions cited in the second book here and in notes 26 and 28–29 were taken from speeches given in 1919. On Andrea's career, see Ambrosio Romero Carranza, *Itinerario de Monseñor de Andrea* (Compañia Impresora Argentina, Buenos Aires, 1957); Auza, *Aciertos*, esp. vol. II: pp. 11–12, and vol. III: pp. 146–50, 273.

26. Andrea, *La perturbación*, pp. 119–21.

27. On education, see Shipley, "Porteño Worker," p. 211; on the competition for work, see Hobart A. Spalding, Jr., "Education in Argentina, 1890–1914: The Limits of Oligarchical Reform," *Journal of Interdisciplinary History*, 3:1 (Summer 1972), p. 60.

28. Andrea, *La perturbación*, p. 115; Monseñor Miguel de Andrea, "Orientaciones sociales," *Instituto Popular de Conferencias*, 3 (15 June 1917), p. 84.

29. Andrea, *La perturbación*, pp. 64–5, 111–14; ibid., "Orientaciones," pp. 82, 85, 88. In his speech of 1935 in *El catolicismo social y su aplicación* (Domingo Viau y Cía., Buenos Aires, 1941), p. 152, Andrea continued to ask that women should ideally remain at home.

30. Niklison, "Acción social," p. 17; Jose Pagés, "Los ensayos sindicales de inspiración católica en la República Argentina," *Anales de la Comisión de Estudios y Conferencias de la Corporación de Ingenieros Católicos* (1944), pp. 84–7; Recalde, *La iglesia*, pp. 81–3, 85.

31. Pagés, "Los ensayos," pp. 98–100; Spalding, *La clase*, pp. 502–4; Néstor Tomás Auza, *Los Católicos argentinos: su experiencia política y social* (Ediciones Diagrama, Buenos Aires, 1962), pp. 78–84; Niklison, "Acción social," p. 112.

32. *Boletín de Servicios de la Asociación del Trabajo*, 3 (5 Dec. 1922), p. 562.

33. J. M. G., "Los derechos civiles de la mujer," *Criterio*, no. 17 (28 June 1928), p. 525.

34. On Bunge's career, see José Luis de Imaz, "Alejandro E. Bunge, economista y sociólogo (1880–1943)," *Desarrollo Económico*, 14 (Oct.-Dec. 1974), pp. 545–67; Auza, *Aciertos*, vol. II: pp. 47–9, 61, 71–6. His elitist views are apparent in Alejandro E. Bunge, *Una nueva Argentina* (Editorial Guillermo Kraft, Buenos Aires, 1940), pp. 51–60, and "La palabra de la economía nacional," *Revista de Economía Argentina* (Nov. 1930), pp. 305, 316. Bunge's views hardened over time. Fearing the decline of the Christian family and the white race in Argentina, he questioned whether the "excessive intervention of the woman in all branches of work" had caused the birthrate to fall, in *Una nueva*, p. 45.

35. Information for this and the following paragraph comes from Alejandro E. Bunge, "La formación del sentido económico en la mujer argentina," *Revista de Economía Argentina* (Oct. 1921), pp. 295–309, esp. 296–7, 300.

36. Celia LaPalma de Emery, *Discursos y conferencias de Celia LaPalma de Emery: Acción pública y privada en favor de la mujer y del niño en la República Argentina* (Alfa y Omega, Buenos Aires, 1910), pp. 34–6, 154. Also see Niklison, "Acción social," pp. 71–3.

37. LaPalma de Emery, *Discursos*, pp. 46–8.

38. Ibid., pp. 112–14, 154–5, 185–202.

39. Ibid., pp. 183–204. Also see "Consejo Nacional de Mujeres," *Boletín del Museo Social Argentino* 1:6 (1912), pp. 161–7; Cecilia Grierson, *Decadencia del Consejo Nacional de Mujeres de la República Argentina* (n.p., Buenos Aires, 1910); Carlson, *¡Feminismo!*, pp. 87–106, 139–41.

40. Delfina Bunge de Gálvez, *Las mujeres y la vocación*, 2nd edn. (Editorial Poblet, Buenos Aires, 1943), pp. 28–35, 63–4, 92–3, 104. This work originally appeared in 1922. On her background, see her sister Julia Valentina Bunge's memoir, *Vida, época maravillosa, 1903–1911* (Emecé Editores, Buenos Aires, 1965), and Lily Sosa de Newton, *Diccionario biográfico de mujeres argentinas*, 2nd edn. (Editorial Plus Ultra, Buenos Aires, 1980), p. 72.

41. Bunge de Gálvez, *Las mujeres*, pp. 34, 38–9, 47–8, 104.

42. Manuel Gálvez, *Entre la novela y la historia* (Librería Hachette, Buenos Aires, 1962), pp. 316–17.

43. Bunge de Gálvez, *Las mujeres*, pp. 34–6.

44. Ibid., pp. 80–1, 94–6, 100–1. On the right and the vote, see Deutsch, *Counterrevolution*, pp. 193, 207–8.

45. María Rosario Ledesma de García Fernández, *Una época a través de mis escritos* (Talleres Gráficos Zaragoza, Buenos Aires, 1949), pp. 13, 75.

46. Ibid., pp. 14–16, 23, 38–9, 43. The statements cited here and in notes 47–48 were made between 1916 and 1922.

47. Ibid., pp. 15, 27, 40, 43–4.

48. Ibid., pp. 42–51; María Rosario Ledesma, "Más sobre feminismo," *El Pueblo*, 23 June 1920.

49. Niklison, "Acción social," pp. 94–95. Feminists accused such programs of providing the rich with cheap servants. For more details on Catholic programs for women, see McGee, "Activists."

50. Niklison, "Acción social," pp. 274–7; Auza, *Aciertos*, vol. III: pp. 262–70.

51. *El Pueblo*, 26 Feb. 1920; Osvaldo Bayer, *Los vengadores de la Patagonia trágica* (3 vols., Editorial Galerna, Buenos Aires, 1974), vol. 1: pp. 48–50; Niklison, "Acción social," p. 188; Auza, *Aciertos*, vol. II: pp. 144–5; Navarro, "Hidden," pp. 171–2.

52. Celina de Arenaza, *Sin memoria* (Buenos Aires, 1980), p. 24. Data on the Center comes from Arenaza, pp. 24–5; Celina de Arenaza, interviews, Buenos Aires, 4 and 15 July 1981; *La Nación*, 12 Apr. 1921; *El Pueblo*, 15–16 Dec. 1919; Ledesma de García Fernández, *Una época*, pp. 16, 25–6, 76.

53. Niklison, "Acción social," p. 271; Arenaza, interview, 15 July 1981; Ledesma de García Fernández, *Una época*, pp. 16, 18, 24, 39, 76.

54. Andrea, *La perturbación*, p. 111.

55. Andrea, quoted in Elisa Esposito, "La Federación de Asociaciones Católicas de Empleadas," *Boletín de la Acción Católica Argentina* (Apr. 1951), pp. 111–12. Also see Esposito, pp. 109–12; Archivo de *La Prensa*, File 46, 948; Arenaza, *Sin memoria*, p. 25; *La Prensa*, 5 July 1935 and 22 Nov. 1972; Andrea, *El catolicismo*, p. 23.

56. Andrea, *La perturbación*, p. 165.

57. On gender as a metaphor, see Joan W. Scott, "Gender: A Useful Category of Historical Analysis," *American Historical Review* 91:5 (Dec. 1986), pp. 1053–75.

58. On Peronist ideology, see, among other works, J. M. Taylor, *Eva Perón: The Myths of a Woman* (University of Chicago, Chicago, 1979); Nicholas Fraser and Marysa Navarro, *Eva Perón* (Norton, New York, 1980); Bergquist, *Labor in Latin America*, pp. 149–82; Carlos H. Waisman, *Reversal of Development in Argentina: Postwar Counterrevolutionary Policies and Their Structural Consequences* (Princeton University, Princeton, 1987), pp. 164–206; Paul H. Lewis, "Was Perón a Fascist? An Inquiry into the Nature of Fascism," *The Journal of Politics*, 42 (1980), pp. 242–56.

59. John J. Kennedy, *Catholicism, Nationalism, and Democracy in Argentina* (University of Notre Dame, Notre Dame, 1958), pp. 205–6; Arenaza, *Sin memoria*, pp. 32–3; Ledesma de García Fernández, *Una época*, p. 79; Delfina Bunge de Gálvez, "Una emoción nueva en Buenos Aires," *El Pueblo*, 25 Oct. 1945. I thank Fortunato Mallimaci for giving me a copy of the latter. On Peronist relations

with the church and the right, see, among other works, Cristián Buchrucker, *Nacionalismo y peronismo: La Argentina en la crisis ideológica mundial (1927– 1955)* (Sudamericana, Buenos Aires, 1987), pp. 279–399; Floreal Forni, "Catolicismo y peronismo (l)," *Unidos* 4:14 (Apr. 1987), pp. 211–26; Maria J. Lubertino Beltrán, *Perón y la iglesia (1943–1955)*, (2 vols., Centro Editor de América Latina, Buenos Aires, 1987); Noreen Frances Stack, "Avoiding the Greater Evil: The Response of the Argentine Catholic Church to Juan Perón, 1943– 55" (Ph.D. diss., Rutgers Univ., 1976).

## 12  Josephine Hoeppner Woods ◆ The "Chola"

*As North American companies began investing in Latin America, increasing numbers of women accompanied their husbands to the field. Some, like Josephine Hoeppner Woods, made the most of the experience and studied the host culture closely, learning as much as possible. As the wife of a mining engineer, Woods called more than a dozen mining camps home in the Peruvian and Bolivian mountains in the 1930s. She recorded her impressions and observations in detailed letters to friends and family and later reworked them into the highly readable* High Spots in the Andes *(1935). Woods clearly enjoyed her Latin American visits, and her memoirs demonstrate that an observant amateur can come to informed conclusions about foreign cultures.*

### The "Chola"

The "Chola" is a woman with some foreign blood, be it ever so little; although 90 percent Indian, she is no longer Indian but a Chola. Here in the plaza, which was also the marketplace, the Chola sits on the ground, usually a sheepskin under her, and her many, many voluminous skirts become useful as well as picturesque; whatever she has to sell is spread out in front of her; generally a certain Chola sells only eggs, another onions and still another only slices of pumpkin. . . .

In one corner of the plaza was the *recova*, a large warehouse-like structure where the Indians brought their vegetables, fruits, eggs and whatnot, often from very long distances, on llamas and not infrequently on their backs. Whenever I saw a train of llamas or burros wending its way down the steep mountainside, I grabbed my camera and hurried to the plaza: the unloading of the llamas or burros, the brisk selling at the *recova*, the scurrying back and forth of the high-hatted, billowing-skirted Cholas, carrying their wares in the *llijillas* [shawls] on their backs and followed by a seemingly endless rabble of *niños* (children), heterogeneously garbed, mostly ragged and dirty, but as picturesque as their mothers. . . .

I could even estimate, fairly accurately, the wealth of the Chola from the amount of jewelry she wore (and the Chola wears no spurious jew-

From *High Spots in the Andes: Peruvian Letters of a Mining Engineer's Wife* (New York: G. P. Putnam's Sons, 1935), 44–48, 51–53, 70–71, 93, 100, 131–32.

elry), calculated with her number of *polleras* (skirts). I presume no Chola wears less than three *polleras* and I was told . . . that one Chola counted fourteen of them on herself. . . . The *pollera* is made of a thick, fuzzy, woolen material, called *castilla* . . . pleated in wide pleats on a yoke, as many pleats as is possible, thus making the skirt very full; the length is about halfway from ankle to knee and "they say" the skirts are never taken off—the newest one is put on top and eventually the oldest one drops off. . . .

The Chola, nor the Indian woman, knows not bloomers nor "panties." The "high-class" Chola costume is beautiful and very expensive: besides the many voluminous skirts (the *castilla* costs a dollar a yard up to as much as three, and each skirt requires at least eight yards; the "ultra first class" Chola disdains even *castilla* and has heavy silk or velvet, which means many more yards) she has a basque, costing from ten to twenty-five dollars, a pair of very high-topped boots with excessively high heels, a stiff, painted white Panama hat and a most gorgeous, beautifully embroidered, heavy silk shawl. If she should change her garb as often as we do, it would take a millionaire to keep her in skirts alone.

The babies—and there are so many of them—have their legs tightly swathed together and are thus bandaged up to their armpits . . . [and] are invariably carried in a shawl, called a *llijilla*, on the mother's back; these mothers seem to love their babies very much until they are able to toddle and then, with a younger one to look after, the older ones apparently look out for themselves. Most of the little girls are dressed in exact replica of their mothers, enormously full skirts, tight basque, and all! The little boys are more nondescript, ofttimes literally a bundle of rags.

All the women and girls wear their straight black hair in two braids down the back. . . . It is an unusual sight to see a Chola well combed—they have queer, little, homemade wooden combs, and, believe this or not, but I saw two Cholas combing each other's heads and with evident relish picking the lice off these wooden combs and *eating* them! It is a common sight to see a mother delousing her offspring by hand, and I have been repeatedly told that the "hand picked" lice are always eaten by the mother or, if the child is "real good," it may get them! . . .

Miss Danskin showed me a small hill where the Chola goes to pray to the Virgin, that she may be given a child, for the Cholas believe a childless woman cannot enter heaven. . . .

If an expectant mother dreams of snakes, she will have a son; of frogs, a daughter; of a condor, her [son] will be a great man.

Another superstition: When a girl is born, the midwife procures needle and thread and goes through the motions of sewing up the child's mouth—to prevent her from talking too much when she grows up. . . .

[At the Cliza market] we became the unwilling and astonished on-lookers at a birthday party; we saw an Indian woman, presumably the midwife, pick up the newly born infant, take it to the irrigation ditch, a few feet away, dip her hand in the water and give the baby its first bath. I am sure to all three of us, involuntarily, came the image of an up-to-date maternity hospital in its spotlessness. . . . In contrast, here on the road-side, but a few feet away from the smelly stock corrals, an Indian woman *dar á luz* (gave light, give birth) to a mite of humanity with neither mother nor nurse in white, and the mother, perhaps, carried her few hours'-old baby that same day to her home. . . .

## Life in the Mining Camps

### The Cancha

About three quarters of the way up, there was a *cancha* [pit] where the ore is sorted by women, the waste ore being dumped over the mountain-side. The women work in this open *cancha* in all kinds of weather, push-ing wheelbarrels loaded with heavy ore, or sorting ore ready to be put in the wheelbarrels, bundled up to their ears, yet barefooted. . . .

### Comadre's Day

Carnaval, corresponding to our Mardi Gras . . . is followed by Comadre's (Godmother's) Day, which, to the Gringos at least, is the most colorful and most exciting of all the holidays. I told you about the one hundred and fifty to two hundred women who sorted ore, but I did not add that they were considered better workers than the men but received smaller pay; that almost every one had a baby each year with usually a different father for each baby; the Company maintained a nursery at the *cancha* where these women worked; a nurse with other helpers looked after the babies while the mothers sorted ore. The father takes no responsibility whatsoever for the support or care of the child; the boy babies become miners, the girls, ore sorters, and thus the cycle of workers is perpetuated.

These "*cancha* women," as they are called, begin months ahead to plan for this day: they elect a chairman, appoint committees, send for artificial flowers, serpentine, confetti, plenty of liquid refreshments in-cluding beer, whisky, crème de menthe, *chicha* [corn beer], and *leche de tigre* (tiger's milk), appropriately named for it is alcohol and hot milk. . . . The Company furnishes the printed programs and the prizes for the lottery; the prizes consist of basques, hats, *polleras* . . . and handsome shawls or *mantas*, the most coveted prize of all. The prizes are numbered and duplicate numbers put in a box while the names of the women were put in another box; a "Gringita," usually an American child, draws the numbers. . . . Whenever a *pollera* or *manta* is drawn, there is much applause and a round of drinks.

A committee of three women came to our home about ten in the morning of Comadre's Day to escort Clarence and me to the elaborately decorated *cancha*. . . . We, with the Manager and his wife, other Heads of Departments and their wives, were given "grandstand" seats to witness the big drawings. . . . After the drawing . . . Clarence was appropriated by one of the women "bosses," the doctor gallantly offered me his arm and thus pairing off, we revelers, accompanied by three or four bands and followed by the whole camp, marched and countermarched through the streets, stopping often for the paraders to dance the *cueca*, a charming native dance in which the waving of handkerchiefs, much bowing and pirouetting play a prominent part. After what to us seemed hours and hours of parading and intermittent dancing, the *cancha* women and their guests . . . climbed the Administration steps to the dining room, the overflow in the immensely long hall and on the steps, where all were served with a *copa de champaña*, and it was during the "champagne-respite" that we Gringos made our escape to our homes for a much-needed rest. But not so with the natives; they "whooped 'er up" until five. At seven, the same committee came for us again and, "willy-nilly," we had to go with them to the schoolhouse, where dancing continued all night. The Gringas were very popular with the *cancha* women, who danced with us even more than with our husbands, mostly the *cueca* . . . it was really lots of fun. . . .

I think I can truthfully say that this Comadre's Day was one of the most strenuous merrymaking days of my whole life. The next morning the camp . . . was completely "dead to the world"; the plaza was deserted and not a soul was stirring. But by noon little cliques began to gather and at two the parades with banners and much music again started, but luckily we were expected to be only spectators from now on; as participants our little part had been played. . . .

*The Strike*

Finally, on January the 13th, matters came to a crisis; there had been many, many rumors of *huelgas* (strikes), so many that we had ceased to pay any attention to them, but this morning the Mill Superintendent told Clarence that the strike would take place at two that afternoon. . . .

Shortly before the clock struck two, men could be seen coming from the mill, the *maestranza* (shops), from everywhere, converging to the plaza, and at two, in a more or less orderly procession, the thousand men (not counted) started for the Administration. At the first indication of trouble, the women of the neighborhood gathered at my home, because from our porch there was an unobstructed view of the Administration Building and then, too, we all felt there was safety in numbers. We watched the men climb the outside steps, saw them go inside, could see them part way going up the inside steps, saw a large part of the crowd deploy on the veranda and then we heard a shot and a few seconds later another, followed by two blasts of dynamite, . . . and each and everyone one of us "went to pieces.". . . .

At this juncture, "Jorge," the French secretary, appeared, assuring us, even shaking his wife to convince us, that our respective husbands were all safe and unhurt and fortunately Clarence did come in a minute or two and was followed by the other husbands almost immediately; then, somewhat calmed but still excited, we women with our men watched the frenzied mob drag the half-fainted, torn and bleeding Manager down the steps, through the plaza, and toward the railroad tracks. The women and children, mingling in the crowd, were worse than the men: they threw missiles of anything they could lay hands on, they spat at him, they called him vile names in Quechua. . . . Then he was lost to our view but we learned that he was half-carried, half-dragged a kilometer or more down the railroad track. . . .

During all this excitement and hubbub, the *intendente* (sheriff) and his handful of soldiers were conspicuous by their absence, and only when the train was made up and ready to depart did they appear from behind a hill and they escorted the Manager's wife to the train; she was a good sport, held her head high, disdaining the mob. . . .

After the train had departed and the crowd was straggling back from its degrading pursuit . . . we were all breathing a little easier, when that whole multitude came marching right up to our house! I didn't know but what they intended to take my husband forcibly, too. And they did, but with what a difference! The spirit of the mob had completely changed; now instead of sullen, "hell-bent" faces, there were broad grins; the men, and women, too, threw their hats up in the air and shouted in unison, "Queremos al Señor Woods, queremos al Señor Woods!" ("We want Mr. Woods, we want Mr. Woods!") . . . After much speech-making, the waving of the two flags [American and Bolivian], and patriotic music, the self-appointed "master of ceremonies" in "behalf of his fellow countrymen" declared Clarence *Gerente* (Manager).

## 13  Francesca Miller ◆ The Suffrage Movement in Latin America

*Based on extensive archival research and an exhaustive examination of
the secondary material concerning the evolution of the women's movement in modern Latin American history, Francesca Miller's* Latin American Women and the Search for Social Justice *(1991) is the best work written
to date on the subject. Drawing upon the now-considerable monographic
literature as well as on her own archival work on the international dimensions of women's politics, she has woven together a remarkable story
of female political activity from the late nineteenth century to the present.
In the following excerpt she explains why suffrage was not as important
to the women's movement in Latin America as it was in either the United
States or Great Britain.*

Woman suffrage had not been a central concern of Latin American
feminists for a variety of reasons. First, most Latin American women
lived in countries where there was no history of effective male suffrage
and no legacy of reform achieved at the ballot box. Social and economic
concerns dominated the discussions of the various women's congresses;
the issue of women's right to vote was generally introduced to the agenda
as part of the Socialist women's platform, which called for universal suffrage for both sexes.

Second, Latin American feminists by no means agreed on the value
of the vote to their cause. Some, like Julieta Lanteri-Renshaw—who,
though unable to vote, ran for Congress in Argentina in 1919—equated
the denial of the vote to the denial of full adulthood to women. Many, like
Bertha Lutz, promoted the right to vote as a means to enable passage of
reformist legislation. Others, like many of the teachers who attended the
Mexican feminist congresses, viewed woman suffrage with suspicion,
believing that women should abstain from such a corrupt, masculine realm.
And still others saw the woman's vote as potentially dangerous to the
causes of feminism and reform, believing that the female vote would be
essentially conservative, supportive of the status quo, and under the influence of the clergy.

By 1922, with the example of the North American women's success
and in the wake of the war to "make the world safe for democracy," the

From "Feminism and Social Motherhood" in *Latin American Women and
the Search for Social Justice* (Hanover, NH: University Press of New England,
1991), 86–102, 259–60. ©1991 by University Press of New England. Reprinted
by permission of University Press of New England.

movement to promote woman suffrage throughout the hemisphere was acclaimed by the delegates to the Baltimore conference. One immediate result was the organization of women's societies in a number of Latin American nations that were linked together through the newly formed Pan American Association for the Advancement of Women, which included suffrage as a goal. It is significant that the association was founded at the instigation of the Latin American delegates to Baltimore; it was proposed by Celia Paladino de Vitale of Uruguay and strongly supported by Flora de Oliveria Lima of Brazil and Amanda Labarca of Chile, both veterans of the Latin American and Pan American Scientific Congresses. Elena Torres, a well-known Mexican activist who had sided with the radical Hermila Galindo at the feminist congresses held in Yucatán, was elected the Pan American Association's vice president for North America.

The breadth of the women's concerns was undiminished by the decision to work for woman suffrage, and the final document of the Baltimore convention directly reflected the issues to which Latin American feminists had given priority over the years as well as the influence of the international peace movement and woman's movement. It called for international peace through arbitration, abolition of the white-slave trade, access to public education at all levels, and the right of married women to control their own property and earnings and to secure equal child guardianship; it encouraged organization, discussion, and public speaking among women and freedom of opportunity for women to cultivate and use their talents; it pressed for political rights and promoted friendliness and understanding among all Pan American countries, with the aim of maintaining perpetual peace in the hemisphere.

The immediate goal was to organize national umbrella groups of women's organizations in each country to work toward the goals agreed on in Baltimore. North American suffragist Carrie Chapman Catt was elected president, and she undertook a South American tour to lend her organizational skills and prestige to the establishment of the associations.[1] Bertha Lutz was elected vice president of the Pan American Association for South America and upon her return to Brazil used the network of the League for Female Intellectual Emancipation to establish a new organization, the Brazilian Federation for the Advancement of Women (Federação Brasileira pelo Progresso Feminino [FBPF]), which, unlike the league, was national in scope, with representatives from all twenty Brazilian states, women's professional organizations, and social action and charity groups. The goals of the FBPF paralleled those outlined at the Baltimore conference.

In December 1922 the FBPF attained national prominence by staging a five-day international convention. The timing of the event was propitious; in 1922, Brazil was celebrating the centennial of its independence from Portugal, and a powerful nativist intellectual movement was in bloom. Educated Brazilians wanted to be seen as progressive, as leaders of artistic, intellectual, and political movements, rather than as imitators of the Old World. Lutz and her fellow workers were able to invoke national pride in the inauguration of the FBPF. The international convention was attended by numerous congressmen and government officials as well as by female delegates from all over Brazil. Carrie Chapman Catt inaugurated her tour of South America at the convention. The international women's movement also was represented by Ana de Castro Osorio from Portugal and Rosa Manus from Holland. Edward Morgan, U.S. ambassador to Brazil, gave a luncheon honoring Bertha Lutz that brought together the leaders of the Brazilian feminist movements and the vice president of Brazil, the minister of foreign relations, the director of public education, and various congressmen. Although few if any of the Brazilian officials or Ambassador Morgan could be described as entirely sympathetic to the women's movement, the FBPF began operations in an aura of respectability unmatched in feminist annals.[2]

Despite the clearly upper-class origins of the leadership of the FBPF, the membership encompassed women from many walks of life. At the December meeting, representatives of the Teachers' League, the Rio de Janeiro Union of Employees in Commerce, and the Bureau of Employees of the Young Women's Christian Association spoke on the problems faced by working women, citing poor transportation, excessive hours, low pay, sexual harassment, unhealthy workplaces, and lack of legal protection. The FBPF endorsed the recommendations made by the International Labor Organization in 1919, which called for legal regulation and protection of female employment, and passed the following resolution: "Considering the urgency of insuring legal protection for female labor, which has been subject to inhuman exploitation, reducing women to an inferior position in the competition for industrial and agricultural salaries, as well as in other activities of modern life, it has become necessary to call to the attention of political leaders the need to incorporate protective measures for women into our social legislation."[3]

The FBPF established commissions to address various aspects of women's estate; problems faced by women in the workplace were given high priority, as was the issue of female education. The Brazilian Female Suffrage Alliance (Aliança Brasileira pelo Sufragio Feminino) was established; its officers were the wives of leading political figures. Within the year, woman suffrage associations had been founded in São Paulo, Bahia, and Pernambuco. The focus of the FBPF was women's rights, and the issues of suffrage, equal education, and legal reform dominated the platform; more controversial social issues, such as divorce and sexual equality, were avoided. Although members of the FBPF professed to speak on behalf of all working women, they in fact addressed the problems of the new professional women—teachers, government employees, clerks.[4] The vast majority of Brazilian women were untouched by and unaware of the activities of these upper- and middle-class political activists.

The impact of the Pan American Association for the Advancement of Women was visible in other areas of the hemisphere as well, as was the move to form nationwide "umbrella" organizations. In Cuba, meetings of the National Women's Congress were held in Havana in 1923 and 1925.[5] Like the Brazilian women, the Cubans disavowed the militant political tactics of British and North American suffragists. In the 1920s general political violence was rife in Cuba, and the women's strategy was to link their role as the national keepers of morality with the claim that the female vote would put an end to public violence and stabilize an unsteady democratic system.

A number of Cuban women had been present at the founding of the Pan American Association for the Advancement of Women in Baltimore in 1922, and it was not a coincidence that woman suffrage became a central issue of the National Women's Congress held in 1923, at which thirty-one women's organizations were represented.[6] María Luisa Dolz and Domitila García de Coronado gave the keynote address, "The Social Mission of Women," which emphasized the value of woman's separate political ideals. The two women had been active in Cuban politics since the 1880s; they not only represented an earlier generation of Cuban feminists but [also], because of their ardent support of the Cuban cause during the wars of independence, symbolized the patriotism of Cuban women.

Fourteen resolutions were agreed on at the First National Women's Congress in Havana in 1923:

1.  That all women wage a campaign for suffrage for all women. (The repeated insistence on "all women" was meant to emphasize that the conferees would not restrict the vote on grounds of property ownership, marital status, class background, or race, the latter being a particularly divisive issue in the Cuban context.)
2.  To work for general educational reform, including special schools, and give attention to homogeneous grouping within grades.
3.  To work for reform of civil and penal law with the intent of equalizing the rights and responsibilities of men and women.
4.  To work for the passage of protective legislation for children and to ensure its enforcement.

5. To pay special attention to reformatories and to establish juvenile courts.
6. To intensify the love of plants and animals.
7. To work for the beautification of the city.
8. To create popular state schools as a means of intensifying nationalism.
9. To intensify the fight against drugs, prostitution, and the white-slave trade.
10. To participate in the high echelons of organization and inspection of the educational system.
11. To influence penitentiary reform.
12. To consider the rights of illegitimate children.
13. To revise legislation on adultery.
14. To work intensely and efficiently, with all of the legal tools available and without compromise, to obtain suffrage.

The content of the resolutions raises a number of points about the national Cuban women's alliance. First, in ranging from suffrage to urban beautification to adultery legislation, the resolutions illustrate the diverse backgrounds of the conference participants and reflect the priorities of both progressive and conservative political constituencies within the country. Cuban women, no less than Cuban men, had participated in the fight for independence from Spain, won in 1901; and in the 1920s the women joined the struggle to establish democracy, with universal suffrage and justice for all. The national political crisis aroused common feelings of patriotism and national pride that temporarily obscured social and political differences among the women. Second, it should be noted that the Cuban women were asking for reforms within the educational system, not just for access to higher education, as the Brazilian women had done: the principle of equal education for both sexes from the primary level through the university was embodied in the Cuban constitution of 1901.

At the Second National Women's Congress in 1925, the resolutions were fewer, but women were unyieldingly firm in the call for social as well as political reform:

1. Social equality between men and women.
2. Protection for the child.
3. Equal pay for equal work.
4. Equality of the claims of illegitimate children.
5. Elimination of prostitution.
6. Prohibition of the unequal treatment of women.

In her study of the Cuban women's movement, K. Lynn Stoner states that "no literate Cuban could have been unaware of the women's campaigns,"[7] and that by the mid-1920s woman suffrage was a popular political issue in the country. In this respect more than any other, the situation in Cuba presents a contrast to that in Brazil or Mexico or Argentina, where strong women's movements were also gaining momentum in the period but where enormous problems of communication existed. Although the particular historical circumstances and political configuration that existed in each nation provided the matrix from which the women's movements emerged, more obvious but often overlooked factors were also critical. In contrasting the Cuban situation with that of Brazil or Mexico or Argentina, the relative size of the country and of its national elite should be kept in mind. In 1925, Cuba, whose national territory encompasses 45,397 square miles, had a population of approximately 3.5 million people and one major city, Havana. In contrast, Brazil, the fifth largest nation on earth, with a territory of 3,286,344 square miles, had a population of more than 30 million; in the 1920s it was markedly regional, as was Argentina, with a population of some 11 million and an area of 1,072,745 square miles. Mexico, with 767,919 square miles, counted a population of 16.5 million people in the mid-1920s and had a number of major urban centers in addition to the federal capital district. The logistics of communication in these enormous nations, combined with problems of illiteracy and regionalism, obviated the possibility of national awareness of any issue.

The situation in Mexico provides contrasts to the Cuban and Brazilian experiences. Whereas both Cuban and Brazilian feminists were able to attract the support of members of the national political elite, the revolutionary government in Mexico paid scant attention to the petitions of women working for women's rights. In 1920 the political situation in Mexico, although not as violent as in the preceding decades, remained volatile, marked by revolts and assassination. The struggle between church and state was bitter and bloody, and the leaders of the revolutionary government believed most women to be in sympathy with the church. Those Mexican women who had made some small gains toward political and civil reform, and in industrial employment in the period between 1890 and 1920, found themselves under siege. As men returned to the work force, women were pushed out of their jobs; workers' unions, far from protecting women, proved to be bastions of male supremacy. Virulent antifeminist cartoons appeared regularly in the national press; a typical example published in *Excelsior* in 1925 depicted a Gertrude Stein-like figure seated in what obviously had been Papa's easy chair, smoking a cigar and reading a feminist newspaper while her ragged, weeping children pulled at her skirts, begging for food and attention, and her husband, evidently unmanned at the transformation "feminism" had made in his wife, cowered in the kitchen.

The most vociferous opponents of feminism were members of the Confederation of Catholic Associations of Mexico, founded in 1920 to combine Catholic youth, worker, journalist, and woman's groups. The Union of Catholic Women of Mexico "asserted that women's place was in the home, and equated socialism with free love and feminism."[8] The government, determined to wrest away the power and wealth of the church, began to enforce the articles of the constitution of 1917, which divested the church of its schools, property rights, and jurisdiction over ceremonies such as marriage. In 1926 the Cristero Rebellion against the government broke out in full force; women were deeply involved on both sides of the conflict.[9] Ironically, by the early 1930s, when the rebellion had been quelled, the women who had supported the government's struggle against the church still were unable to realize their political program. Most government leaders continued to view all women as potentially conservative and thus dangerous to their cause. Such distinctions did not seem so difficult to make among men, who had also fought on both sides of the conflict.

Despite the hostility toward feminism and the indifference of the government to women's issues, women played a central role in the campaigns to consolidate the revolution. Women teachers and health-care workers were recruited in great numbers in the government's massive campaign against illiteracy and poverty, particularly in the rural areas of Mexico. Prior to the Revolution of 1910, education and social welfare were primarily under the aegis of the Catholic church. . . . The literacy and health-care campaigns of the 1920s were secular in content and thus presented a direct challenge to church authority. Elena Torres, teacher, feminist, and admirer of Leon Trotsky, was named chief of the Bureau of Cultural Missions. The female educators who filled the ranks of mission instructors were poorly paid, often receiving as little as one or two pesos per day,[10] but they were inspired by the vision of building a truly revolutionary society, where ignorance and poverty were vanquished. Female health-care workers and educators were equally vital to the efforts of the government to improve sanitary conditions and disseminate information. "Sanitary brigades" went into the countryside, and prenatal clinics were established in urban centers. Smallpox vaccinations, lectures on child and maternal health care, and information on tropical and venereal diseases were offered. In 1925 one clinic in Mexico City distributed thousands of copies of Margaret Sanger's pamphlet on family limitation.

The involvement of Mexican feminists in the international arena had a direct effect on the establishment and direction of both the educational and health-care programs in Mexico. In 1918, Elisa Acuña y Rossetti, a schoolteacher and journalist who, with Juana B. Gutierrez de Mendoza, edited the feminist journal *Vesper*, joined Elena Torres and Luz Vera to found the National Council of Mexican Women (Consejo Nacional de Mujeres) in Mexico City. Luz Vera, a teacher and writer, served as secretary and, together with Torres, represented the council in 1922 in Baltimore. In May 1923 the Mexican branch of the Pan American Association for the Advancement of Women held its first national convention in Mexico City with one hundred women in attendance.[11] The women addressed the need for education and woman suffrage and presented research papers showing that Mexican women had lost ground, particularly in employment, since the revolution.[12] Women speakers pointed out that prostitution and alcoholism were on the rise, with especially pernicious effects for poor women and children.

The question of divorce was an issue of profound disagreement among Mexican feminists. The more radical women, like Socialist schoolteacher Inés Malvaez, believed that [President Venustiano] Carranza's Law of Domestic Relations, passed in 1917, should be amended to permit divorce at the will of only one spouse in a marriage. Sofia Villa de Buentello, who was a lawyer and an advocate of equal civil rights for men and women, "feared that lenient divorce laws, in the context of Mexican society, would benefit men and leave women with even less legal protection."[13] Many other women believed that divorce was immoral and should not be discussed. To faithful Catholic women and men, divorce threatened home, family, and church.

The meeting of the Mexican branch of the Pan American Association was but one of numerous women's conferences convened in the 1920s.[14] Mexican feminists had strong ties to the international socialist movement and international feminist associations, as well as a heritage of grassroots women's organizations, including teachers' and workers' associations and workers' unions. The proliferation of conferences and congresses in the 1920s in Mexico showed a breadth of concerns and opinion, as well as demonstrating that an impressive number of women were involved in organizing to discuss and gain support for their programs. Although there are clear ties between the founding of some of the Mexican national associations and the international women's movements—the International Congress of Women in 1918, the Pan American Association in 1923, and the Socialist Congress in 1925—Mexican women always exhibited a strong sense of the native origins of their movement, and even political moderates were careful to distance themselves from the North American feminist movement.

Between December 1924 and July 1925, Sofia Villa de Buentello organized a Congreso de Mujeres de la Raza. Sponsored by the Liga de Mujeres Ibericas e Hispanoamericanas and the Unión Cooperativa, the meeting opened in Mexico City on July 5, with more than two hundred representatives from Mexico, Latin America, and Spain in attendance. The ideologic splits that were to characterize the women's movement in the hemisphere in the following decades were manifest at the *congreso.* Irreconcilable divisions emerged between the Socialist left, led by Elvia Carrillo Puerto and Cuca García, which insisted on the economic basis of women's problems, and conservatives and moderates, led by Sofia Villa, who believed female inequality to be rooted in social and moral conditions. Question of class loyalties and the continuing struggle between the church and the Mexican state further exacerbated the proceedings.

By July 10, Sofia Villa had increasing difficulty in maintaining any semblance of order, and many delegates left. Villa cried out, "This is an international congress, not a socialist or worker Congress; the foreign delegates have abandoned us and now there is no Congress." Elvia responded, "If it is to be said that this Congress, to be international, is for people of class, why have you invited us, the workers? The heart, the very fiber of the country, protests against the parasites that suck the life-blood from it."[15] Even more outrageous to many of the Mexican delegates was the attack of the women of the left on the revolution itself. The radicals denounced the presence of "reactionaries" in government, particularly in the Department of Education. To the assembled women, many if not most of whom were teachers and a number of whom were leaders in the education programs, this proposal struck at their lifework as well as their political beliefs.

Ultimately, fewer than half of the original delegates remained, representing an uneasy collection of women of the left and right wings: the foreign delegates and the moderates who were the original organizers of the congress had departed by July 15. The problems of the congress were seized on by a press already inclined to be hostile to women's political activities. The Mexico City daily, *El Universal,* ran an editorial titled "A Defeat of Feminism," which stated that "if this were an example of women's participation in public life, it was a fraud . . . a scandalous caricature of the National Congress . . . run by women trying to behave like men."[16]

Prior to this time, in Mexico as elsewhere, there existed a generally accepted assumption among politically active women that their common interests as women—in gaining the vote, in health care, in education —cut across class backgrounds and ideological orientations. This assumption of a cross-class, supra-ideological "women's cause" (an assumption that would reemerge in the sisterhood movements of the 1960s and early 1970s) characterized the early *congresos* and the political platforms agreed on by feminists in Cuba, Mexico, Brazil, and Argentina, even though the political allegiances of the conferees were often disparate. The breakdown of this coalition based on gender, illustrated at the 1925 *congreso* in Mexico City, was apparent throughout the hemisphere in the 1930s.

In the 1920s women in Mexico, Brazil, Argentina, and Cuba continued their organizational efforts at the local and national level, but they also took the opportunity to carry their platform to the inter-American meetings, which had not convened since 1910. Both North and South American feminists hoped that if they could win support for their cause at the diplomatic table they could bring pressure on their national governments to consider reform at home.

The first evidence of the direct impact of the women's efforts on the International Conferences of American States came at the Santiago meeting in 1923. Chile, with its sizable community of activist women, provided a favorable setting for introducing the women's issues. Moreover, the Chilean meeting was in many respects a departure from pre-World War I conferences. The old emphasis on commercial exchange had given way to heated political discussions that challenged the growing dominance of the United States in hemispheric affairs. The early Pan American meetings, convened between 1881 and 1910, had been primarily devoted to establishing conventions that would enhance inter-American commercial opportunities. They exhibited little of the fiery idealism expressed by Simón Bolívar, who had dreamed that "the assembling of a Congress of American nations will form a new epoch in human affairs."

The invocation of the ideals of Pan Americanism by the feminists added a new dimension to the inter-American conferences. The International Conference of American States held in Santiago in 1923, the first since the onset of World War I, took place in an atmosphere of controversy. The desire of the women to insert feminist issues and matters of broad social reform into the program coincided with the widespread desire of many in both North and South America, male and female, to use the conferences to challenge U.S. imperialist activities in Central America and the Caribbean.

A sizable number of "unofficial" female delegates attended the Santiago meeting. At their instigation, Maximo Soto Hall, a member of the Argentine delegation, introduced a motion pertaining to the rights of women in the hemisphere. It included the recommendation that the member states appoint women to their official delegations and suggested that the individual nations undertake a study of their laws with the intent of abolishing the inequality of the sexes. The motion passed but was advisory rather than binding.

The next International Conference of American States met in Havana in 1928; there were no official women delegates. But women from throughout the hemisphere foregathered in Havana for the inter-American conference. Their organizational efforts were evident in the diverse constituencies they represented: They spoke for the Consejo Feminista Mexicana, the WILPF [Women's International League for Peace and Freedom], the National Woman's Party of the United States, the Club de Madres of Buenos Aires, and many others. They were hosted by the Alianza Femenina Cubana and the Club Femenino de Cuba.

By the end of the conference the women had secured an audience before a plenary session, presented an Equal Rights Treaty for the consideration of the governments of the hemisphere,[17] and successfully lobbied for the creation of an officially designated body, the Inter-American Commission of Women (IACW), which was charged with the investigation of the legal status of women in the twenty-one member states. The IACW was "the first government organization in the world to be founded for the express purpose of working for the rights of women."[18]

The choice of the Pan American meetings as a forum for the discussion of women's and feminist issues proved politically astute. Whereas many of the women found little support from their national governments for their programs in the 1920s, their success at the inter-American meetings gave them political leverage back home. The Latin American women provided the precedent of using inter-American congresses as a forum for the debate of feminist issues with the scientific congresses at the turn of the century; their leadership is also evident in the insistent inclusion of issues of social justice in the Pan American women's platforms. Moreover, although the hope of effecting reform at the transnational level was a characteristic of the period, the transnational arena held particular appeal for Latin American feminists, who had historically identified with the forces of change in their own societies.[19] The inter-American conferences provided the opportunity for a different strategy, demonstrated by the presentation of the Equal Rights Treaty to the assembled diplomats in Cuba in 1928. Had the treaty been agreed on, it would have been introduced to the national governments of each member state for ratification; the political opponents of equal rights could no longer prevent the issue from being considered.

The first task undertaken by the IACW was the investigation of the legal status of women in all countries of the hemisphere. Their work drew attention to the legal inequities suffered by women, and as the symbolic representative of numerous women's organizations in the Americas, the IACW was able to lend support to women's efforts within their national communities by providing information and acting as a communications center—the support was never financial. A rare instance of direct action occurred in Havana in 1928, when the women attending the Sixth International Conference of American States took the opportunity to parade in support of the Cuban woman suffrage movement.[20]

It was in this period that full suffrage was first granted to women in a number of Latin American nations. Three time periods are discernible: the earliest, 1929–1934, during which the governments of Ecuador, Brazil, Uruguay, and Cuba granted woman suffrage; the middle, 1939–1945, when El Salvador, the Dominican Republic, Guatemala, Panama, and Costa Rica did likewise; and the postwar period, 1947–1961, when the remaining nations conformed. The following chart gives the dates when woman suffrage was enacted in each state:

| *Pre-World War II* | | *World War II* | | *Post-World War II* | |
|---|---|---|---|---|---|
| Ecuador | 1929 | El Salvador | 1939 | Venezuela | 1947 |
| Brazil | 1932 | Dominican | | Argentina | 1947 |
| Uruguay | 1932 | Republic | 1942 | Chile | 1949 |
| Cuba | 1934 | Panama | 1945 | Haiti | 1950 |
| | | Guatemala | 1945 | Bolivia | 1952 |
| | | Costa Rica | 1945 | Mexico | 1953 |
| | | | | Honduras | 1955 |
| | | | | Nicaragua | 1955 |
| | | | | Peru | 1955 |
| | | | | Colombia | 1957 |
| | | | | Paraguay | 1961 |

The enactment of female suffrage should not be interpreted as a signpost that the women's program had triumphed in a particular time and space. The meaning of the vote and the reasons woman suffrage was enacted in a particular nation at a particular time vary greatly. Moreover, irregular transitions in power and the suspension of civil liberties, including elections, characterized the political scene in many Latin American nations during the 1930s. Effective universal suffrage, male and female, did not exist anywhere until after World War II.

Examining the ways in which women gained suffrage underscores the political diversity of the hemisphere. In the earliest period there was no consistent pattern of achievement of the franchise; woman suffrage was enacted by reform administrations, by one-party systems that sought to further consolidate their power through incorporating the female vote, and by conservative governments. In each country, women had to work within the national political context to gain their ends. But if the means to the end was not consistent, the program was: in Latin America, woman suffrage was almost universally portrayed by its advocates as the means to a more moral society, with a platform that emphasized social motherhood issues and peace more than gender equity.[21]

The fact that woman suffrage had been passed in the United States in 1920 provided impetus to the woman suffrage movement in Latin America; it also demonstrated that the female vote was far from revolutionary in its impact. Female suffrage could be viewed as a step toward democracy, and a safe one, particularly if women were indebted to the incumbent government for their enfranchisement and if the vote was restricted to those who could fulfill certain literacy and property requirements.

In 1929, Ecuador became the first nation in Latin America to grant woman suffrage. The political coalition in power that promulgated the female vote was deeply conservative and sought to broaden its political base in the event of a renewed threat from the group of young Socialist officers who had staged a successful military coup in 1925. The Ecuadorean establishment saw women as congenitally conservative, loyal to the Catholic church, and politically malleable; certainly, few feminist voices had been raised in Quito or Guayaquil to challenge this view.

In contrast, in Brazil, Uruguay, and Cuba the enactment of woman suffrage was the result of years of hard work and carefully planned campaigns; the women were prepared to act when an advantageous political situation arose. In Brazil the revolution of October 1930 brought to power men who had promised to enact a reform agenda. The Federação Brasileira pelo Progresso Feminino, well organized and with a nationwide network, immediately took steps to ensure that their platform would be part of those reforms. Their first victory came in the electoral reform decree of February 24, 1932, which granted woman suffrage. Bertha Lutz, appointed to the government commission charged with drafting a new national constitution, and Carlota Pereira de Queiroz, elected to the Constituent Assembly from São Paulo, ably represented the women's program.

Working with other members of the FBPF, Lutz prepared the Thirteen Principles, which included woman suffrage and equality before the law; the right of married women to retain their nationality; equal pay for equal work; paid maternity leaves; the right of women, whether married, single, or widowed, to hold all public positions; and the appointment of qualified women to administer welfare programs that dealt with maternity, child care, female labor, and homemaking. The FBPF's Principles also reflected their long commitment to legislation that would protect female workers by incorporating the central tenets of the labor platform: minimum salary, the eight-hour day, paid vacations, and compensation for illness, injury, disability, and retirement.[22] The efforts of the Brazilian women were successful; the Thirteen Principles were incorporated into the constitution of 1934. One year later, María Luiza Bittencourt wrote to the IACW to report that she had been elected to the state legislature of Bahia, and that "eighteen of the twenty states in Brazil have elected women to their legislatures, and the new president of the State of Rio de Janeiro has appointed women to the portfolios of Labor and Education in his cabinet."[23] The political opening in Brazil proved short-lived; in 1937, President Getúlio Vargas proclaimed the *Estado Novo*, and neither Brazilian women nor Brazilian men participated in open elections again until 1946.

Uruguay was, in theory, the first of all Western Hemisphere nations to recognize female suffrage: the constitution of 1917 stated that women had the right to vote and hold office at local and national levels. However, the principle of woman suffrage required a two-thirds majority in each of the legislative houses to become law. By 1932 popular pressure for reform, including reform of the electoral process, was acute: a rapidly expanding population, which included thousands of European immigrants, a strong and articulate labor movement, and liberal politicians joined in demanding an opening up of the political process. The Uruguayan economy, which depended almost exclusively on the export of its range products for revenues, was reeling in the aftermath of the Great Depression. A decree of December 16, 1932, provided for women's participation in the elections scheduled for 1934; those elections were not held, but the new constitution of 1934 stated that "national citizens are all men and women born within the nation . . . and every citizen is as such a voter and qualified to hold office." The reluctance of the government to grant political rights to immigrant male workers, who were the most numerous—and potentially most disruptive—group of residents, is reflected in the stipulation that "foreign men and women, when married, and of good repute, have the right to vote, if they are employed in a profession or hold property and have resided in the Republic for fifteen years." In short, when the government in Uruguay could perceive the female vote not as an opening for feminists, many of whom had traditionally aligned themselves with the Socialist or Anarchist parties in Uruguay, but as the incorporation into the political process of native-born Uruguayan women who would buttress the class interests of the ruling elite, female suffrage became law.

In Cuba the configuration of events surrounding the passage of woman suffrage in 1934 presents both contrasts and parallels to the situations in Uruguay and Brazil. As was true in those countries, the Cuban woman's movement was well organized, with long roots, but Cuban women also laid claim to a history of direct political participation for their role in the Cuban independence movement. Historian K. Lynn Stoner writes:

> In 1934, Cuba became the fourth Latin American country to extend the franchise to women. Cuba's rapid passage of women's suffrage coincided with a crisis in the Cuban democratic system which President Gerardo Machado's government, stricken by economic decline during the Great Depression, guilty of repressive action against the population, and suspected of becoming a dictatorship, created. Suffragists gained influence during this period because of the turmoil and because of their importance as a legitimizing force. . . . Cuban suffragists could not play one established part off against another, as United States and British suffragists had done, nor could they treat the franchise as an issue separate from a national crisis. . . . The overthrow of Gerardo Machado was for Cuban women what World War I was for British and American women: the crisis that forced respect for female political and national action.[24]

Since the National Women's Congresses of 1923 and 1925, numerous women's associations in Cuba had worked for suffrage. The Alianza Nacional Feminista, the Partido Nacional Sufragista, and the Partido Democrata were joined by women attending the International Conference of American States in Havana in 1928 in a parade calling for the government to grant woman suffrage. In 1930, Cuban women and their supporters received further support from the members of the IACW, which held its first meeting in Havana in that year. In the increasingly violent political situation in the early 1930s, politically active Cuban women threw their support behind the opposition. Recognition of the potential legitimizing value of women's support was apparent in the attempts of successive administrations to establish woman suffrage between 1928 and 1934; the formal extension of the franchise to women was incorporated in the provisional constitution of February 3, 1934. In the first elections in which women participated, in 1936, six women were elected to the House of Representatives, and several others took office as mayors and members of municipal councils.

In other countries, partial suffrage was enacted. The Peruvian constitution of 1933 allowed women to vote in municipal elections but retained the definition of "citizen" to mean propertied males; in Chile, in 1934, a law opened local elections to women and "male and female foreigners who had resided in a district more than five years." In Argentina, which boasted one of the strongest women's movements in Latin America, a bill to grant the vote to women passed the Chamber of Deputies in 1932 but failed to pass the Senate and never became law. The Argentine province of San Juan passed a local female suffrage law, and, in 1934, Dr. Ema

Costa became the first Argentine woman elected to a provincial legislature. San Juan's proximity to Chile and its distance from the federal government in Buenos Aires were factors in this achievement.

In its 1936 survey of woman suffrage, the IACW reported that the constitutions of the Dominican Republic, Colombia, and Guatemala "definitely limit the suffrage to male nationals." The report noted that "in the Dominican Republic, however, Dominican women were allowed by a decree of November 22, 1933, to go to the polls at the 1934 election and indicate whether or not they wished the suffrage. Over ninety thousand women took advantage of this privilege and only nine voted no; but so far no action has been taken on this plebiscite."[25]

In Mexico, women continued their campaign for the extension of political rights to women. The Mexican constitution of 1917 granted voting rights to all citizens, which the constitution defined thus: "All Mexicans are citizens of the Republic who fulfill the following requisites: Are eighteen years old if married, twenty-one if not, and have an honorable means of livelihood." From the time of the *congresos femeninos* in the Yucatán to the meetings of the 1920s, Mexican women had tried to insist that this constitutional definition of citizen did not exclude them. Although their earlier efforts on behalf of woman suffrage and a feminist agenda had met with resistance from the federal government, the election of Lázaro Cárdenas as president in 1934 was greeted with enthusiasm by women activists. Cárdenas had spoken out on his commitment to fulfilling the promise of the Revolution through incorporating peasants, indigenous peoples, urban workers, and women into the national agenda. He stated: "A sound basis for social revolution will not be achieved until the constitution is reformed to grant equal rights."[26]

Soon after taking office, Cárdenas appointed Palma Guillen as minister of Mexico to Colombia, making her the first Mexican woman to hold a high diplomatic appointment. Apropos of this appointment, Margarita Robles de Mendoza, who was president of the Consejo de Mujeres and represented Mexican women on the IACW, challenged Cárdenas with the need to extend citizenship to all Mexican women. The question was referred to the Department of Government, which, in 1935, responded that there were no reasons to deny Mexican women citizenship in the republic. In his address to Congress later that year, Cárdenas said, "A necessary consequence of this plan to unify the working masses has been the recognition of the National Revolutionary Party that the working woman has the right to take part in the elections, since the constitution puts her on an equal footing with man."[27] A constitutional amendment giving women the vote was drafted, with strong support from

Cárdenas; in 1938 it was passed by the Senate and the House and referred to the states for ratification. Ratification was not forthcoming, and it was to be another fifteen years before Mexican women won full suffrage.

It is evident that there was no one road to woman suffrage in Latin America, and it is apparent that woman suffrage carried different meanings in each country. The class interests of those in power are clearly reflected in the ways in which female suffrage was defined or limited. Cárdenas wanted to bring working women into the electorate to broaden the constituency of the National Revolutionary party. The Uruguayan government wished to use the vote of native-born Hispanic women to increase its mandate and simultaneously to weaken any threat from foreign-born radicals. In Brazil, suffrage was won by a coalition of upper- and middle-class women who used their personal connections to the incumbent government to gain their ends; property and literacy requirements were such for both male and female voters that only 5 percent of the Brazilian populace was in effect enfranchised prior to 1946.[28]

It would seem that the women's movement in Latin America would have found a powerful ally in the labor movement. The first major political party to include universal suffrage for men and women in its platform was the Socialist party, and, as we have seen, many of the early women activists were members of the Socialist or Anarchist parties. By 1900 much of the labor platform had been incorporated into the agenda of Latin American feminists. The political crises in Brazil in 1932 and in Cuba and Uruguay in 1934, which gave women the opportunity to enact their program, were in fact partly created by the push by labor for the extension of political rights to broader sectors of the national populace. However, the attitude of the revolutionary party in Mexico, which espoused the principle of social justice and yet remained hostile to woman suffrage, is emblematic of the attitude of the Latin American political left toward the woman's movement.

The political left, like the political right, tended to view women as highly conservative, politically malleable, and subject to the influence of the church, despite eloquent evidence to the contrary. Peruvian poet Magda Portal was a founding member and the first secretary general of Peru's Alianza Popular Revolucionaria Americana (APRA). In 1924 a group of young Peruvians, including Portal, who were living in exile in Mexico, outlined the APRA program. Revolutionary in intent in the 1920s and 1930s, APRA sought to integrate the Indian into Peru's social and economic structure and to end the monopoly of political power by landowners, the clergy, and foreign corporations. APRA also had a significant international dimension, with supporters throughout Spanish America, especially among university students in Argentina, Bolivia, and Chile. Portal summarized the APRA program as "anti-imperialist, for the unity of the peoples of America, and for the realization of social justice." Though Madga Portal's attitude toward gender discrimination changed over time and through her own experience, in 1933 her alienation from *feministas* was explicit: "But the *aprista* woman, who professes our ideology, does not want to conquer her rights through an open fight against man, as *feministas* do, but to collaborate with him as her companion."[29]

Portal exemplified the attitude of the political left toward woman suffrage in her essay written in 1933, *El aprismo y la mujer*: "What class of women ought to have the right to vote? The cultural level of the Peruvian woman, her prejudices, her unquestioning dependence on masculine influence, and often, on clerical influence, makes the female vote a measure to better support conservative ideas than revolutionary ones. . . . Consequently, the woman *aprista*—the woman worker, the woman of conscience—believes that the female vote must be qualified."[30]

Portal's alienation from feminism (she labeled feminists *las damas patrioticas civilistas*) and her tutelary attitude toward working-class women who needed to be educated in the principles of *aprismo* in order to vote did little to endear her or her ideas to either working-class women or other intellectual women in Peru: Women need tutoring; men don't. Portal was not an original political thinker, and her assessment of the probable effect of woman suffrage was part of the received political wisdom in Latin America in the 1930s.

## Notes

1. Papers of Carrie Chapman Catt, The Arthur and Elizabeth Schlesinger Archives on the History of Women in America, Radcliffe College, Cambridge, Mass.; see also Mary Wilhelmine Williams, *People and Politics in Latin America*, rev. ed. (Boston: Ginn and Company, 1945), 791, 815.

2. Susan Kent Besse, "Freedom and Bondage: The Impact of Capitalism on Women in São Paulo, Brazil" (Ph.D. diss., Yale University, 1983), 246.

3. *Boletín da Federação Brasileira pelo Progresso Feminino,* I (November 1934), cited in Besse, "Freedom and Bondage," 231.

4. Besse, "Freedom and Bondage," 231.

5. K. Lynn Stoner, "From the House to the Streets: The Cuban Women's Movement for Legal Change, 1898–1958" (Ph.D. diss., Indiana University, 1983), 111.

6. Stoner notes that the organizations ranged from the conservative "Catholic Damas Isabelitas to the more liberal Club Femenino [and] debated no less than thirty-nine social and political issues important to women." The agendas of the Cuban women's conferences are cited in Stoner, "From the House to the Streets," 111–112

7. Stoner, "From the House to the Streets," 113.

8. Shirlene Ann Soto, *The Mexican Woman: A Study of Her Participation in the Revolution, 1910–1940* (Palo Alto, Calif.: R & E Research Associates, 1979), 83.

9. Ibid., 83.

10. Ibid., 75.

11. Ana Macías, *Against All Odds: The Feminist Movement in Mexico to 1940* (Westport, Conn.: Greenwood Press, 1982), 106. See also Francesca Miller, "The International Relations of Women of the Americas, 1890–1928," *The Americas: A Quarterly Review of Inter-America Cultural History*, 43 (October 1986): 179.

12. Dawn Keremetsis, "Women Workers in the Mexican Revolution (1910–1940): Advance or Retreat?" (unpublished paper, 1981).

13. Macías, *Against All Odds*, 106.

14. Shirlene Soto discusses a number of women's congresses, as does Ana Macías. Soto, in *The Mexican Woman*, p. 76, writes: "The most spectacular change in the women's movement in Mexico from 1920 to 1934 was in the increased number of women's organizations and conferences. Hundreds of women, recognizing the value in national and international organization, joined together."

15. Soto, *The Mexican Woman*, 79.

16. Ibid.

17. The Equal Rights Treaty was drafted by Alice Paul of the National Woman's Party of the United States and presented to the Havana Conference by Doris Stevens.

18. James Brown Scott, *The International Conferences of American States, 1889–1928* (New York: Oxford University Press, 1931), vii.

19. Francesca Miller, "Latin American Feminism," in Seminar on Women and Culture in America, in *Women, Culture and Politics in Latin America* (Berkeley and Los Angeles: University of California Press, 1990).

20. Alice Park, 1928 Diary, Alice Park Collection, Archives of the Hoover Institution on War, Revolution and Peace, Stanford, Calif.

21. This idea is discussed in the work of the scholars cited above and in my own research; see also Jane Jaquette, "Female Political Participation in Latin America," in *Women in the World: A Comparative Study* (Santa Barbara, Calif.: ABC Clio Press, 1976), for an early statement of this thesis. Elsa Chaney in *Supermadre: Women in Politics in Latin America* (Austin, TX: University of Texas Press, 1979) put it thus: "The whole struggle for the vote, just emerging as an issue at the time of these meetings, often was viewed almost exclusively as a vehicle for obtaining social reforms in favor of women, children, the old, the sick, juvenile delinquents and prostitutes."

22. Bertha Lutz, *Trexe principios basicos: Suggestões ao ante-projecto de constituição,* cited in Besse, "Freedom and Bondage," 133. See also June Hahner, "The Beginnings of the Women's Suffrage Movement in Brazil," *Signs: Journal of Women in Culture and Society*, 5 (1979): 200–224.

23. María Luiza Bittencourt, "Report from Brazil," in Beatrice Newhart, "Woman Suffrage in the Americas," *Pan-American Union Bulletin,* 70 (April 1936): 425.

24. Stoner, "From the House to the Streets," 106.

25. Beatrice Newhart, "Woman Suffrage in the Americas," *Pan-American Union Bulletin*, 70 (April 1936): 426.

26. Soto, *The Mexican Woman*, 85.

27. Newhart, "Woman Suffrage in the Americas," 427.

28. Rollie E. Poppino, "Brazil: A New Model for National Development," *Current History*, 62 (February 1972).

29. Magda Portal, *El aprismo y la mujer* (Lima: Editorial Cooperativa Aprista "ATAHUALPA," 1933), 56.

30. Portal, *El aprismo y la mujer*, 17.

# 14  Larissa Lomnitz and Marisol Pérez-Lizaur ♦ Kinship Structure and the Role of Women in the Urban Upper Class of Mexico

*Because the vast majority of Latin Americans live in poverty, upper-class women have not been the preferred subject of social scientists. They are frequently dismissed as superficial women who spend their days talking on the phone, playing cards, shopping, and generally wasting their time. Lomnitz and Pérez-Lizaur, teachers of cultural anthropology at the National University of Mexico, took exception to this analysis and turned the question on its head. They asked if the seemingly useless activities of elite women had importance. They concluded that the extended family— the core social institution— actually reaped benefits from the duties performed by what they termed the "centralizing women."*

In 1970 we began a study of kinship structure in an upper-class family in Mexico City that ranged over five generations of men and women, including 118 nuclear families.* These were the descendants of Carlos Gomez (1825–1876), a small-town merchant of the state of Puebla, who had three children by his first, criollo wife, and six by his second, Indian wife. From this nuclear family emerged a number of branches, within

From *Signs* 5, no. 1 (Autumn 1979): 164–68. Reprinted by permission of the University of Chicago.

*The study [1979] is based mainly on intensive participant observation. The authors have participated over the last eight years in countless family rituals and informal social gatherings and have met and spoken to most of the living members of the stock. We also have had the assistance of a "key informant," a young woman whose family belongs to the wealthier branches of the stock, who has introduced us to many members of her family branch. To a lesser extent we have done formal, though unstructured, interviews with individuals felt to possess knowledge on particular aspects, mainly older "centralizing women" and young entrepreneurs. Finally, we have tried to complete and ratify the historical material with archival sources, written historical literature, and the press. For the theoretical analysis of our data, we are consulting, among others: Robert T. Aubey, "Capital Mobilization and the Patterns of Business Ownership and Control in Latin America: The Case of Mexico," in *Entrepreneurs in Cultural Context*, ed. Sidney M. Greenfield, Arnold Strickon, and Aubey (Albuquerque: University of New Mexico Press, 1979), pp. 225–242; Feo R. Calderon, "Los ferrocarriles," in *Historia moderna de México. El porfiriato. Vida económica*, ed. Cosío Villegas (Mexico City: Hermes, 1965); CEPAL/NAFINSA, *La politica industrial en el desarrollo económico de México* (Mexico City: NAFINSA, 1971); Abner Cohen, *Two-Dimensional Men* (London: Routledge and Kegan Paul, 1974).

which socioeconomic stratification developed. One of the "mestizo" sons, who migrated to Mexico City in the 1880s, became one of the earliest native Mexican industrialists and big businessmen. Capital formation among this wealthy branch began during the latter years of the Porfirio Díaz administration, particularly during the period 1890–1910. Descendants of this entrepreneurial branch remained in the upper class, while the descendants of employees became members of the middle class. The mechanisms that maintained the notable internal cohesion and solidarity among members of this kinship group, over and beyond the differences in socioeconomic status and genealogical distance, are the subject of this brief research report.

The various branches and extended families of this kinship group are scattered today throughout Mexico City. Some branches have become "lost" through emigration or through deliberate severance of the personal ties with the family. Among the remaining members there is a strong sense of membership in a prominent family group, with membership defined both through kinship and a system of exchanges and interactions. Interaction among family members takes various forms: exchange of information (family gossip), symmetrical exchange of goods and services (exchange of presents on specific occasions, partnership deals between economic equals, economically relevant information), and asymmetric exchanges (patron-client relationships). The relative intensity of the flow of exchange determines the strengths of the kinship relation, the actual (as opposed to formal or genealogical) closeness between kin. For example, an individual may have a number of first cousins, but the actual social ties he or she maintains with each depend on the amount of social contact, exchange of information, joint business ventures, and informal assistance that transpire between them.

Economic linkages with the family enterprises appear to be a key factor in the persistence of family cohesion. Since the early stages of Mexican industrialization, the family enterprise has been dominant, a model which relies heavily on the loyalty and social or political connections of family members. At the head of the enterprise stands the father-entrepreneur surrounded by his sons and trusted relatives, many of them from the less wealthy branches of the family. This entrepreneur often owns one or two major industrial concerns in addition to many more smaller businesses and real estate investments. A pool of trusted relatives may be called upon to take charge of each business interest in his behalf. Family allegiance is relied upon to ensure that these caretakers from the poorer branches of the family will serve the entrepreneur loyally and will never leak information to outsiders. Among the less wealthy relatives, membership in the family thus does not only involve the pride and prestige of being associated with a powerful kindred but also a livelihood which, however dependent, is permanently assured so long as loyalty is maintained. Even in the wealthy branches, most young men begin their business careers as employees in some family business and work their way up or eventually break away to set up their own firms. Although most exchanges between a rich entrepreneur and his less wealthy kin-employees are of the patron-client type, there is also a wide range of reciprocal dealings and partnerships between the lesser businessmen across the economic spectrum of the family. The major entrepreneurs of the family have had as many as thirty-nine dependents working for them, plus countless other relatives who were business associates of one kind or another. Today, the intrusion of modern foreign corporations forces these businessmen to adopt more competitive management methods, often to the exclusion of relatives. Yet, family solidarity is as high as ever, less so in the old patron-client pattern and more so in the form of partnerships on equal footings.

Information, the most elementary and basic type of exchange within the clan, involves a wide spectrum of facts, ranging from family gossip to knowledge about relatives and ultimately to clan ideology. Women have always played a large role in the transmission of such information, which is one of the main mechanisms of clan solidarity. Prominent female figures, who devoted their lives to creating and transmitting a clan ideology, established information networks over certain branches of the family kindred, often across generational and socioeconomic boundaries. The personal prestige of these "centralizing women" was based on their authoritative knowledge of the family history, including the personal backgrounds and relationships among individual members, within an ideological framework of family values and family solidarity.

Formerly, the actual exchange of information was carried out in the course of social visiting and family reunions; nowadays, much of it is transmitted over the telephone. Ritual family reunions are of course still very frequent—christenings, first communions, birthdays, saints' days, graduations, send-offs and welcoming receptions, marriages, births, visits to the sick, and funerals, not to mention the major occasions connected with the life cycle or with the Catholic calendar. Some social occasions (i.e., funerals and visits to the ill) are open to all family members, others are by invitation to most (e.g., weddings), and some are restricted to certain branches or to an extended family only, which serves to define relative status within the family ranking order. Participation in such public or quasi-public reunions is ritualistic since it symbolizes an individual's belonging to the family group. Women are prominent in the organization and promotion of all such reunions as well as of informal social gatherings between close relatives: visits in the home, dinner parties, games, theater parties, and so on. The kind of gossip exchanged during such events is not restricted to personal affairs; on the contrary, business gossip is prominent—who is moving into a new home, who is doing well or not so well in business, and so on. Women are conversant with a wealth of details concerning the business affairs of family members, past and present, which constitutes vital background information on those deals initiated or formalized during family reunions. These "centralizing women" often also act as brokers for needy relatives or relatives looking for jobs.

In recent years, women's role in the family business has become more important, especially as a contributor of capital. Female members may maintain ownership of their share of the family business even after marriage, while those who marry into the family are generally expected to contribute their personal capital to the family enterprise. Nevertheless, women are still expected to remain passive partners and housewives even when they are noted for their business abilities. Women, socialized toward a housewife's role from early childhood, may listen, learn, and eventually express their opinions, but they are only allowed to participate indirectly through their husbands, brothers, or sons in decision making in business affairs. Motherhood, of course, is still considered the female's main concern. Until recently, the family ideology promoted having a large number of children; now, it is acceptable for a woman to have fewer children so long as they are "well looked after." Although the dirty work involved in child care may be done by servants under the mother's supervision, the family's concept of good motherhood includes breast-feeding, sitting up at night if baby cries, changing the diapers, helping children with their homework, and teaching them the principles of religion.

Girls are brought up to become good wives, and in the upper-class ethos this means acknowledging the intellectual and economic superiority of the husband; fitting her own interests and tastes to those of her husband, even in such areas as fashion; and enforcing the family ideology at all times. The girl is taught family values, including the importance of actively furthering close social relations within the wider family group, affine as well as consanguineal. She is to visit and look after the sick, promote parties and reunions, congratulate relatives on their birthdays or saints' days, buy presents suitable for every occasion, and bring assistance to relatives in need. Indeed, the business of asserting and reasserting one's status and position in the family is almost a full-time occupation for a woman. Eventually, she will be expected to welcome to her home all the business associates and influential people who must be entertained in the interest of her husband's or her relatives' business affairs, or to attend parties for business reasons. At all of these occasions, she is expected not to sit idly but to further the family interests by befriending the right people and making useful contacts.

Kinship relations in the upper class of urban Mexico are conditioned by the structure of a social network based on the flow of information, goods, and services among socially recognized relatives. Mutual recognition as relatives is based on this flow of exchange and is reasserted continually in the arena of family rituals, where women played and still play a prominent part. Such findings help us understand kinship in complex societies, particularly the interaction between kinship and class, the nature of the kindred, and the specific role of women in business and in the social system of the urban upper and middle class.

## 15  Republic of Cuba ◆ Law No. 1263:
## The Revolution Protects Motherhood

*The Cuban Revolution has never developed a policy regarding popula-
tion control because it has always held that husbands and wives should
determine the size of the family. It neither urged women to have large
families by offering privileges or prizes, as did Stalinist Russia, nor did it
discourage reproduction by limiting the number of children, as is practiced currently in China. The revolution did address itself to improved
health care and developed a series of short-range objectives that included
close attention to preventative and curative maternity care. Legislation,
such as the 1974 Maternity Law for Working Women reproduced here,
demonstrates why even critics of Fidel Castro accept that Cuba has become a leader in hemispheric health-care reform.*

I, OSVALDO DORTICÓS TORRADO, president of the Republic of
Cuba,

HEREBY PROCLAIM: That the Council of Ministers has approved
and I have signed the following:

WHEREAS: Studies made on problems pertaining to working women,
especially those relating to maternity, counsel the enactment of new legislation in order to grant the maximum guarantee to all maternity rights
which, although recognized and provided for by Social Security Law
No. 1100 of March 27, 1963, should be reconsidered on the basis of
present-day medical and scientific principles;

WHEREAS: It is a primary interest of the revolutionary government
to give special attention to the working mother since, in addition to her
valuable contribution to society in the procreation and education of children, she also fulfills her social duty by working;

WHEREAS: A successful pregnancy as well as the delivery and the
future health of the child require the adoption of adequate measures on
the part of the pregnant woman, as an unavoidable duty toward her child
and society;

WHEREAS: To secure the above-mentioned measures, it is necessary to ensure medical attention and rest to the working woman during
her pregnancy, the breast-feeding of the newborn during the first months

From "Maternity Law for Working Women" in *Women and the Cuban Revolution: Speeches and Documents by Fidel Castro, Vilma Espín and Others*, ed.
Elizabeth Stone (New York: Pathfinder Press, 1981), 133–39. ©1981 by Pathfinder Press. Reprinted by permission of Pathfinder Press.

of life which will protect it from disease and favor the development of strong emotional bonds between mother and child, and the systematic medical examination of the child by a pediatrician during its first year of life;

WHEREAS: In our country all medical and hospital services, including pharmaceutical and hospital dietary services related to maternity, are guaranteed free of charge to all the population. This makes it necessary to establish additional legislation on the enjoyment of said rights by the working woman or the wife or the companion of a worker;

THEREFORE: By virtue of the authority vested in them, the Council of Ministers resolves to dictate the following:

# LAW NO. 1263
# MATERNITY LAW FOR WORKING WOMEN

## Chapter 1: Scope and Protection

*Article 1.* The present law comprises the working woman and protects her maternity, guaranteeing and facilitating, in a special manner, her medical attention during pregnancy, her rest before and after delivery, the breast-feeding and care of the children, as well as a financial aid in those cases specified in these provisions.

## Chapter 2: Paid Leave

*Article 2.* Every pregnant working woman, regardless of type of work, will be obliged to stop working on the thirty-fourth week of pregnancy and will have the right to a leave of absence of eighteen weeks, which will include six weeks before delivery and twelve weeks after delivery. This leave will be paid as determined by this law, provided that the working woman meets the requirements stated in Article 11.

The Ministry of Labor, at the proposal of the Central Organization of Cuban Trade Unions, will regulate exceptional situations in those places of work whose special characteristics, according to medical and scientific criteria, make it necessary that working women take prenatal leave for longer periods than those established by this law.

*Article 3.* In cases of multiple pregnancy, the working woman will be obliged to stop working on the thirty-second week of pregnancy, extending to eight weeks the period of her paid leave before delivery.

*Article 4.* If delivery does not take place during the period established for the prenatal leave, this leave will be extended to the date on which delivery takes place and the extended time period will be paid for up to two weeks.

*Article 5.* If delivery takes place before the expiration of the prenatal leave, this leave will cease and the working woman will begin her postnatal leave.

*Article 6.* If delivery takes place before the thirty-fourth week of pregnancy, or before the thirty-second week in the case of multiple pregnancy, the leave will include only the postnatal period.

*Article 7.* The working woman will be guaranteed a postnatal leave of six weeks necessary for her recovery, even when, because of adverse circumstances of accident or acquired or congenital diseases, the child dies at birth or during the first four weeks after birth.

*Article 8.* If the working woman, because of complications during delivery, requires a longer period of recovery beyond the postnatal leave, she will have the right to receive the subsidy for illness as established in the Social Security Law.

## Chapter 3: Accidents of Pregnancy

*Article 9.* Accidents of pregnancy are those complications relative to pregnancy or diseases acquired during pregnancy which require absolute bed rest by doctor's order, with or without hospitalization.

Accidents of pregnancy which occur before the thirty-fourth week will give the working woman the right to the subsidy for illness as established in the Social Security Law.

## Chapter 4: Financial Aid

*Article 10.* The financial aid that the working woman will receive during her maternity leave will be equal to the weekly average of salaries and subsidies she has received during the twelve months immediately prior to the leave. This aid will never be under ten pesos a week.

*Article 11.* In order to have the right to receive the paid maternity leave established by this law, it will be indispensable that the working woman have her records in order, exception made in the case of administrative negligence, and have worked not less than seventy-five days in the twelve months prior to the leave. However, even when the working woman does not fulfill these requirements, she will have the right to receive the complementary leaves established in the following chapter.

## Chapter 5: Complementary Maternity Leave

*Article 12.* During pregnancy and up to the thirty-fourth week, the working woman will have the right to six days or twelve half-days of paid leave for her medical and dental care prior to delivery.

*Article 13.* In order to guarantee the care and development of the child during the first year of life, the working woman will have the right every month to one day off, with pay, to take her child for a pediatric checkup.

## Chapter 6: Unpaid Leave

*Article 14.* The working mother will have the right to an unpaid leave for the purpose of taking care of her children, under the terms and conditions established by this law.

INTERIM PROVISIONS

*First*: The present law will be applied to all working women who, at the time of its promulgation, have fulfilled thirty-four weeks of pregnancy and have still not taken their maternity leave, and to those who are already on leave according to Social Security Law No. 1100 of March 27, 1963, as regards the extension of the leave to twelve weeks after delivery and one day off, with pay, every month for pediatric visits. Additional payment to cover the extended postnatal leave will be given as established in this law.

*Second*: The extra hour of rest period for child care established by Law No. 1100 of March 27, 1963, will remain for those working women now enjoying this benefit.

*Third*: Working women enjoying unpaid leave, as established in Instruction No. 1 of the Labor Justice Office of the Ministry of Labor, dated September 23, 1968, will maintain the same labor rights established in said instruction, until the expiration of their leave.

FINAL PROVISIONS

*First*: The Ministry of Labor is authorized to dictate as many provisions as required for the execution and application of this law.

*Second*: Title II of Law No. 1100 of March 27, 1963, Instruction No. 1 of the Labor Justice Office of the Ministry of Labor, dated September 23, 1968, and all other provisions and rulings which oppose the fulfillment of this law, are hereby abrogated. This law will go into effect on the date of its promulgation in the *Official Gazette of the Republic*.

THEREFORE: I command that this law be fulfilled and enforced in all its parts.

SIGNED, at the Palace of the Revolution, in Havana, on January 14, 1974.

OSVALDO DORTICÓS TORRADO
Fidel Castro Ruz, *Prime Minister*
Oscar Fernández Padilla, *Minister of Labor*

# Regulations of Law 1263
# Ministry of Labor, Resolution No. 2

WHEREAS: Law No. 1263 of January 14, 1974, in the first final provisions authorizes the passing of as many provisions as required for the execution and enforcement of said law;

THEREFORE: By virtue of the authority vested in me,

I RESOLVE:

FIRST: To dictate for the execution and enforcement of Law No. 1263 of January 14, 1974, the following [regulations]:

## Responsibility of the Administration in Workplaces

*Article 1.* The administration in all workplaces will be responsible for payments of all financial aid stipulated in Law No. 1263 of January 14, 1974.

*Article 2.* The administration will have the obligation of granting maternity leave after the thirty-fourth week of pregnancy—or after the thirty-second week of pregnancy in case of multiple births—once the working woman presents the medical certificate required.

*Article 3.* The fulfillment of the paid leave stipulated in Articles 2 and 7 of the law will take place in three parts: The first, at the beginning of the prenatal leave; the second, at the beginning of the first six weeks of the postnatal leave; and the third, at the beginning of the last six weeks of the postnatal leave, when applicable.

*Article 4.* In exceptional cases when delivery does not take place within the six-week period of the prenatal leave, the said leave will be extended until delivery actually takes place; payment for the additional period will never be over a term of two weeks, after which it will be considered an unpaid leave.

*Article 5.* The payment of [the] two weeks stipulated in the preceding article will be made jointly with the payment of the six weeks of the postnatal leave.

*Article 6.* If delivery takes place before the expiration of the prenatal leave, the financial difference between this date and the original expiration of the leave will be deducted from the postnatal leave, as stipulated in Article 5 of the law.

*Article 7.* In order to grant the rights stipulated by the law, the administration will be responsible in all cases to demand the medical certificates or assistance notes to medical services issued by establishments of the Ministry of Public Health.

*Article 8.* The administration will have the obligation to guarantee that the working woman who resumes her work upon expiration of the maternity leave will have the right to occupy the same post she had before.

## The Amount of Payment

*Article 9.* In order to calculate the average weekly income, referred [to] in Article 10 of the law, the salaries and subsidies received by the working woman during the twelve months immediately prior to the start of the maternity leave will be added up and its result divided by fifty-two weeks.

*Article 10.* The procedure to calculate the amount of payment established in the previous article will be applied in all cases, including those working women with a work record of less than one year. Trial periods in the case of new workers will be included for the purpose of calculation.

*Article 11.* A temporary working woman with a work record will have the right to a paid maternity leave and receive the payment even when the start of the same does not coincide with her cycle of work. The amount of payment will be calculated in the same way as for other working women.

*Article 12.* The right to paid leave will be granted to the pregnant woman with seventy-five or more workdays, from the time when she should have been properly accredited as a worker even though she was not because of administrative negligence.

*Article 13.* Working women who have not worked during the period established in Article 11 of the law will have the right to pre- and postnatal leaves, without payment, as established by the law. However, all other complementary leaves will be paid.

## Unpaid Leave

*Article 14.* If the working woman cannot work because she must take care of her children, she will have the right to an unpaid leave of up to:

a) Nine months, if the leave starts with the expiration of the postnatal leave or any time after it. This leave will expire when the child is one year old.

b) Six months for all working mothers with children under sixteen years of age.

*Article 15.* Rights previously established will be granted initially for a maximum period of three months, renewable every three months if the original motive for the leave is still valid.

*Article 16.* If a woman returns to work according to the terms established for the unpaid leave, she will have the right to occupy her former post.

*Article 17.* The administration, after hearing the opinion of the trade union local, may extend the leave when exceptional circumstances so advise, but in no case may the extension be for more than three months after the expiration of the terms established in Article 14. After this period of time, or after the extension if such is the case, the working woman will be separated and her post occupied, following the existing evaluation norms.

*Article 18.* In order to receive the leave regulated by paragraph b of Article 14 of these regulations, it will be indispensable for the working woman to have been hired by a workplace and have actually worked two thirds of the workdays of the semester prior to the date of the request for leave.

In cases of new workers the trial periods will be included for the calculation of payments.

*Article 19.* Unpaid leave may be granted in short periods, of not less than one week, and will be accumulative until the maximum time period established is reached. If between one leave and another, the working woman works uninterruptedly for a period similar to the one established in the previous article, she will have the right to a new leave.

SECOND: All provisions which are contrary to the dispositions of the present regulations are hereby abrogated. These provisions will become effective on the date of its publication in the *Official Gazette of the Republic.*

SIGNED, in Havana, Ministry of Labor, on the fifteenth day of January, 1974.

OSCAR FERNÁNDEZ PADILLA
*Minister of Labor*

## 16 Economic Commission for Latin America and the Caribbean ◆ A Typology of Poor Women

*The goal of "Women and Development" programs is to facilitate the ef-
fective and permanent integration of more than half of the population
into development planning. Since the Pan American Union in the 1920s,
international agencies have taken the lead in advocating a women's rights
agenda. The Economic Commission for Latin America and the Caribbean, an arm of the United Nations, has been particularly involved in
development programs, for which it gathers information concerning how
women actually live. During the past decades, numerous research projects
and diagnoses have been produced and, to some extent, have laid the
foundations for a new phase. Experts in the development field make sug-
gestions and formulate policies, based on data collected, to improve living conditions for women. Most recently, the emphasis has been on directly
involving women in this process of change rather than on relying on outside experts to suggest what improvements should be made.*

Since International Women's Year [1975] and during the subsequent
United Nations Decade for Women [1976–1985], there has been a
proliferation of studies on the situation of women in the world. Some of
these studies have tried to cover the wide range of phenomena of discrimination which affect women, but latterly attention has centered on
certain topics such as education, employment, and income. This new orientation has meant that the analyses are increasingly objective and measurable and also make it possible to consider women in the context of
their respective social strata and appreciate the diversity and complexity
of such strata.

In this work it is proposed, in addition to examining some background
details about the aspects of Latin American women in question, to formulate a typology which will take account not only of their differential characteristics in comparison with men but also the social aspects underlying
sexual differences, and to describe the characteristics of women from the
lower occupational strata. . . .

Up to now, no one has attempted to define exactly what is meant by
poverty. Some studies have noted the difficulty in defining the poor,

From the Economic Commission for Latin America and the Caribbean, "Some
Types of Poor Women in Latin America" in *Five Studies on the Situation of Women
in Latin America*, CEPAL series, No. 16 (Santiago, Chile, June 1983), 87, 98–
109. United Nations publication, Sales No. E.82.II.G.10. Notes and some tables
omitted. Reprinted by permission.

either because poverty is viewed from a consumerist perspective, as a specific situation, or because it is defined in relative terms, i.e., in the light of social inequalities. When poverty is considered as a situation, emphasis is placed on the existence of a group called "poor" who do not possess the resources to satisfy their basic needs. In contrast, the concept of poverty as a relative state means raising the question of social inequalities and the interdependence between groups which are poor and those which are not poor.

For the purpose of this paper, poor women will be considered as those belonging to the lower occupational strata, whether residing in the country or the city, whose place in the labor market is determined by their occupation and their occupational category. These are the most important variables which will be borne in mind. In this way, it is possible to come close to defining what may be called the class situation of poor women. Insofar as information is available on education and income, these data will be incorporated as a means of describing each class situation.

One of the objectives of this paper . . . is that of separating and distinguishing between different situations of poor women. The most suitable way of doing this seems to be to construct a typology which will make it possible to show the internal variations of the group on the basis of two variables: their form of insertion in the labor market and their place of residence (urban or rural). We should not lose sight, however, of the fact that the resulting types are abstractions of a much richer reality and therefore to some extent distort the true characteristics. It should also be borne in mind that this typology will not cover all the possible types, but only those considered to be the most representative in numerical terms and the most frequently seen in the majority of countries of the region.

The layout of the properties in the typology would be as follows:

|  | *Economic sector* | *Residence* | |
|  |  | *Rural* | *Urban* |
| --- | --- | --- | --- |
| | Not incorporated | 1 | 2 |
| Lower occupational | –agricultural [primary] | 3 | 4 |
| strata of the | –secondary | 5 | 6 |
| activities indicated: | –tertiary | 7 | 8 |

Crossing the two variables (economic sector and residence) gives eight possible types of poor women. In order to operationalize what we have called the lower occupational strata, we have considered as poor women wage-earners, unpaid family workers, and own-account workers in agriculture, stock-raising, fishing, mining, and similar occupations, all of which make up the type of lower strata in primary activities. Women employed as drivers of means of transport, artisanal spinners, other types of craft workers, manual workers, and female day workers correspond to the lower occupational strata in secondary activities. Finally, women employed in domestic and service jobs make up the lower occupational strata in tertiary activities.

There would also be two types of women of the poor strata who do not work and whose qualification as poor women would be defined by the occupational status of the husband. Such is the case of the majority of women who are theoretically of working age, since female participation in employment in 1975 only amounted to 19.6 percent. . . . Let us first of all analyze the case of rural housewives, who at first sight seem to offer a more homogeneous set of characteristics than those of urban housewives.

**The Rural Housewife**

This type is generally not found in its pure form, since the mothers, wives, or daughters of peasants are also brought into agricultural work on a sea-sonal basis or as what may be called an extension of household work. This covers such activities as taking care of small kitchen gardens, grind-ing corn, fetching water from the well, and collecting firewood, fruit, or herbs, all tasks which are carried out in addition to the household work proper and the work of bringing up the children.

For the most part, official surveys omit the productive work carried out by women in rural areas, treating it in most cases as domestic work of no economic value.

The life and organization of household work of rural women who do not carry out social work would therefore depend on the place of the male head of the family (father, husband, or son) in the productive system. Tentatively, the following categories may be distinguished: wage-earning agricultural laborer, smallholder, sharecropper on a big estate, bonded laborer, or, finally, a combination of the first two categories.

Moreover, they could be grouped according to whether they are part of what may be called a "traditional" system of land tenure or a "modern-capitalist system." Outstanding in the first group are the bonded laborers on large estates and the smallholders and, within the second group, the wage-earning agricultural laborers.

In the case of the bonded laborers and the smallholders, it may be assumed that the women sporadically carry out domestic work in the houses of the landowners and also take part in agricultural activities at times when the demand for labor is greatest, in view of the seasonal nature of the crops grown, i.e., during harvest time, the fruit-harvesting period, the wine harvest, and so on.

In the second case, the wife or daughter of the wage-earner also takes part in productive agricultural labor, in the production of goods, or in paid household work. The census information shows differences between countries [Argentina, Chile, Mexico, Dominican Republic, and Guatemala], however, with regard to the participation of labor in the primary sector, and also in the case of women.

From this information, it may be inferred that the majority of women who live in the country do not carry out a productive activity which is reflected in the census figures, and in this regard, it is perhaps right to refer to agriculture as a male productive activity.

Bearing this situation in mind, no special account will be taken of the type of woman who lives in the country and works in the primary sector, although it should be noted that the total work load to which she is subjected is considerably greater (apart from her work in the fields, she also has to carry out her household tasks) and that the rudimentary nature of household facilities and fittings makes the execution of household tasks more difficult.

### The Female Agricultural Worker

The group of women of the lower strata working in the primary sector is numerically the smallest. They are generally own-account workers or unpaid family workers, the proportion of wage-earning women being very small. Furthermore, they also have the lowest educational levels. In the [five] countries selected, their average level of education did not bring them any higher than functional illiteracy, except in Argentina, where the level was equivalent to that of four years of schooling in 1970.

It should be stressed, especially in the case of rural women, that the consideration of women apart from their family unit may lead to errors. It is in the rural family that both the division and the complementarity of roles are seen most clearly, and the poor rural family is also a small production unit in which each member has well-defined functions according to sex and age.

### The Urban Housewife

The difficulty of finding common patterns for poor urban women who do not work makes the analysis of their situation more complex. At all events, note may be taken of the heterogeneity of their living situations and the difficulty of considering them apart from their family of origin and of procreation. Clearly, any attempt at systematization must include these factors, in addition to diversity of social strata to which they belong. In this respect, two extreme cases may be cited by way of example: that of the marginal slum dweller and that of the wife of a worker in the modern secondary sector. Between these two cases there is a wide range which may be considered to represent the poor urban woman who does not participate in the labor market.

In spite of these reservations, however, some common aspects can be identified. One of these is that their position as housewives and mothers presupposes a series of well-established functions. In this case, the difference between household work and the production of goods and services for the market is clearer. They are responsible for all the household work, and this is accepted as an unavoidable obligation. This household work, generally of a routine nature, has been learned by observing the activities of the woman's own mother. Possible innovations are due only to school influences (if there is a certain minimum level of schooling) and to the influence of the mass media, such as radio and television. Some influence may also be exerted in this respect by communication with other housewives and the sharing of common experiences.

Another fundamental aspect of the situation of this type of urban housewife lies in the fact that the income received by the husband, father, or companion is not sufficient to take care of the minimum requirements for food, clothing, and housing, and the possibilities of making ends meet depend on the woman's skill in managing the family budget.

More background information is required, however, to be able to determine more accurately the aspects of the life and organization of urban housewives in order to bring out both the common features and the differences in this sector.

## The Female Manual Worker

Female manual workers of the secondary sector have been considered as the most modern and dynamic group, in that their work in this sector gives them greater exposure to the mass communication media, better communication and contact with workers in the same situation, and therefore a fuller view of the society in which they live and the role they play in it.

Although their level of education is higher and their occupational qualifications better, however, this does not mean that they have a greater awareness of their position in the social structure. It is well known that women are frequently used to smash movements aimed at gaining better conditions, because they are the persons who are most afraid of losing their jobs and therefore accept more unfavorable conditions. More information is needed, however, to justify pronouncements regarding variations in the labor- and trade-union attitudes of female manual workers.

In this group, women choose occupations which are an extension of their domestic functions: thus, most female manual workers work in the textile industry and clothing manufacture.

It is interesting to note that, contrary to what might be expected, this sector of female industrial workers does not increase in relative terms in the same proportion as in the other production sectors. On the contrary, during the decade under examination there was a drop in its relative size, except in Guatemala, where there was a slight increase in the participation of this stratum.

Once again, the double task facing working women is to be noted. Although in some enterprises—the biggest and most modern—there are child-care centers and nurseries, this is not the case in most of them, so that workers are obliged to make various arrangements for their children to be looked after during the working day. This responsibility is often entrusted to older children or the goodwill of relatives or neighbors, and as always the female worker is also responsible for the organization and execution of the household work for herself and her family group. Efforts have been made to enable female workers to acquire take-out meals for their families at low cost, but these attempts have been isolated and apparently not very successful.

Within the range of strata listed, however, this is the stratum in which women are in the best relative position, since in the case of medium-sized and large enterprises they enjoy certain basic services, while they also receive relatively higher wages compared with those of peasant women and women in the poor services strata.

## Housemaids

Among women who work in the services sector and belong to the lower strata, two main types may be described: housemaids and street vendors. Attention will be focused here on the first type, which covers rather more than 90 percent of the women of the lower strata who work in the tertiary sector.

This stratum is the biggest of those considered so far. It covers the activities of almost one third of the women who work, and although it has tended to go down during the decade, it has done so only very slightly. The average number of years of schooling differs from one country to another, from one year in Guatemala to five years in Argentina in 1970. Thus, it is below the average level of the female manual worker, although higher than that of the female peasant.

Most of the women who migrate from rural areas are absorbed into the economy through domestic work. It is interesting to note that this sector contains the largest number of working women under twenty years of age. This is because housemaids, like street vendors, require little or no training, and this can be carried out while actually working. Moreover, the demand for housemaids is quite elastic and also very fluid, so it is possible to pass directly from domestic work in one's own house to domestic work for others, thus enabling women to reduce or increase the number of hours they work relatively easily. On the supply side, domestic work is that in which the labor is cheapest, because of the lack of qualifications and training already referred to, and the continuous flow of women from rural areas to the cities.

Two basic kinds of domestic service are to be distinguished: "living-in maids" and "living-out maids," depending on whether or not they live in the dwelling of their employers. The first type of work involves longer hours and closer integration with the people for whom the maid works. This means that a housemaid has less possibility of organizing an independent life or forming her own family group. The "living-in" form of work predominates in domestic service.

The constant interaction with the persons for whom a housemaid works leads her to identify herself with the values held by these persons and to displace her own class interests, and this, in view of the difficulty of linking up with other workers in the same situation, makes it difficult for housemaids to perceive where their own interests lie.

In the case of "living-out" maids, the situation may be different, since they live in contact with persons of their same social stratum who thus naturally modify their view of society.

Reference has already been made to the low social and economic significance attached to household work, not only when women carry it out for their own family units, but also when they carry it out for other persons. It is the lowest kind of work as regards occupational prestige, satisfaction, and remuneration. Certain information indicates that in Greater Santiago the wages of housemaids corresponded, in relative terms, to only 41 percent of the average national income in 1970, compared with 47 percent in the case of manual workers and 139 percent in the case of nonmanual workers. The wages of housemaids are far below the national daily average, and around 1972 they were only 50 percent of the minimum legal wage for manual and nonmanual workers.

## Native Street Vendors

The difficulty in obtaining adequate information on all the Latin American women who spend part of their time in selling their agricultural and handicraft products means that it is only possible to note some important features taken from studies of an anthropological nature. Most of these tend to highlight only the specific aspects encountered in each community, thus losing sight of the more general aspects common to all of them.

An essential feature is that most of the Latin American women who may be included in this category belong to the indigenous population.

Their activity consists mainly in traveling once or twice a week from the community to which they belong and in which they and their families work in agricultural activities to the trading centers where their agricultural and handicraft products can be sold. Sometimes they only act as intermediaries, since they buy the products and then sell them in the markets nearest to their place of origin.

The training needed to carry out these activities is gained by watching the mother and other adults. One of the most important aspects, which affects the prestige of the vendor and the effectiveness of her work, is the need to have a good knowledge of Spanish and to be reasonably good at figures. It has also been noted that many vendors give up wearing their native dress and adopt city styles as a sign of higher status.

Since this type of commercial activity of native women is independent, it gives them a certain freedom in making decisions. They can decide with whom they are going to do business and also how they are going to fix their prices. At the same time, the arrival at the market of other vendors gives them an opportunity to exchange experiences and communicate with people of other areas or communities, although it has been noted that there is competition among them to gain a certain steady clientele and to occupy the best places for the sale of their products. . . .

The organization of these women's domestic activities during their absence one or two days a week may be the responsibility of older daughters. If their children are too small, the women take them with them when carrying out their trading activities.

Unfortunately, more detailed information is not available regarding the patterns followed by this type of insertion of rural women in the labor field. A fuller study of their situation is needed, which could serve to determine the effects that this type of activity may have when those carrying it out decide to migrate to the city.

## 17  Barbara Seitz ◆ From Home to Street: Women and Revolution in Nicaragua

*The increasing importance of the women's agenda in Latin America is apparent in the national liberation movements of Nicaragua, Guatemala, and El Salvador, where female participation reached higher levels than ever before. The Nicaraguan Revolution took place during the rising tide of the new popular feminism and pledged "No revolution without women's emancipation: No emancipation without revolution." Despite this promise, in 1982 Tomás Borge, minister of defense, publicly declared that the revolution had failed to confront women's liberation energetically enough and that the fate of Nicaraguan women was essentially the same as before the FSLN victory in 1979. Because of this failure to address women's concerns some feminist writers, such as Maxine Molyneaux, criticized the Sandinistas for not rooting out the patriarchal behavior that continues to be a problem. In this essay, Seitz asks her readers to take the long view and see the progress made in Nicaragua—progress that Nicaraguan women believe is real and has improved their lives considerably.*

Presently the poorest nation in the hemisphere, Nicaragua spent the 1980s struggling to achieve stability after a decade of rebellion characterized by nationwide strikes, clandestine activities, and guerrilla warfare which eventually involved every segment of the population. On July 19, 1979, the popular revolution led by the Frente Sandinista de Liberación Nacional (FSLN) defeated and expelled Anastasio Somoza Debayle (1967–1979), a repressive dictator who diverted wealth to his own pocket while perpetuating the poverty of the masses, who lacked educational opportunities, medical care, and a political voice.[1]

With Somoza's removal and the institution of a new government in 1979, freedom from oppression and potential for personal growth became new possibilities. However, after such impressive accomplishments as a national literacy campaign, which reduced the illiteracy rate from 50 percent to 13 percent in twelve months,[2] a malaria reduction effort that dramatically curtailed the disease's incidence, and the establishment of a national health-care system, which vastly improved the general level of health, the nation ran headlong into political conflict with the United

From *Women Transforming Politics: Worldwide Strategies for Empowerment,* ed. Jill M. Bystydzienski (Bloomington: Indiana University Press, 1992), 162–74. Reprinted by permission of Indiana University Press.

States. Made anxious by Soviet-Nicaraguan military relations, the United States attacked the port of Corinto on October 10, 1983, put in place an economic blockade, and began to fund an army of counterrevolutionaries known as the "Contra" to undermine the nation's economic, social, and political welfare. Contra attacks concentrating on small communities, schools, [and] health personnel and facilities forced diversion of attention from reconstruction to defense. The 1980s became a decade of radical change, of social transformation, and of progress mixed with recession and the psychological and physical devastations of war.

In a context of extreme economic and political-military pressure, elections were held in February 1990. Observed by hundreds of representatives from around the world, these elections were universally judged a model for all democratic nations. The outcome awarded victory to Violeta Chamorro, widow of the revolutionary hero Joaquín Chamorro, internationally honored journalist and editor of the opposition paper *La Prensa*, who was murdered by Somoza's National Guard. Chamorro and the UNO (Unión Nacional de Oposición, or National Union for Opposition) coalition of fourteen political parties, united only by their opposition to the Sandinista party, won by a narrow margin over the incumbent FSLN. In this election many Nicaraguans voted for an end to U.S. economic and military aggression—in other words, against the status quo of hunger and war. Many, especially women, voted for an end to the military draft and continued deaths of their children.

Integrally woven into the fabric of these developments has been the struggle of women for emancipation and empowerment. In this chapter, I describe the heritage of Nicaraguan women and the course of their movement for equality. The information contained herein derives from personal observations and numerous interviews I conducted during six visits to Nicaragua over the past four years, supported and complemented by documentation from published sources.

I examine the struggle of Nicaraguan women in the context of the restrictions and responsibilities placed upon women by their culture and the long-standing contradiction between the ideal "vision" and the reality of most women's lives. In the first part of the chapter, I recount the traditional ideal of women as domestic caregivers and of their subordinate role in decision making and in family and couple relationships. I contrast this with their critical role as wage earners and examine changing attitudes toward women's participation in the labor market. The second part follows the emancipation movement from its identification with the revolution to its present dilemma in the face of government policies favoring a return to tradition.

## The Historic Contradiction

Traditionally in Nicaragua, the identity of the Nicaraguan woman has been tied to her relationship with other people (her children and especially her husband) whom she nurtures. This is especially obvious in her work activities according to the traditional division of labor, which assigns women ideally to operations in the private domain *en la casa* (in the home) and men to the public domain, popularly referred to in Nicaragua as *en la calle* (in the street). For generations women's self-image depended upon this vision. A young female medical doctor described her grandmother's objections to her daughters' holding jobs and granddaughters' picking coffee, activities which she described as *andando en la calle* (walking in the street) when a woman's place, she said, is *en la casa*.[3] This "ideal" system ties women to their home and family in a subservient position, while men are to occupy positions of leadership in all spheres, particularly the public/political one.

Prior to the revolution, men actually held decision-making authority in both private and public domains, with limited female participation. Women's authority resided principally with home and children. But even here, officially, according to Somoza's Family Code and the law of *patria potestad*, the father had sole rights over his children, and his wife was regarded largely as his property. Men were to work at jobs for pay; women were to stay at home, be loyal and loving spouses, bear children, and nurture them out of love for the family. One woman described it this way: "Before the triumph, women were marginal. Women didn't have the power to develop themselves in their labors equally as men in their work, because it was understood that women were only for the home, for being in the home, nothing more. For the kitchen, for caring for the children, for marrying. From early childhood they taught us this."[4] Except for the very rich who were cared for by female servants, all young girls learned to help and perform household chores. In a developing nation these can easily consume the greater portion of the day, especially when combined with child care. Boys, and especially men, were not expected to participate in these tasks.

In historically Catholic Nicaragua, centuries of tradition have associated women with the figure of the Madonna, the pure and virtuous mother. Adopting this idea of woman, called marianismo, Nicaraguan women identify strongly with the image of the devoted mother. In fact, they often think that giving a man children will gain or hold his affection.[5]

In the Nicaraguan countryside nearly every woman I saw who was between eighteen and forty-five years of age was either pregnant, had a babe in arms, or both. Many have ten children or more, and 21 percent of mothers are under the age of twenty. These Nicaraguan women belong to the set of mothers described [in 1988] by UNICEF as a target group needing assistance for their own and their children's sake:

> A significant improvement in the state of the world's children . . . depends most of all on the state of the world's mothers. . . . The everyday hardship and discrimination which women face—in food, in education, in health care, in work, and in rewards—is the single most important barrier to the improvement of their own and their children's health.
>
> With less education and status, less access to technology or training, and few resources of either cash or credit, women in almost all communities are expected to be not only wives and mothers but . . . income earners, homemakers and health workers, fuel gatherers and animal feeders, food providers and water carriers. It is too much.

The plight of these mothers is extreme in a country ravaged by economic scarcities, war, and a whole range of problems shared by developing nations.

Because Nicaraguan women identify so closely with their roles as wives and mothers, living to a large degree through others, the war held especially excruciating consequences for them. Mothers lost sons and daughters, wives lost husbands, some of whom remain missing in action. Women lived in a constant state of anxiety for loved ones, fathers, husbands, brothers, sons, and daughters, currently serving or soon to be called to service, then mobilized to the mountains where they might not be heard from for months.

Most Nicaraguan couples live in common-law marriages, registered neither with church nor state. Nicaraguan Catholics are not the orthodox variety found in the United States, bound by the letter of the law. Like other Latins in Europe and the Americas, Nicaraguans seek the "spirit" of the law and feel excused from certain "rules," for example, a church wedding, by virtue of circumstance. For most Nicaraguans church weddings are considered unaffordable, as they entail the purchase of a wedding dress, ring, and making a contribution to the church. "Wedding rings," I was told, "are only necessary for church weddings."[6] And though civil marriage is cheap and required by law in addition to any church ceremony, most couples opt to live without formal contract. Perhaps Catholic tradition has influenced couples' decisions not to enter a civil contract since the church does not recognize a civil marriage. An opinion expressed by a young man in Managua maintains that it is a truer sign of love that people stay together without force of legal contract. He, therefore, thought it best not to formalize his relationship with his partner, mother of their two children.[7]

In any case, relationships in Nicaragua operate under a set of assumptions about appropriate behavior founded on the female and male concepts of marianismo and machismo. *Marianismo*, which requires women to be virtuous and humble, serves to support the male regime of machismo. *Machismo*, a system of male superiority and dual standards, exists in traditional Nicaragua in an extreme form. Dual standards greatly restrict women's freedom and make them highly accountable to men, who, in turn, enjoy freedom of movement and action with virtually no accountability.

The vast majority of women with whom I spoke agreed that it is to be expected that husbands will have a certain number of affairs each year, and they see this as inevitable: "One accustoms herself that the man has that freedom, and one sees it as natural. That the man leaves, and yourself, no."[8] In contrast, Nicaraguan women have no interest in obtaining the sexual freedoms cultivated by their men. They see such behavior by women as not only outrageous but in strict violation of their duty as women to be at home waiting for their husbands. A young woman medical doctor put it quite bluntly: "It has not gotten to the point where one says, 'I am a man,' and then [the woman responds] 'Because you are free, I want to be, too.' No, the woman knows well what is her place. She must be waiting for the man. She has to be in her house."[9] If they cannot control their husbands, the wives at least hold themselves strictly accountable.

That women were held more accountable by the society was substantiated by the divorce laws on the books from the days of Somoza until 1988.[10] These old laws blatantly discriminated against women. A man's saying that his wife committed adultery was sufficient proof for obtaining a divorce; but in order for a woman to obtain a divorce, she had to establish that her husband was living in residence with another woman or that the relationship was public knowledge.

Women, especially before the revolution, were expected to stay close to home with their children and even to ask permission to go out in the evenings. A *campesina* (peasant) woman told me that before the revolution, if a woman wanted to attend a meeting in the evening, her husband might say no and then she could not go.[11] On the other hand, if a man does not feel like informing his wife about his activities away from home, he feels justified in maintaining silence. The wife should assume trust and not question him. Women learned at an early age about the female side of machismo, that women's place is in the home. Only if economic pressures make it impossible to stay home are women to work outside the home, and then only to supplement the family income.

Thus it came to pass that despite the traditional ideal that the woman's place is in the home, Nicaraguan women entered the labor market. Even before the revolution more women in Nicaragua worked outside the home than in most other Latin American nations, providing an important condition for a women's liberation movement. To understand how the Sandinista government would take the unprecedented steps it had to empower women and accept the cause of women's emancipation, we must look to the nation's exceptional history.

Somoza maintained control for his elitist power structure through brutal repression of the masses, carried out by his corrupt and violent National Guard forces. The resulting mass poverty caused family disintegration. Men without work, unable to fulfill their traditional responsibilities to wife and children, frequently abandoned their families, going off to search for jobs. Women found themselves alone, with responsibility for home and children. Consequently, larger numbers of women in Nicaragua came to participate in the labor force than in other Latin American countries where repression was less acute. Forced self-reliance, independence, and participation in the labor sector ripened Nicaragua for a strong women's movement.

Under Somoza, in 1963, according to census statistics, 20 percent of all households nationally, and 25 percent in Managua, were headed by women. Similarly, in groups, not families, living together, 20 percent nationally, and 25 percent in Managua, were headed by women. In 1979 labor force statistics from the Organization of American States reporting economically active population (1950–1965) and projections (1970–1980) by country and sex for all of Central America showed Nicaragua leading the rest of Central America in the percentage of females in the total work force.

These working women were not, however, voluntarily electing a career; rather, there has been a consistent and direct correlation between civil status (women heads of households) and employment, and economic necessity and employment. Women heading households have constituted the largest portion of working women, and this is a large percentage of all Nicaraguan women. In 1978 women headed roughly a third of all households. More recent figures indicated that in 1983 in Managua 49 percent of all households were headed by women and in 1981 that 83 percent of all women who worked headed households. Surely, a majority of the remaining 17 percent of working women were compelled to supplement their husband's income, leaving a scanty few who worked for satisfaction rather than economic necessity. Given the continuously deteriorating national economy, from comments made to me by women and my observations of changing life-styles, it is apparent that today more women are working or seeking employment in the face of layoffs and massive unemployment than ever before and that the primary motivation remains economic necessity.

Attitudes toward women working, however, have changed radically. A growing number of women are choosing to be single professionals, others to be single-parenting professionals, and still others to be married career professionals.[12] When asked about their commitment to their careers, these women confirm that they would elect to continue working even if there were no necessity. Women and young girls agreed that Nicaraguan women will continue to work and in greater numbers regardless of what happens to the economic state of the nation in the future.[13] Many young girls talk about working when they grow up and are making educational plans for realizing their choice of career.

In summary, women in Nicaragua traditionally defined themselves in terms of motherhood and those whom they nurture. Their primary sphere of activity and limited authority was the home, especially homemaking and childrearing. They have lived in a context of machismo, which idealizes women but places them in subservient positions, restricted in freedom of movement and held accountable to men in virtually every aspect of their lives. Despite the ideal of woman as domestic nurturer, for generations Nicaraguan women have worked outside their homes out of economic necessity, often as heads of households.

The official and societal view of women in Nicaragua changed markedly with women's full participation in the revolution and under the Sandinista government, which supported the women's movement and recognized the need to address and respond to women's issues. To understand these events and envision the future direction of the women's movement, the role of women in the process of the revolution and in the context of the new government must be explored.

**The Movement for Emancipation**

The commencement and growth of the women's movement in Nicaragua paralleled the course of the revolution. Linda Lobao (1987) compared the involvement of women in guerrilla movements in Cuba, Colombia, Uruguay, El Salvador, and Nicaragua in terms of the extent of female participation, women's social class origins, and functional roles. She found that in Cuba a small number of women (about 5 percent of troops) served essentially support and relief roles, being actively mobilized only after the insurgency with the establishment in 1960 of the Federation of Cuban Women. In Colombia in the mid-1960s, women did not take part to any significant degree in the EPL (People's Liberation Army), founded supposedly by educated middle-class people. In the Tupamaros Uruguayan movement, women from primarily the middle class constituted 25 percent of the membership by 1972 and served in support and combat capacities. In El Salvador, women make up 40 percent of the FPL (Popular Forces of Liberation) and Revolutionary Council and hold positions as high-ranking commanders. There, women came primarily from the middle class (in the late 1960s), joined by rural working women and then by urban working women (in the late 1970s) to participate in support and combat activities on a seemingly equal status with men.

In Nicaragua, women took part in every phase of the revolution to overthrow Somoza and made up 30 percent of the FSLN guerrilla membership at the time of the final offensive. Women of all classes were encouraged to take part. Despite cultural norms which reserved the realm of politics for men only, "women of all ages broke the taboo . . . to take up their spot in the combat trenches." As early as 1965, women (e.g., Gladys Baez) were imprisoned for political activities, and from 1967 onward women functioned as an integral part of the FSLN, including fighting in the mountains as guerrillas. They participated in strikes, demonstrated in the streets, and helped hide undercover combatants and weaponry. Numerous names of female heroes of the revolution are well known: for example, Luisa Amanda Espinoza, Arlen Siú, Doris Tijerino, Gladys Baez, and the women of Cuá. Women like Dora María Téllez, leader of the extremely important western front, commanded units and led major offensives, such as in León where four of seven commanders were women.

The FSLN appealed to women and recognized their immediate and long-term needs. Already in 1969, the FSLN declared itself committed to upholding the rights of women: "The Sandinista Popular Revolution will abolish the discrimination that women have suffered with respect to men; it will establish economic, political, and cultural equality between women and men." The program went on to outline at least seven means by which the FSLN would accomplish this, including guaranteed maternity leave and guaranteed rights for illegitimate children, special services for mothers and children, the elimination of prostitution and of women's servitude in general, the institution of child-care centers to assist working mothers, and the elevation of the "political, cultural and vocational level of women via their participation in the revolutionary process." Widespread participation by lower-class women in the revolution attests to its identification with their needs.

The experience of women in the revolution has influenced heavily both men's and women's attitudes toward women, especially regarding women's work and leadership capacities. Women look back upon the revolution as a time of awakening. [One woman relates that] "when the Frente Sandinista began . . . women also within the lines . . . fought in the role of men; that is when the women realized that we can work the same as a man, that we can develop equally as a man. . . . They were heroines. They showed us, they gave us really an idea that the woman in the world, in life, can work, can be equal to a man in work."[14] Today, many women argue they could never return to the repressive prerevolutionary life-style because they are now "awake" and could never again be fooled into tolerating such injustice.

The participation of women in the revolution became both a means and a rationale for their emancipation. Many men saw it as a justification for change, pointing out that women had "earned" the right to equality through their heroism, for they had proven themselves capable of any task performed by a man. Men voiced a duality of perspectives on women's relationship to the revolution. On one side, they idealized women as pure virgins and devoted mothers and saw themselves as their defenders. At the same time, life experience taught them to expect women to be strong and self-reliant in difficult times.

This combination of respect, concern, and protectiveness is heard in the singer's voice in "Venancia," a song by Luis Enrique Mejía Godoy wherein the singer warns Venancia, who is risking her life running messages for the Frente, to "be careful." The composer describes Venancia in terms of her humble peasant origins, her relationship to a brother killed for his affiliation with the revolution, and her courage. The singer tells her, "Your smile, Venancia, is the banner in our struggle." For male combatants the image of the committed woman, plus the macho sense of duty to defend, added purpose to the struggle.

Respect for women blends with love in the song, "Mujer, mujer" by the Grupo Pancasan (1985), which describes women [as] *hecho de amor y besos* (made of love and kisses) and courageous in combat:

| | |
|---|---|
| *Vos asistes para alcanzar la gloria* | You help to achieve the glory |
| *Vos ganastes tu lugar en la historia.* | You [have] earned your place in history. |

Yet even in the setting of the battlefield the association between women and new life is suggested:

| | |
|---|---|
| *Dulce combativa guerrillera* | Sweet guerrilla fighter |
| *Al frente del combate . . .* | To the battlefront . . . |
| *. . . sembrar la Primavera* | . . . to plant the Spring |
| *Propiendo con su sangre.* | Propagating with your blood. |

Based on a tradition of respect for women's strength of character and dedication to family, today's male image of women derives more from an extension of qualities formerly attributed to women than from a complete transformation of men's view of women. One encounters the commonly heard comment that women have "earned" their new rights, something quite different from saying that women have intrinsic rights. In this same context a former combatant, a vigorous supporter of women's rights, can describe the revolution as a woman whom one can never completely conquer.[15]

With the customary Latin American respect for motherhood, the Nicaraguan government has shown appreciation for women who lost children in the revolution. These Madres de Héroes y Mártires (Mothers of Heroes and Martyrs) are the recipients of many social welfare and recreational programs. These women fulfilled their social and patriotic duty to the highest degree, propagating, rearing, and sacrificing children who otherwise might have provided them with companionship and material assistance during the rest of their lives. How indicative of the close identification of women with children and family that no similar programs of recognition honor the fathers of those killed in combat!

In Nicaragua, the first organizations of women with political-social objectives were based on the common concerns of mothers. In neighborhoods, women formed Mothers' Clubs to pursue responses to the situation. Mothers of political prisoners staged strikes. During the 1960s, with the support of the FSLN, the Patriotic Alliance of Nicaraguan Women helped prepare women to join with men in the struggle to confront Somoza. Gladys Baez, who worked with this group in the late 1960s, described their activities: "We organized peasant and working women. We worked to set up safe houses, raised money and agitated for better conditions in the prisons." Thus women became involved first out of familial concern as mothers, and later in a formal network for the cause of the revolution.

In 1977, under the direction of the FSLN, the Association of Nicaraguan Women to Confront the National Problem (Asociación de Mujeres Ante el Problemática Nacional, AMPRONAC) was founded by mainly upper- and middle-class women in concert with men. Like the Luisa Amanda Espinoza Association of Nicaraguan Women (AMNLAE) today, it was concerned with achieving a society which offers full participation to women and men equally.

*The Role of AMPRONAC*

In 1978, AMPRONAC called, among other things, for the repeal of all laws that discriminated against women, equal pay for equal work, and an end to the commercialization of women. The organization was also instrumental on a national scale in demanding freedom of association. Its members visited ministers, passed out leaflets, and held public meetings. During a demonstration associated with a hunger strike, in which women of various political-party affiliations participated, one woman was killed by Somoza's National Guard. Later, many women suffered arrest and torture.

This dynamic group raised women's consciousness and was instrumental in the formation of the Sandinista government, which recognized many of their demands. Because of their forcefulness in projecting their perspective, the struggle became cooperative. Instead of women merely acting as supporters in the traditional nurturing role, they actively forged their nation's future and promoted solutions to women's problems, assuming parallel roles with men.

## The Role of AMNLAE

The Luisa Amanda Espinoza Association of Nicaraguan Women, AMNLAE, was founded with the establishment of the new revolutionary government and was named for the first woman FSLN militant to die in combat against the National Guard in 1970. Initially, this organization, closely aligned with the FSLN, strove principally to integrate women into the work of the revolution. Gradually, after surviving near disbandment in 1981, when the need for its existence was questioned, the organization became more assertive in addressing specific women's issues and in the formation of the new Nicaraguan constitution. In 1988 its name was changed to "Movement," rather than "Association," of Nicaraguan Women.

An important aspect of the women's movement in Nicaragua has been its consistently integrative rather than separatist approach. For women, the initial and long-range objective remained the emancipation of society, the integration of men and women as equal partners in every facet of life. Hence the tenth anniversary slogan, "Together in everything!" The AMNLAE seeks for the Nicaraguan woman "the full development of her human potential," an objective which it proposes can only be achieved by defending and deepening the revolutionary process which would emancipate society from exploitation and oppression.

The AMNLAE operates principally in three areas: education, integration-participation, and legislation. Before women could be emancipated they needed to acquire an education, which under Somoza typically was unavailable to them. They needed to learn about their rights, their bodies, ways to improve their health, and to be offered a medium through which to develop themselves personally and in their common interests with other women.

The AMNLAE has worked for "the promotion of the political, professional, cultural and technical advancement of Nicaraguan women, and their integration into grassroots and labor organizations." Serving as a coordinating body, [the] AMNLAE facilitates the work of women in various sectors and mass organizations, such as trade unions and the Mothers of Heroes and Martyrs.

The AMNLAE has enjoyed remarkable success in achieving legislative reforms. With regard to division of labor, [the] AMNLAE has helped to influence gradual changes in attitudes concerning women's role. The government in 1981 and 1982 enacted new laws, the "Law Regulating Relations between Mothers, Fathers, and Children," and the "Law of Nurturing." Both parents are assigned equal responsibility for childrearing, and all members of the household, including adult men and young boys, are to assist in the performance of household tasks. It is not unheard of today for a husband or son to help the wife/mother with jobs that formerly were considered exclusively hers. Shaping future generations, women active in [the] AMNLAE today teach their sons to participate equally in domestic labor.

Under the Sandinista government, alimony and child support became newly legislated rights. Common-law marriages, the most typical kind, and "illegitimate" children, the majority of all children, were now recognized, giving many times more women and their children protection under the law. In Managua, [the] AMNLAE opened a Legal Office for Women where women can seek the services of legal advisers concerning their rights, including the right to seek child support, a newly legislated obligation of parents who leave children with a former spouse. Legal counsel is also available at most of the Casas de la Mujer (Women's Homes).

The Women's Homes serve the needs of mothers, teaching women about their reproductive health, family planning, and prenatal, infant, and child care. Recognizing that abortion is the second main cause of maternal deaths, [the] AMNLAE made family planning and contraceptive education a high priority and worked to counsel young women against the common notion that having children is a means to capture and/or hold a man's affections. Parents are urged to limit their families to the number of children they can clothe, feed, and educate.[16]

## Conclusion

Women in Nicaragua have successfully challenged the age-old tradition of machismo and have won, to varying degrees, individual rights, which should be awarded to women as birthrights. By means of their valiant and indispensable role in the revolution, women defended and affirmed their capacity to function equally with men. Experience gained during decades of forced labor in the job market and organizational skills forged and refined during the revolutionary struggle served to empower a strong and vocal women's movement. The most powerful expression of the movement, AMNLAE, came to represent Nicaragua's women to the legislature and to coordinate the activities of many other grassroots women's groups. Women's vision in Nicaragua has been integration on equal terms with men. Significant progress toward fulfillment of the vision has been made in the public domain and also in the private sphere, where macho values and behaviors are most difficult to confront.

The prospects for continued progress in the emancipation of women depend largely on women's ability to control their reproductive lives. Recent reports from Nicaragua indicate that the new government's policy will be to ban contraception, except the rhythm method, and to eliminate sex education from the schools, serious blows to the work of women over the past eleven years. Official government policy seems allied with the Nicaraguan Catholic church's view, which was expressed in a sermon I heard in August 1990. The theme was that women's place is in the home, caring for children and performing the traditional domestic chores. The future role of [the] AMNLAE remains unclear, but the resiliency of its members is indisputable. If not able to continue to function in an official capacity, they will certainly continue to exert influence and work for reforms through mass organizations. In the words of the campesina AMNLAE volunteer Elba Aguilera Nervaez, mother of ten and local community leader, and echoed by Orbelina Soza Meirena and the spirits of thousands of Nicaraguan women, whatever else happens, "Seguimos adelante. No cansamos." "We keep moving forward. We do not tire."[17]

## Notes

1. The FSLN, the Frente Sandinista . . . is named for a popular hero, César Augusto Sandino (1893–1934), a peasant who led a guerrilla movement which forced the eventual withdrawal of the U.S. Marines from Nicaragua in 1933 and who was subsequently assassinated by Anastasio Somoza García (1896–1956). Somoza García, who had studied at the Pierce School of Business Administration in Philadelphia, set up a military dictatorship in Nicaragua in 1936. His eldest son, Luis Somoza Debayle, took over in 1957 after his father's assassination and governed until 1967, when a younger brother, Anastasio Somoza Debayle, succeeded him. Educated at West Point and more violent in personality, Anastasio relied on military power and a deliberately corrupted National Guard for strength.

2. In all, over eighty thousand teachers and over one hundred thousand individuals participated in the process, which taught approximately four hundred thousand formerly illiterate Nicaraguans the basic skills of reading and writing. The volunteer instructors were 60 percent women, supported by outreach groups of the national women's organization, AMNLAE. Middle- and upper-class urban volunteers worked in rural areas where they learned to appreciate the hardships and culture of the peasants, or campesinos.

3. Interview with Ivette Amor Quiñonez Cruz, Region II, Nicaragua, August 3, 1989.

4. Interview with Orbelina Soza Meirena, Region II, Nicaragua, August 9, 1989.

5. An objective of the women's movement today is to rid women of this belief. This was pointed out to me by the director of AMNLAE, Region II, on August 9, 1989.

6. Conversation with Auxiliadora Alvarado, witness for a civil marriage which she said required no new dress or wedding ring.

7. Conversation with Ismael Gonzalez, Managua, August 1, 1989.

8. Interview with Ivette Amor Quiñonez Cruz, Region II, Nicaragua, August 7, 1989.

9. Interview with Ivette Amor Quiñonez Cruz.

10. Undoubtedly soon to be completely revised through the efforts of the women's organization, AMNLAE.

11. Interview with Elba Aguilera Nervaez, Region II, Chinandega, Nicaragua, August 2, 1989.

12. Examples, respectively, include Antonica Alvarado Puente, associate director, Ricardo Morales School, and ex-director, School of Heroes and Martyrs, Region II, Nicaragua; Angela Guardado Bravo, teacher and mother of an adopted child; and Ivette Amor Quiñonez Cruz, mother of two young children and sole medical doctor serving a population of eighteen thousand rural Nicaraguans.

13. Interviews with women and children during July and August 1989.

14. Interview with Orbelina Soza Meirena, Region II, Nicaragua, August 9, 1989.

15. Interview with Ignacio Delgado, August 1990.

16. Interviews with Ivette Amor Quiñonez Cruz, medical doctor, and Orbelina Soza Meirena, of AMNLAE, Region II, August 1989.

17. Interview with Elba Aguilera Nervaez, Region II, Nicaragua, July 31, 1989.

# 18  Thomas Niehaus ◆ Interview with Indiana Acevedo, July 21, 1992, Managua, Nicaragua

*In this example of testimonial literature—a highly respected form of ex-pression and the latest trend in Latin American women's studies because it permits ordinary people to record their life stories—Indiana Acevedo, a Nicaraguan housewife, talks about how she developed political aware-ness and why she chose a Christian base community rather than a politi-cal party as the vehicle for her activism. The systematic collection of such interviews would yield a gold mine of information for future social historians. The Reverend Thomas Niehaus is an Episcopal priest and former director of the Latin American Library at Tulane University; his research interests include Liberation Theology, Christian base communi-ties, and street children in Latin America.*

## Background

C hristian base communities (Comunidades eclesiales de base, or CEBs) began in the 1960s in Latin America. Almost all are Roman Catholic and are founded on the principles of liberation theology—that is, on issues of peace and justice. They are small groups usually in poor areas of both the cities and countryside. In many ways they function as parishes, but with emphasis on lay leadership. In many countries most of the leaders are women.

In many Latin American countries, the CEB experience has often been the first time that Latin American rural peasants or urban poor have orga-nized for social action. This has led to consciousness-raising that has been a threat to some governments and to some conservative Roman Catholic hierarchy. Many liberal clerics support the CEBs, seeing them as the van-guard of the post-Vatican II church. They comprise only about 5 percent of the Latin American Roman Catholic church but are a significant and vibrant minority.

The CEB movement has migrated to other countries, including the United States, where it has a small representation and is similar to the house-church movement. Christianity began with small group meetings in private houses, and throughout its history it has returned to that model; for example, various Protestant groups since the sixteenth century have been organized around small groups of laity.

The important point for our purposes is that the CEB movement is new and has opened up a significant role for women in Latin America. The following document is an interview with a woman who is a base community leader and has been working in the communities since 1977. Involvement in the base communities changed her from a passive housewife to a social activist with a career of her own.

**Interview**

My name is Indiana Acevedo. I am forty-two years old. I was born in the city of Rivas [Nicaragua]. I have lived in Managua for twenty-five years. I moved from my hometown to Managua looking for work. I am the mother of six children, three grown up and three still at home. One has graduated from the university, [with] a five-year degree. I am married [although separated for four years].

I finished the second year of high school. I later took other courses. I work as a nonprofessional social worker in a school that includes elementary and secondary levels. We deal with social problems of all types, with young people with very, very serious problems: drugs, alcoholism, prostitution. And I am working there as a social worker in the school.

I have been a member of the base communities for fifteen years, and I have worked with different groups, activities with women, teenagers, and children, adults, groups of poor people that seize land for housing [*asentamientos*], with Christian groups, with all types of groups.

*Can you tell us about your first experience with the base communities? Did this experience change your attitude about the possibilities in Nicaragua?*

I was a traditional person like the majority of us in Nicaragua. I had my life, my home. That was in 1976 or 1977. Then there were some young people [*muchachos*] who had a group in our parish. I was interested, and went there to find out what was happening. I went to Mass like all of the traditional people, and then the young people asked me if I wanted to join, and I stayed to observe, nothing more. The time came for my children to enter catechism class, so that meant more contact with the people in the parish.

I was falling in love with the parish life, and how it worked. This offered me a change in my life because, imagine, I was a housewife locked up in my house, and I offered my support. Later I became more and more involved. The reading of the Bible . . . its truth woke me up to how the people of Israel were liberating themselves from a situation of oppression they were living through. And at that same time we were living through the dictatorship of [Anastasio] Somoza, and so these seemed very similar to me, the situation with Israel and our situation. In reading the Bible one discovers oppression, but one also discovers forms of struggle.

I was raising my consciousness about what was happening in Nicaragua. Thus in light of the Bible, not just the Gospel but also the Old Testament, I was discovering the struggle and the hopes of the people. I was discovering myself. It was a critical consciousness-raising, and this led me to take on more responsibility. But all of this was done through discovering my own faith, because what had been for me something merely traditional became something that gave meaning to my life. I was saying to myself, "This is what God is asking of me, right?" God is asking me to do something, and not just stay in the house. God is making demands on me, and on the basis of those demands I was getting involved in things.

Then I got into serious problems. I was involved in public protests; we demanded things; we made public declarations. It was an era of much persecution for those who made demands and protested. I was one of those whom they pursued. It was an experience of struggle and making demands that was very important in my life, because this changed everything. My entire meaning system collapsed. I adopted other attitudes, which made me more involved in things, and made me more reflective and critical. This threw me into the political life of my country. But always the most important part was that I have done this because of the demands of my faith. That is what I feel: that what God wants me to do is give to others what I have discovered. Not to keep it inside me, but to turn it into service to others. I have always been convinced that what moves me is . . . well, something that I cannot describe, but the more it moves me, the more it drives me on.

I have been doing this for years, and everyone has their low times. Sometimes I have said to myself, "Enough! I don't want to continue doing this." I thought of getting some other type of work. But I found other ways of working. My style of living is very demanding, because I work from 8:00 to 1:00 every day, and then starting at 2:00, I do volunteer work for the base communities. I have groups here in the barrio, groups of young people, a group of adults, one for children. And I also go to other barrios to help out with groups that seize land for housing. I am also working on the Commission for the Quincentenary. So this makes me very busy. I am always doing many things.

*Can you tell us more about the groups within the base communities in the barrio? What are they like?*

Well, one is the group we call the "Root Group." It is one of the oldest in the community. There are fifteen in the group, and we are all women. We begin our meeting with a Bible reading—or, I would say, a rereading, because we have read it so many times. . . . Then after the reading we discuss the most important needs of the barrio.

*Could you give us an example of a discussion topic that was very important for the group?*

One reading that struck the group occurred before the triumph of the revolution [ca. 1978]. It was on the mothers of the Maccabees. They were women who struggled; some were lookouts, and others worked.* But nowadays one Bible reading that moves me and other members of the base communities is when Jesus says, "I come so that you [might] have life, and have it more abundantly" [John 10:10]. This is a wonderful passage.

Now that we are reflecting on the new situation in the country [since the fall of the Sandinista government], one of the readings is the Beatitudes: "I was hungry, and you fed me. I was sick, and you came to visit me. I was in prison, and you came to see me. I was naked, and you clothed me."†

In the base community we have a small project for malnourished children. In the past two years this problem has greatly increased. With the international help of our friends in Holland, we set up a community kitchen [*olla*], where some fifty or sixty children eat every day. The food they eat comes from the money provided by the project, but the services provided come from our base community.

There are many people out of work nowadays. And many of our women are housewives, women who can bake, wash, and iron. They have no skills except domestic skills. So we have a sewing school, where we teach women to design clothes, or remake old clothes. The women receive a certain level of technical skills.

There is another group in the base community, and it is for the young people. In recent years the index of drug addiction has increased greatly. We adults have been concerned, because the young are the future of our country, and a high percentage of our population is made up of young people. There is a concern to instill in the youth values so that they do not get involved in drugs, prostitution, or robbery. Those things lead to the decomposition of the society.

---

*The seven Maccabee brothers were tortured and killed by the tyrant king Antiochus because they refused to give up their Hebrew religious practices. Their mother stood up to the tyrant and died along with them. "O mother, who with your seven sons nullified the violence of the tyrant, frustrated his evil designs, and showed the courage of your faith!" 4 Maccabees 17:2. A short version of the story is found in 2 Maccabees 7:1–42, especially verses 20–42. The full story is found in 4 Maccabees 8:1–18:24, especially 14:11–18:24.

†Matthew 25:42–43. This list is not the Beatitudes, which are sayings such as: "Blessed are the poor in spirit . . . blessed are the peacemakers," as spoken by Jesus in the Sermon on the Mount, Matthew 5:3–12.

Another part of my work is to support the poor when they take over land for housing. Our purpose is to help the poor people discover that they have a right to housing. They have a right to the land, and God gave us the land, not so a few can dominate it, but it is for all. I help those who are looking for places to set up housing. I tell them how to get water in their housing areas, how to legalize their use of the land. I help orient them rather than actually do the work with them.

In one of these areas we are struggling to get a little school started. There are 530 houses with an average of some two thousand or twenty-two hundred people. The most recent census lists some three thousand people. That was last year. The children have problems getting to school now because they have to cross the highway. It is behind the American embassy, and there is a lot of traffic. It is right next to the embassy. It is a very good spot for the housing. In the beginning the ambassador came to the community and said that they couldn't put their houses there because the land belongs to the embassy. But the people said, "As far as we know, Nicaragua belongs to us; and where are we supposed to live?" They said they would not leave. The ambassador offered to build them houses if they would leave the area. But they rejected that, telling him to build the houses but to give them to other people who need them. And so it is a very good project we have there, and that is what happens when the people wake up.

These are examples of my work that I can give you.

*Tell us about your work as a social worker in the school. What are the ages of the children?*

I work mostly with high-school students. My job is to visit the families. The school requires that students come to our center when they are abused, abandoned by their parents, addicted to drugs, or are extremely poor. The center is open from eight to five every day. They eat there.

My job is to deal with the most serious cases, and to establish a relationship with the parents. In the school itself I talk with the children, give them some orientation, and present workshops on the effects of drugs, alcohol, and prostitution. We work with certain groups, because there are 350 young people in the center. We set up groups according to their addiction, and those who work with them are social workers and psychologists. Of course, there are teachers also. In the morning the students go to academic classes, and in the afternoon they attend informal talks or they learn technical skills.

This is very difficult work. They test us. But once they come around, we try to get their families to care for them. That is my work. I also teach religion in the secondary school. What I like best is to visit the families, because it gives me a broader view in trying to understand the children's problems.

*In your experience, what has caused the growth in the participation of women in the last fifteen years? Has the role of men changed also, or is it a situation in which the women have done more; that is, the men have done their part in fighting in the army, but the women have given them support which they had not done before?*

The participation of women in our country has been very significant in both periods, because before the revolution, in the Somoza period, women had a very important role because the men were being pursued and under much pressure. It was always thought that only men carried out war, that only men can do strong acts. Then women had a very important role because they were underestimated by the Somoza forces. The women were the ones displaced in the rural areas. While the men were carrying out clandestine warfare, the women were displaced. Finally the Somocistas realized that the women were also supporting the struggle because, as women, we could feign being pregnant and what we were hiding were guns. We could put a bun in our hair and hide messages in it, carrying them to the front. There was no reason to suspect us. We developed an attitude of enthusiasm, especially for surviving. And this is what the women did.

And so when the triumph of the revolution came, you can imagine how many women were involved in the political and military affairs of the country. And then there was the Ten-Year War [the Contra War], in which both men and women fought. Many women played a very important role in the mountains and in the factories. While all the men were mobilized in the army, the women ran the factories. We had few factories, but those we had were important. And those of us who remained in the city kept it going. And so women developed a high level of military skill. They developed a social sense in many fields, a very strong consciousness-raising.

As you know, in Latin America we live in a situation of strong machismo. There is a deeply rooted machismo in this country. Nevertheless, we women were successful because of the high quality of our participation, which the men appreciated. They gave us a role. In the ten years of the Contra War, we were able to give women dignity and to vindicate them. It wasn't a gift. We earned it.

But there have also been some very difficult situations with men. In my case, for instance. My husband was very traditional, and did not understand these things. His wife was outside the house, away for two days because she had a job to do. Well, he couldn't begin to understand this. He was used to my being in the house and doing all the things he wanted done. But then as I discovered my rights, I told him: "These are my rights. You can't invade my person, because I am me and you are you." This is also something we achieved: to discover ourselves as persons, and to assume our own personalities. These were wonderful discoveries.

Now women are in all areas of the society, and we achieved equal pay for equal work. We demanded that. We have been recognized publicly on a worldwide level. Women have a significant role in our country. In the old days very few of us went to the university. It was almost all men. Even our parents told us that the male children were the ones who were to study, and the girls—well—they were to be typists and secretaries, at a lower level. There were no incentives for us, as there have been now for the last ten years.

Women can now prepare themselves on a higher educational level. So things became more equal. Nevertheless, there were consequences for us, very significant ones. Many marriages failed. Families broke up. Families' ties were broken. But that is a consequence of assuming one's own history and assuming your own personality.

I am one of those cases. My husband said to me: "I cannot live with this woman any longer. I do not control her anymore. I do not want a wife who pays no attention to me. I will look for a woman who pays attention to me." I don't want to give the idea that an agreement should always be reached, nor do I think that things should be imposed on us. This is a consequence. But when one's consciousness has been raised, it gives one a certain security that it is all worth it, and these things have their consequences. I have been separated from my husband for four years, but I am not lamenting over it, because you can't do that. Ideologically it does not have an effect. One just goes on and improves.

So women have a very important role in our country. There is a very high percentage of families that are headed by women. I dare not give you an exact figure, but it is very high. These are women who struggle to survive with their children. In this country the woman's role is to be both mother and father.

*In your visits to families, have you noted that many men have left their families?*

First of all, the men have an attitude of "I don't care," or "What do I have to lose?" This takes away their sense of parental responsibility. This is one of the factors. Women are left with two, three, four, five, or six children or more, and they have to assume this responsibility. There is a tremendous irresponsibility with regard to parenthood in this country.

Another factor is that, as women become more aware, they discover themselves, and they demand respect from the men, who in turn confuse respect with authority. That is the cause of the problem. The truth is that the men are very traditional. A man has two or three women, and if his wife figures out he has the other two women, then we'll see what happens, right? This is just incredible!

So there are many married women who are heads of families. The woman may go out to look for a job. Many men do not like that. He wants her there at home under his control. The woman rebels, and goes out to look for a job, or she rebels and joins an organization. I myself have worked with women's organizations during the last ten years. I worked with the Mothers of the Heroes and Martyrs. Thus women in these organizations are raising their consciousness. I wish that men could just realize that, in spite of their high level of consciousness-raising with respect to the revolution, when it comes to their attitude toward women, their whole scheme of consciousness-raising falls flat.

When a woman joins one of these organizations, she does not remain the same. She changes, because in our women's organizations we help them to discover themselves, to discover themselves as persons. Many husbands tell me, when I go to visit their houses, "You are ruining my home with this stuff you are doing with my wife."

Our work is very rewarding, but also very costly. It fills one with hope. Only a nation that becomes aware of itself can transform itself little by little.

## 19  Daniel Castro ◆ "War Is Our Daily Life": Women's Participation in Sendero Luminoso

*Abimael Guzmán, leader of Sendero Luminoso, advocates a Maoist solu-
tion to the traditional inequities present in Peruvian society. He has stated
that "women are one half of heaven" and, therefore, has assigned to
them a leadership role of unprecedented proportions in a Latin American
guerrilla movement. Peasant women have participated in combat in Peru
and Bolivia since colonial times. In the 1780s they fought against Spain
in the large Andean rebellion led by Tupac Amaru, and, in the struggle
for independence in the early 1820s, they enlisted in the patriot cause. In
this selection, Daniel Castro takes the little existing writing about women's
roles in Sendero Luminoso (Shining Path), places it within a historical
context, and offers some original conclusions about women guerrilla
fighters.*

On September 3, 1982, nineteen-year-old Edith Lagos was killed in a
confrontation with members of Peru's Guardia Republicana.[1] A few
days later more than thirty thousand people attended her funeral in
Ayacucho in an act of open defiance to the authorities' ban of a public
funeral.[2] The frail-looking, petite Lagos had become a tragic and romantic rallying figure in a context where there were none.[3] A member of the
Partido Comunista del Perú-Sendero Luminoso (Communist Party of Peru-
Shining Path, or PCP-SL) since the age of sixteen, Lagos symbolized the
aspirations of many of the Sierra youth who were, then, still trying to
understand the full significance of the bloody rebellion initiated only two
years earlier in the remote Sierra village of Chuschi.[4] More significant
still, the apotheosic posthumous tribute paid to Lagos was a clear recognition of the important role played by women in Sendero's organization.

Unlike other Latin American revolutionary movements, Sendero's
preoccupation with the role of women has resulted in its recruitment of
large numbers of women and their participation as leaders and rank-and-
file members. Juan Lázaro estimates that 35 percent of the military leaders, particularly at the level of underground cells, are women,[5] but, given
the clandestine nature of the organization, it is difficult to pinpoint with
exactitude the percentage of women currently active in the organization.
However, it is eminently clear that women play an active role in the political and military campaign of Sendero. This is reflected in the number
of women arrested by the government in its attempts to stem the tide of
violence. In 1985 there were 100 women arrested by the police, but in
1986 this number increased to 790.[6] In later years, as the armed struggle

has intensified, there has been an exponential increase in the number of women arrested, with as many as 600 being detained in a single day.[7]

The tradition of women's participation in the political life of Peru goes back to pre-Inca times when women occupied positions of leadership in the *ayllus*, the clans that acted as the building blocks of society. The coming of the Incas dictated a transformation of roles when men were chosen to represent the *ayllus*, while women "retained in many cases the economic power in the Andean communities."[8] The coming of the Spaniards caused a dislocation of the most basic cultural and social relationships; the indigenous people, and women in particular, fell into the category of legal minors. The only women who were granted the right to own land were the members of Inca nobility, forcing the women commoners to work as domestic servants and field hands in order to survive.[9]

The passive role to which women were relegated in the first two centuries of the colony came to an abrupt end with the active participation of women in the wars of resistance and rebellion in the eighteenth century. In the insurrection of Juan Santos Atahualpa in the Central Sierra of Peru in 1742, there was a "separate fighting unit of some fifty *serrana* women, captained by one 'Doña Ana,' a *zamba* (mixed Indian-black) from Tarma."[10] In 1780–81, Micaela Bastidas was instrumental in Tupac Amaru's rebellion against Spanish exploitation, and so significant was her role that Tupac Amaru's defeat is widely attributed to his refusal to listen to her advice and attack Cuzco at a time when Spanish forces were in a state of disarray.[11]

The tradition of women's participation in popular struggle continued through the wars of independence in the early 1820s and was sustained in the wars of resistance against the Chilean occupation of Peru during the War of the Pacific (1879–1883).[12] Thus, the large participation of women in Sendero is but the culmination of a long historical process of Andean women's struggle for social equality and recognition in a male-dominated society.

As the avowed repository of a long tradition of Andean resistance and rebellion, Sendero has managed to address specific problems affecting women throughout the country in general and in the Andes in particular. Ideologically, this concern can be traced to the writings of José Carlos Mariátegui, who founded the PCP in 1928. These ideological postulates became inordinately important in the reemergence of the reconstituted party in the Andean context of Ayacucho in the sixties and seventies. Writing in 1924, Mariátegui celebrated the gains made by women in the twentieth century, and in a burst of unbounded optimism he claimed that "gradually we have come to the juridical and political equality of both sexes." He supported his pronouncement with the examples of women who occupied prominent positions in the world political scene of his time.[13] He specifically singled out the role played by the British Labourite and Cabinet member Margaret Bondfield and the Soviet ambassador to Norway, Alexandra Kollontay [*sic*], a former people's commissar of the revolutionary Soviets. In the midsixties the Movimiento Femenino Popular (People's Feminine Movement, or MFP, one of Sendero's many "mass organizations"),[14] chose Kollontai's *Love in a Communist Society*, and her essays "Social Relations and Class Struggle" as well as "Communism and the Family" as texts for studying and discussing the role of women.[15]

The MFP emerged as the representative group of the female faction of the Frente Estudiantil Revolucionario (Revolutionary Student Front, or FER) at the National University of San Cristóbal de Huamanga (UNSCH).[16] Its purpose was to educate and to incorporate peasant women from the surrounding area into the revolutionary movement that was beginning to be articulated under the leadership of a philosophy professor by the name of Abimael Guzmán.[17]

Aside from being the home of UNSCH, Ayacucho provided fertile ground for the evolution of a revolutionary movement; it ranked as Peru's second most impoverished province and it was characterized by a foreign observer as a "Fourth World" enclave in a "Third World" country.[18] It lacked the most elementary services, it reputedly had one physician per eighteen thousand inhabitants,[19] and the caloric intake of *Ayacuchanos* amounted to 420 calories per day, well below half of the World Health Organization's prescribed minimum of 850 calories. Ayacucho also led the nation in illiteracy, in adult and infant mortality, and, in the twenty years between 1961 and 1981, it experienced a decrease in population from 4.1 to 3 percent of the country's total while receiving only 1 percent of the national budget earmarked for internal expenditures.[20]

In addition to the conditions of misery obtaining in Ayacucho, the majority of the population was either rural or was engaged in one form or another of agriculturally related occupations. Accepting Mariátegui's characterization of Peruvian society as semifeudal and semicolonial, and recognizing the success of the Chinese revolution under the guidance of Mao Zedong, Guzmán posited that in Peru the peasantry represented the truest revolutionary force in the country. Thus, all political work by the nascent organization was oriented toward the political preparation and development of the peasantry for the unavoidable armed conflict that would resolve the class struggle once and for all.

The incorporation of women into its program of preparation for the armed struggle became one of Sendero's main priorities; women were considered not just as supporters but also as potential and real combatants.[21] Sendero's analysis of objective conditions helped them to determine that Peruvian women and particularly peasant women bore the quadruple brunt which, according to Mao, characterized all semifeudal and semicolonial societies: the burdens of political, societal, marital, and religious oppression.[22] From this perception it followed that women could only be truly liberated when the capitalist structures of class exploitation were destroyed. This conclusion concurred with Mariátegui's position that women were first and foremost members of a class rather than members of a particular gender. Consequently, their goal should be to gain total social and political emancipation rather than partial liberation along gender lines.[23]

In 1975 the "democratic" faction of the Movimiento Femenino Popular, the faction favoring emancipation, won out in the ideological struggle against the faction favoring "bourgeois" liberation solely along gender lines. The MFP published a call to develop the women's movement,[24] while at the same time outlining the party's priorities in resolving the problems affecting women.

By addressing the problems faced by women in Peru—specifically peasant women—from a class perspective, the PCP-SL has provided a platform where women can be seen and heard and from which they can participate in the war against the official Peruvian state initiated by Sendero in 1980. While female participation in the official political parties, including the electoral left, is purely nominal,[25] women occupy positions of leadership and responsibility in the higher ranks of Sendero's political organization. In 1975 the highest ranking member of MFP was Augusta la Torre, who served as president of the organization. It is widely rumored that she was an active member of the central committee of the party until the time of her death.[26] Although information on the rank of various female members of Sendero is the result of speculation, generally based on the knowledge of their positions before the organization became clandestine at the end of 1979, it is nevertheless evident that many women occupy important positions within the organization.

Laura Zambrano ("*Camarada* Meche"), Margie Clavo Peralta ("Doris"), and Fiorella Montaño ("Lucía") are among the most prominent Senderista leaders arrested and rearrested at various times between 1984 and 1987. There is widespread agreement that all three of them have occupied, at different times, leading positions in Sendero's political/military *buró* in Lima.[27] Of the three, Laura Zambrano is the best known, having admitted her membership in Sendero. She first gained a reputation as a fiery leader of the SUTEP [United Teachers' Federation of Peru] in the strikes of 1978 and 1979. In 1984 she was arrested and tortured, but public pressure prompted her release for lack of evidence. She was soon rearrested and confined to the Miguel Castro high-security prison in

Lima with more than seven hundred suspected Senderistas. Police raids in early 1991 uncovered documents and other evidence that point to the existence of an extended central committee, the majority of whose members appear to be women.[28]

Sendero is applying the same lack of sexual discrimination that exists in recruiting members to the choice of targets singled out for attack. In February of 1992, the day after she had organized a march denouncing Sendero,[29] María Elena Moyano, deputy mayor of Villa El Salvador and head of El Vaso de Leche (a breakfast program for impoverished children), was shot to death and blown up in a graphic warning to those who might want to oppose Sendero.[30] The escalating violence provided Peru's President-elect Alberto Fujimori with a viable excuse to dissolve Congress and to suspend the constitution, assuming virtual dictatorial powers on April 5, 1992, for the alleged purpose of combating and eliminating Sendero.[31]

As the crisis in Peru worsens and the violence increases exponentially, it becomes more difficult to predict with certainty the final outcome. . . . However, the significance of women in this open war is being brought into sharper perspective every day. Without women and their participation, Sendero would not have been able to sustain such a prolonged and relatively successful attack on the Peruvian state. The long historical tradition of women's struggle in the country has steeled them for war on both sides of the trenches, and there is no indication of any willingness to retreat. Under these circumstances the Peruvian government cannot underestimate the importance of women in this ongoing civil war. . . . The resolve of Senderista women and their willingness to fight to the end in order to gain total emancipation is evident in the words of Laura Zambrano: "For the combatants of People's Guerrilla Army, our center of gravity is to fight, war is our daily life, we fight to conquer power for the Party and the people. . . . We have been steeled in the harshness of life, in sacrifice and in defiance of death, we incarnate revolutionary heroism."[32] The level of dedication exemplified by Zambrano can only find an equivalent in the women of China and Vietnam. From this perspective, the war in Peru has radically transformed women's perceptions of themselves and their role in society, and, regardless of the outcome, the future does not augur well for the survival of the traditional patterns of gender oppression.

**Notes**

1. The circumstances of Edith Lagos's death remain shrouded in controversy. Some versions claim that she died during the confrontation, shot by the police, while others claim that she was captured alive and killed while in police custody.

2. See Juan Lázaro, "Women and Political Violence in Contemporary Peru," *Dialectical Anthropology* 15:2–3 (1990): 243.

3. See Gustavo Gorriti Elenbogen, *Sendero: Historia de la Guerra Milenaria en el Perú* (Lima, 1990), 1:362.

4. The evening of May 17, 1980, a group of masked individuals burned the electoral registers and the ballot boxes in Chuschi, a highland village in the department of Ayacucho. They were going to be used the next day to carry out the first democratically held election after twelve years of military rule.

5. Lázaro, "Women and Political Violence," 234. Caution must be exercised in coming up with any definitive figure, because at best it can only be the result of estimates based on the number of women arrested or on media reports.

6. José González, "Sendero de mujeres," *Si*, Lima, (April 6, 1987), 81.

7. Carol Andreas, "Women at War," *Report on the Americas* 24:4 (December/January 1990–1991): 21.

8. Lázaro, "Women and Political Violence," 234.

9. Irene Silverblatt, *Moon, Sun and Witches: Gender Ideologies and Class in Inca and Colonial Peru* (Princeton, 1987), 119–120.

10. Steve J. Stern, "The Age of Andean Insurrection in 1742–1782: A Reappraisal," in Steve J. Stern, ed., *Resistance, Rebellion, and Consciousness in the Andean Peasant World, 18th to 20th Centuries* (Madison, WI, 1987), 46.

11. Andreas, "Women at War," 25.

12. Florencia E. Mallon, "Nationalist and Antistate Coalitions in the War of the Pacific: Junin and Cajamarca, 1879–1902," in Stern, *Resistance, Rebellion, and Consciousness*, 262.

13. José Carlos Mariátegui, "La Mujer y la política," in *Temas de educación*, sixth ed. (Lima, 1980), 123.

14. The *organizaciones de masas* are organizations working in concert with the Communist party. However, their members do not necessarily have to be party militants.

15. Andreas, *When Women Rebel*, 179; and Lázaro, "Women and Political Violence," 243.

16. The group was formed in the mid-1960s at the National University of San Cristóbal de Huamanga in Ayacucho. Established in the 1650s, the university was closed for lack of funds following the War of the Pacific. It was reopened in 1959 under the Prado administration. It was the FER's publication "Por el Sendero Luminoso de Mariátegui" that gave the party its present nickname.

17. Abimael Guzmán Reynoso earned a degree in philosophy with a thesis entitled "Concerning the Kantian Theory of Space." For his graduation from law school he wrote "The Bourgeois-Democratic State." He began teaching philosophy at UNSCH in 1962. There, he was also in charge of the education program designed to train teachers; it is important to note that approximately 55 percent of all Peruvian women pursuing a professional career train as teachers. In 1979, prior to his disappearance from public view, he was arrested by the Peruvian police in a roundup of potentially dangerous Communist leaders suspected of supporting a national work stoppage in January of that year. The next time he was seen in public was during his arrest by the Antisubversive Unit of the National Police (DINCOTE), September 12, 1992. As the recognized leader of the Communist Party of Peru-Sendero Luminoso, Presidente Gonzalo, as he is most commonly known to his followers, has been sentenced to life in prison by a military tribunal.

18. Cynthia McClintock, "Sendero Luminoso: Peru's Maoist Guerrillas," *Problems of Communism* (September-October 1983): 26.

19. A priest working in Ayacucho places the number at one physician per thirty-nine thousand inhabitants. Nicholas Shakespeare, "In Pursuit of Guzmán," *Granta* (Spring 1988): 182.

20. Carlos Iván Degregori, "Sendero Luminoso": I. *Los Hondos y mortales desencuentros*. II. *Lucha Armada y utopía autoritaria* (Lima, 1988), sixth ed., 9–15.

21. Lázaro, "Women and Political Violence," 241.

22. González, "Sendero de mujeres," 83. See also Gabriela Tarazona-Sevillano with John B. Reuter, *Sendero Luminoso and the Threat of Narcoterrorism* (New York and London, 1990), 77–78.

23. Mariátegui, "Las reivindicaciones feministas," in *Temas de educación*, 130.

24. Movimiento Femenino Popular, "Manifiesto: Bajo las banderas de Mariátegui Desarrollemos el Movimiento Femenino Popular" (Lima [?], 1975).

25. In 1985, 3 women were elected to the Senate as opposed to 57 men (5 percent) while in the lower chamber women occupy 10 out of 180 seats (6 percent). During the elections women represented 20 percent of the senatorial candidates and 10 percent of the candidates to the Chamber of Deputies. *Programa Nacional de Promoción de la Mujer (1990–1995)* (Lima, 1990): 163–164.

26. Augusta la Torre was married to Abimael Guzmán until her death in 1988 or 1989. However, she had distinguished herself as a political activist before her marriage to Sendero's eventual leader.

27. See González, "Sendero de mujeres," 80, 82; Lázaro, "Women and Political Violence," 243; "Las caras del terror: La cúpula senderista," *Caretas* (March 4, 1991): 32–33.

28. "Las caras del terror," 32–33.

29. Simon Strong, "Where the Shining Path Leads," *New York Times Magazine*, May 24, 1992.

30. Villa El Salvador is one of the most remarkable success stories in the evolution of shantytowns on the outskirts of Lima. From a straw-mat squatter settlement, it has been chosen as the recipient of several world prizes as a model of planning and development.

31. James Brooke, "A Lethal Army of Insurgents Lima Could Not Stamp Out," *New York Times*, April 7, 1992.

32. "Nuestra vida cotidiana es la guerra. Entrevista exclusiva a Laura Zambrano Padilla," *El Diario* (Lima), March 14, 1988, 9.

## 20 Carolyn Lehmann ◆ Bread and Roses: Women Who Live Poverty

*The Casa Sófia project in Chile takes one step further women who already had been mobilized during the Pinochet era into arpillera workshops and soup kitchens and challenges them to see themselves as women first—not as mothers. While consciousness-raising may seem old hat to a North American, in Latin America to be a woman is to be a mother, a concept at the heart of the Marianist paradigm: there, woman and mother are interchangeable. To suggest otherwise is what makes Casa Sófia potentially revolutionary. If the condition of Latin American women is to change, then that process must begin with how these women perceive and define themselves. In this vein, Casa Sófia works to meet the desperate need of poor urban women for literacy and mental health. Carolyn Lehmann, a founder of the organization, worked for twenty years in Chile as a Maryknoll missioner and feminist educator.*

### Feminist Popular Education

Feminist popular education is different from popular education as developed in Latin America since the mid-1960s. Traditional popular education is gender-blind in that it treats men and women and the realities of their daily lives in the same manner. Writings on this subject (almost all by male authors) make this abundantly clear.[1] Latin American feminists have been critical of the gaps and misnomers present in popular education, but they also recognize that the grass-roots movement is crucial. Feminist popular education extends, shapes, and strengthens both the theory and the practice of popular education from the standpoint of women's lives: sexual, spiritual, and political. Popular education in general overlooks physical abandonment, violence against women, and authoritarianism in the home. It assumes that these problems belong to the private world.

The one-sidedness of much of popular education can be illustrated by one simple example. There are countless grass-roots groups organized in Santiago and throughout the country composed, for the most part, entirely of women. They are often mobilized by umbrella organizations motivated by the political parties and the church. They carry on such

From *Popular Culture in Chile: Resistance and Survival*, ed. Kenneth Aman and Cristián Parker (Boulder, CO: Westview Press, 1991), 115–23. Reprinted by permission of Westview Press.

activities as first-aid campaigns, family gardens, and soup kitchens. These groups capitalize on the fact that the *pobladoras* [residents] see themselves first as mothers. The mother's role is to fill the daily soup pot; the *pobladoras* will run the soup kitchens, and the government will not have to use its resources to solve the hunger problem.

When women have gone through a gender-specific consciousness-raising process at a women's center, however, they begin to organize and participate in meeting their specific needs as women. For example, women of Casa Sofía put together a theater group to reach other *pobladoras*. "Our purpose is to present the lived reality of the *pobladora* as it is. In doing this, we are able to transmit some of what we have learned. We recognize now that we have many values; that we have power and can do much more than just be housewives. We want to show other women that they also can do more—more than the daily chores. Who we are now as women has nothing to do with what we were before. We are changed people."[2]

Feminist popular education enlarges the horizons of other pedagogies, which ignore women. It develops programs in which women learn with women. Men have long been the "gatekeepers" of knowledge, but today it is women who are the "door-openers" in our lives, with the power to inspire and motivate. In this setting, it is women who have the capacity to be the group motivators, guides, companions, and educators. It is they who empower other women; who have the joy and privilege of witnessing an enormous growth in awareness. Women strive to transmit and increase knowledge, particularly knowledge that has been silenced and denied to women. Body is reconnected to reason, emotion to spirit. They provide for one another both bread and roses. They make use of relaxation, exercise, music, touch, and massage as well as intellectual knowledge. The next section describes how this happens through mental health and literacy programs at Casa Sofía. More important, some of the *pobladoras* will testify to these programs in their own words.

### Casa Sofía

Casa Sofía opened in April 1985 as the first women's center in the *poblaciones* of Santiago. It is a rented house in an ordinary neighborhood, located on a busy street and easily reached by public transportation. Nestled in urban poverty, it is a place where women of the neighborhood come to leave behind their burdens, tell their stories, discover their worth, and help one another recapture their dignity and plan a new future. It is a place where *pobladoras* are safe to open their eyes, express rage, find deep friendship, and charge the unfolding drama of their own growing consciousness. Women begin to live a process that moves outward, beginning with the sharing of experiences and moving to: (1) an awakening of consciousness and analysis of reality; (2) a change of attitude and a new perception of oneself; [and] (3) a distinct way of acting and achieving goals for oneself and beyond oneself—an eventual transformation of society.[3]

Casa Sofía was the final stage in work that had been going on for years in the southern and western zones of Santiago. In 1980, Peggy Moran and I had begun the first popular mental-health support groups for women in a Chilean *población*. Monica Hingston, an Australian, joined the team in 1984. Prior to Casa Sofía, the groups generally met in local Catholic chapels. These chapels were the only safe places to meet in a political environment in which meetings were either forbidden or suspect (depending on whether the government had decreed a state of siege or a state of emergency). As the number of groups multiplied, coordination and organization grew more complicated. (In the *poblaciones*, telephones and automobiles were not available.) In spite of the political risks involved and with virtually no financial assistance, we decided to open a "popular" center exclusively for women. Our hope was that a single central location and space of our own would provide greater opportunities for the work to flourish. After the first year, when the center became somewhat more established, a number of international organizations helped to sustain it financially.

Since its founding, Casa Sofía has become well known locally and nationally and has even acquired something of an international reputation. The networking of women's groups in Santiago and elsewhere has facilitated this. The International Women's Tribune Center based in New York has published a directory of women's centers in Latin America that includes Casa Sofía. The guest book at the house lists visitors who have come from many parts of the world.

*Popular Education for Mental Health*

Even in the early years of a brutal dictatorship, the issue of mental health had already become a central focus for many women. At first their hope was that this nightmare had only temporarily intruded into their lives. It took years to realize that the situation was relatively permanent and that they needed to prepare for the long haul. The ragged edges began to show in everyone's lives. In 1979–1981 an extensive research project was carried out by twenty people living and working in Pudahuel, in the western zone of Santiago. They found that mental anguish and fear were major health problems.[4] The grass-roots community was already aware of this, but now it was confirmed by professionals. A group of psychiatrists wrote:

"Chile is a sick country. The political, social, and economic conditions that this country lives in generate insanity."[5] Another report said: "Political repression, growing unemployment, labor instability, a decline in the quality of life, a general lack of participation in political and social decisions: All are conditioning factors for the critical deterioration of the mental health of the Chilean people."[6]

There were few or no public resources for professional help in the area of mental health; thus, female educators began to introduce mental-health programs. In this field, feminist education is simultaneously political and personal, embodied and spiritual. The struggle for mental health has come to be seen as an equilibrium inside oneself, as a balance within ourselves as women and between ourselves and the cosmos. It is therefore necessary for us all—men and women—to reject our dualistic and divisive social system.

Women's responses to life's difficulties, often termed neurotic by the predominantly male medical profession, are natural protests against a system that violates and oppresses. The real modern illness is disconnection, and the tasks of women and feminists are to remake and reweave connections. The connections inside of ourselves, the connections of friendship among women, the connections of ideas and theories with reality, the connections of wisdom born of suffering: All of these and more are important resources for women attempting to form networks for better mental health.

Our popular mental-health support groups are designed by and for women. The objectives are: (1) to learn about our mental health; (2) to understand ourselves better as women; and (3) to discuss and find collectively alternative solutions to our problems. Women who participate in the groups gain new strength as well as other benefits. They undergo obvious personal growth, become liberated from a multitude of fears, and offer and receive the support of friendship.[7] The group leaders or facilitators are *pobladoras* who were once participants. Regina, for example, is a group facilitator who attended the program as a participant four years ago. As she conquered her fears and anxieties, she was able to make concrete changes in the way she dealt with her husband and her children. She loves to talk about how she began to believe in herself as a worthwhile person who has dignity and importance. She is now an educator capable of inspiring her sisters living the same poverty she lives.

> [*Regina*] There was a time when the only thing I wanted was to die. I just didn't want to live. I didn't find any meaning in life, and I certainly didn't like myself. Any small problem made me suffer and be depressed. But never again. For me to be happy is to have learned that I have dignity, that I'm capable of doing many things and to earn a living. That

was the first and greatest step in my life. That's the first thing that women learn in these support groups: that they are persons, nothing less. A woman discovers she has rights that no one ever told her about. It's like learning to walk again, little by little. Now, as a group facilitator, I see myself reflected in each new woman who arrives for a group. Then, I wonder, how can I succeed in helping this woman to see another world? You feel very, very satisfied when this happens. You can actually see the changes in the women, and you feel wonderful. It's beautiful: Women who live such extreme poverty, and yet we come alive to new ideas.[8]

Within this support-group process, women most experience liberation in the area of sexuality. Women living poverty suffer in the cruelest manner from an ignorance of their own sexuality and from a lack of love for their own bodies. With motherhood as the major role assigned to women by the culture (as Teresa Valdés repeatedly observes), *pobladoras* especially have internalized this social message and understand their fulfillment solely in terms of maternity and motherhood. But interestingly, they see no connection between the role of being a mother and a woman's body and sexuality.[9] Women refer to their bodies as machines: "I used to look at myself in the bathroom mirror and say: 'Who am I? Who will I be?' It was like I was just floating in the air. I was just a machine who attended children and husband, washed the clothes, did everything in the house: all automatic like a robot, a machine. And I thought this was what you were supposed to do in order to be a good mother."[10]

The changes women experience in their lives are directly related to their roles as wives and mothers. The opportunity for women to participate in support groups at centers such as Casa Sofía is a crucial prerequisite for these changes. It is through their bodies that women come to modify their concepts and their actions. The shift is transformational, from seeing oneself only as a mother to perceiving what it is to be a woman. This new dimension of self-discovery is the foundation, first, for personal change and then for creative action within the social sphere.

[*Mari Petra*] Through the support group I began to overcome all the violence of my life by throwing myself into life. I put up a sign that advertised that I was able to give injections. I discovered my own personality. Before, everything and everyone dominated me. I now see myself as a woman, with worth and dignity.[11]

[*Nora*] In my home they notice that I'm completely changed. What they don't understand is that I'm in a process of enriching myself. They don't like the fact that I'm no longer submissive. For example, if I have a hundred pesos, I'll make a cake for the women in my group rather than feel I have to use the money in the house. My sons say to me: "You have things to talk about now. You know more things and have wis-

dom." How we women have been victims! . . . But not anymore. I know
I have value now and don't have to be last; now I'm first, second, and
third.[12]

## Literacy Course for Women

As it exists in Casa Sofía, this course attempts to break through the literacy frontier. It begins with questions and reflects on male-dominated society, always beginning with the experiences of the women themselves. Literacy is essential for the future Chilean *pobladoras'* desire for themselves and their nation.

The history and evolution of Chile's literacy campaign can be traced back to the beginning of the twentieth century. The Ministry of Education defines as illiterate all persons older than fifteen who cannot read or write. In 1907, 60 percent of the population was listed as illiterate. By 1970, 88.3 percent of the population was said to be literate.[13] In fact, UNESCO declared in the 1970s that Chile was among the five countries in the world that have most succeeded in overcoming illiteracy. It is interesting to note, however, that in 1983, although 88 percent of the population was literate, only 27 percent of adults actually read books, and of those one third could not remember the title or theme of the last book they had read.[14]

Literacy programs for women should have a special focus. Such a course was created by Peggy Moran and Monica Hingston in their book *Mañana Sera Distinto* (Tomorrow will be different). In their view, learning to read and write words is much more than a matter of vocabulary. It involves both word and action and, hence, reflections on relationships in our world. A feminist literacy process relates the speaking of a word to the transformation of reality and begins with words that point directly to women's reality. Moran and Hingston develop a process of consciousness-raising that facilitates a better understanding of a patriarchal culture from which women have been excluded or in which they have been dominated. At the same time, the women are able to achieve a basic literacy level within four months. This program is powerful and moving to witness as it functions within the *población*. It gives women the possibility of making decisions about their lives. It is a powerful example of bread and roses.

The program is based on seventeen key words (known as generative words) necessary to learn Spanish. A sketch with one of these words is shown to initiate the reflection and dialogue. The first word is *mamá* (mother). Discussion questions are suggested for the word. The women answer the questions out of their life experience; the wisdom that is tapped and shared is a new resource for them.

[*Adriana*] My life has been very sad. I was born in the countryside and never went to school. I was physically disabled and wasn't worth a thing. I was just a bother for everyone. Only when I began to assist at the Casa Sofía programs did I begin to liberate myself. Before that I was completely closed in on myself and sometimes never left my room. I was almost crazy, no one to talk to and no friends. First, I began with the support group, and when the literacy course started I was the first one there. That was the absolute ultimate for me, the most beautiful thing in the world . . . because now I write and write. That I would be able to pick up a pencil and be able to say, to write to you that I love you, that I care for you: That is wonderful. All of my feelings that I've had inside for so long that I was never able to express, now I can write them down. My whole personality has changed, and I have a totally new understanding about life.[15]

[*Elena*] All the problems in my house and with my daughters aren't such a major thing for me anymore. Now I've begun to live for myself. I believe that I'm the happiest woman in the world. Imagine, forty-five years old and learning! Now I want to be able to study for a career. This is so important because all my life I thought I was worthless. To think that I might have died without this knowledge! Now I won't die without knowing.[16]

This is a literacy with powerful links to other issues important to women: economic literacy, cultural literacy, women's rights literacy. It is not an easy matter for women living in poverty to imagine alternatives, much less to act on them. Meanwhile, though, they read and write about and question the way things in society are structured for women.

## Notes

1. For a recent example, see Jorge Chateau and Sergio Martinic, *Educación de Adultos y Educación Popular en la Ultima Década* (Santiago: FLACSO, 1989). [Note that the term "popular education" in this selection should be interpreted from the Chilean point of view, keeping in mind the undertone of class distinctions and specific places, as in *poblaciones*].

2. Casa Sofía theater group meeting, June 27, 1989.

3. Taken from the objectives of Casa Sofía as presented in promotional literature.

4. Cristían Parker et al., *Rasgos de Cultura Popular en Poblaciones de Pudahuel* (Santiago: Vicaría Zona Oeste, 1981).

5. The magazine *La Alternativa* (Chile), July 1986.

6. "Salud Publica, Privada y Solidario en Chile Actual," Working Document No. 44 (Santiago: PET, July 1986).

7. For the methodology of the groups, see Carolyn Lehmann, Peggy Moran, and Monica Hingston, *Rehaciendo Nuestras Conexiones* (Santiago, April 1988).

8. Interview with Regina Viscay, July 1989.

9. Andrea Rodo, "El Cuerpo Ausente," *Proposiciones* 13 (January-April 1987).

10. Interview with Georgina Olea, August 1989.

11. Interview with Mari Petra Marinov, July 1989.
12. Interview with Nora Tarifeno, July 1989.
13. *Las Transformaciones Educaciones Bajo el Régimen Militar*, Volume 2 (Santiago: Programa Interdisciplinario de Investigaciones en Educación [PIIE], May 1984), 439.
14. A study by the Catholic University, quoted in *Jornada de Creación de Hábitos de Lectura* (Santiago, 1983).
15. Interview with Adriana Torres, July 1989.
16. Interview with Elena, July 1989.

# Suggested Readings

## Anthologies

Lavrin, Asunción, ed. *Latin American Women: Historical Perspectives.* Westport, CT: Greenwood Press, 1978.

Pescatello, Ann, ed. *Female and Male in Latin America.* Pittsburgh: University of Pittsburgh Press, 1973.

Safa, Helen, and Nash, June, eds. *Sex and Class in Latin America.* New York: Praeger, 1976.

———. *Women and Change in Latin America.* South Hadley, MA: Bergin and Garvey, 1985.

## Bibliographies

Knaster, Meri, ed. *Women in Spanish America.* New York: G. K. Hall, 1977.

Stoner, K. Lynn, ed. *Latinas of the Americas: A Source Book.* New York: Garland Press, 1989.

## Culture and Images

Cypress, Sandra Messinger. *La Malinche in Mexican Literature: From History to Myth.* Austin: University of Texas Press, 1991.

Franco, Jean. *Plotting Women: Gender and Representation in Mexico.* New York: Columbia University Press, 1988.

## Development

Deere, Carmen Diana. "Cooperative Development and Women's Participation in the Nicaraguan Agrarian Reform." *American Journal of Agricultural Economics* 65 (December 1983).

Dixon-Mueloer, Ruth, and Anker, Richard. "Assessing Women's Economic Contributions to Development." No. 6. *Training in Population, Human Resources and Development Planning.* Geneva: International Labour Office, 1988.

Ellis, Pat, ed. *Women of the Caribbean*. Atlantic Highlands, NJ: Zed Books, 1986.

Sen, Gita, and Brown, Karen. *Development, Crises, and Alternative Visions: Third World Women's Perspectives*. New York: Monthly Review Press, 1987.

Wasserstrom, Robert. *Grassroots Development in Latin America and the Caribbean: Oral Histories of Social Change*. New York: Praeger, 1985.

Wignaraja, Donna. *Women, Poverty, and Resources*. Newbury Park, CA: Sage, 1990.

Yudelman, Sally J. *Hopeful Openings: A Study of Five Women's Development Organizations in Latin America and the Caribbean*. West Hartford, CT: Kumarian Press, 1986.

## Feminist Thought

Ahern, Maureen, ed. *A Rosario Castellanos Reader: An Anthology of Her Poetry, Short Fiction, Essays, and Drama*. Austin: University of Texas Press, 1988.

Lavrin, Asunción. *The Ideology of Feminism in the Southern Cone, 1910–1940*. Working Paper. Washington, DC: The Wilson Center, 1988.

Offen, Karen. "Defining Feminism: A Comparative Historical Approach." *Signs* 14:1 (1988): 119–58.

Saporta Sternbach, Nancy, et al. "Feminisms in Latin America: From Bogotá to San Bernardo." *Signs* 17 (1992): 393–434.

Seminar in Feminism and Culture in Latin America. *Women, Culture, and Politics in Latin America*. Berkeley: University of California Press, 1990.

## Marriage, the Family, and Sexuality

Das, Man Singh, and Jesser, Clinton J., eds. *The Family in Latin America*. New Delhi: Vikas, 1980.

Guy, Donna J. *Sex and Danger in Buenos Aires*. Lincoln: University of Nebraska Press, 1991.

Jelin, Elizabeth, ed. *Family, Household and Gender Relations in Latin America*. London: Kegan Paul International (UNESCO), 1991.

Lomnitz, Larissa A., and Pérez-Lizaur, Marisol. *A Mexican Elite Family, 1820–1980: Kinship, Class, and Culture*. Princeton, NJ: Princeton University Press, 1988.

Martinez-Alier, Verena. *Marriage, Class, and Colour in Nineteenth-Century Cuba*. New York: Cambridge University Press, 1974.

Pescatello, Ann M. *Power and Pawn: The Female in Iberian Families, Societies, and Cultures.* Westport, CT: Greenwood Press, 1976.

## Politics

Chaney, Elsa. *Supermadre: Women in Politics in Latin America.* Austin: University of Texas Press, 1979.
Fisher, Jo. *Mothers of the Disappeared.* Boston: South End Press, 1989.
Lewis, Oscar; Lewis, Ruth M.; and Rigdon, Susan M. *Four Women Living the Revolution: An Oral History of Contemporary Cuba.* Chicago: University of Illinois Press, 1977.
Menchú, Rigoberta. *I, Rigoberta Menchú: An Indian Woman in Guatemala.* Ed. Elisabeth Burgos-Debray and trans. Ann Wright. New York: Verso, 1983.
Taylor, J. M. *Eva Perón: The Myths of a Woman.* Chicago: University of Chicago Press, 1979.

## Rural Women

Beneria, Lourdes. *Women and Development: The Sexual Division of Labor in Rural Societies.* New York: Praeger, 1982.
Beneria, L., and Feldmen, S., eds. *Unequal Burden: Economic Crisis, Persistent Poverty, and Women's Work.* Boulder: Westview Press, 1992.
Borque, S., and Warren, K. *Women of the Andes.* Ann Arbor: University of Michigan Press, 1981.
Boserup, Ester. *Women's Role in Economic Development.* London: George Allen and Unwin, 1970.
Bronstein, Audrey. *The Triple Struggle: Latin American Peasant Women.* Boston: South End Press, 1982.
Stephen, Lynn. *Zapotec Women.* Austin: University of Texas Press, 1991.

## Women's Movement

Andreas, Carol. *When Women Rebel: The Rise of Popular Feminism in Peru.* Westport, CT: Lawrence Hill and Co., 1985.
Carlson, Marifran. *Feminismo: The Women's Movement in Argentina from Its Beginnings to Evita Perón.* Chicago: Academy Chicago Publishers, 1987.
Hahner, June E. *Emancipating the Female Sex: The Struggle for Women's Rights in Brazil, 1850–1940.* Durham, NC: Duke University Press, 1991.

238                                                      Suggested Readings

Jaquette, Jane, ed. *The Women's Movement in Latin America*. Boston: Unwin, Hyman, 1989.

Macías, Ana. *Against All Odds: The Feminist Movement in Mexico to 1940*. Westport, CT: Greenwood Press, 1982.

Miller, Francesca. *Latin American Women and the Search for Social Justice*. Hanover, NH: University Press of New England, 1991.

Molyneaux, Maxine. "Mobilization without Emancipation: Women's Interest, the State, and Revolution in Nicaragua." *Feminist Studies* (Summer 1985).

Stoner, K. Lynn. *From the House to the Streets: The Cuban Women's Movement for Legal Change, 1898–1940*. Durham, NC: Duke University Press, 1991.

**Women Warriors**

Heyck, Denis, and Daly, Lynn. *Life Stories of the Nicaraguan Revolution*. London: Routledge, 1990.

Latin American Working Group. *Central American Women Speak for Themselves*. Toronto: LAWG, 1983.

Martin, Megan, and Willet, Susie, eds. *Women in Nicaragua*. London: Nicaraguan Solidarity Campaign, 1980.

Marshall, Catherine. *Militarism versus Feminism: Writings on Women and War*. London: Virago Press, 1987.

Pérez, Ester R.; Kallas, James; and Kallas, Nina. *Those Years of the Revolution, 1910–1920: Authentic Bilingual Life Experiences, as Told by Veterans of the War*. San Jose, CA: Aztlán Today, 1974.

Randall, Margaret. *Sandino's Daughters: Testimonies of Nicaraguan Women in Struggle*. Ed. Lynda Yanz. Vancouver: New Star Books, 1981.

———. *Sandino's Daughters Revisited: Feminism in Nicaragua*. New Brunswick, NJ: Rutgers University Press, 1994.

Salas, Elizabeth. *Soldaderas in the Mexican Military: Myth and History*. Austin: University of Texas Press, 1990.

Soto, Shirlene Ann. *Emergence of the Modern Mexican Woman: Her Participation in Revolution and Struggle for Equality, 1910–1940*. Denver: Arden Press, 1990.

Thomason, Marilyn. *Women of El Salvador: The Price of Freedom*. Philadelphia: Institute for the Study of Human Issues, 1986.

**Work**

Arrom, Silvia M. *The Women of Mexico City, 1790–1857*. Stanford: Stanford University Press, 1985.

Babb, Florence E. *Between Field and Cooking Pot: The Political Economy of Marketwomen in Peru.* Austin: University of Texas Press, 1989.

Bunster, Ximena, and Chaney, Elsa. *Sellers and Servants: Working Women in Lima, Peru.* New York: Praeger, 1985.

Chaney, Elsa, and Garcia Castro, Mary, eds. *Muchachas No More: Household Workers in Latin America and the Caribbean.* Philadelphia: Temple University Press, 1989.

Fernandez-Kelly, Maria Patricia. *For We Are Sold, I Am My People: Women and Industry in Mexico's Frontier.* Albany, NY: Zulu Press, 1983.

Graham, Sandra Lauderdale. *House and Servant: The Domestic World of Servants and Masters in Nineteenth-Century Rio de Janeiro.* New York: Cambridge University Press, 1988.

Hahner, June. *Poverty and Politics: The Urban Poor in Brazil, 1870–1920.* Albuquerque: University of New Mexico Press, 1986.

# Suggested Films

The films listed below are easily available in the United States and are either dubbed or subtitled.

*Camila* (Argentina). 1984. A young Catholic socialite from Buenos Aires runs away with a young Jesuit priest. They find temporary happiness in a small village but eventually are recognized and condemned to death without trial. Based on an actual case and set in the midnineteenth century.

*Dona Flor and Her Two Husbands* (Brazil). 1976. Based on Jorge Amado's novel of the same name. Details the life of a young widow, her respectable new husband, and her dynamic, sexy, dead first husband who refuses to stayed buried. Stars Sonia Braga. Adult.

*El* (Mexico). 1952. In public, "El" is an upstanding, respectable man. In private, he is a paranoid, authoritarian, ultramacho husband who abuses his wife physically and psychologically.

*Erendira* (Mexico). 1983. Based on a Gabriel García Márquez short story. Erendira is a teenage girl exploited as a sexual slave by her greedy grandmother.

*Frida: Naturaleza Viva* (Mexico). 1983. Portrait of the realist painter Frida Kahlo (1907–1954), whose works starkly showed the difficult lives of Mexican women. She was the wife of muralist Diego Rivera.

*Gabriela* (Brazil). 1983. Based on a novel by Jorge Amado. The story of a barkeeper whose passionate romance sends sparks flying in a small town where sex and politics are the main diversions. Stars Sonia Braga and Marcello Mastroianni.

*Hour of the Star* (Brazil). 1986. Story of Macabea, a young woman from the countryside of northeast Brazil who moves to the sprawling city of São Paulo. It won all twelve of the major film awards at the Brazilian Film Festival.

*Lady on the Bus* (Brazil). 1978. Stars Sonia Braga as a shy young bride who is frigid on her wedding night. Frustrated by her problem, she decides to sample other men while her devoted husband goes slowly insane.

*Love, Strange Love* (Brazil). 1982 (Adult). Story of a young boy sent to live with his mother in a luxurious brothel.

*Lucia* (Cuba). 1968. Shows the lives of three Cuban women from three different eras: an aristocratic spinster from 1895, a bourgeois girl from 1933, and a young peasant woman of the 1960s.

*María Candelaria* (Mexico). 1943. The heroine is an outcast in her small Mexican village because of her late mother's immoral behavior. Her only friends are the local priest and a peasant whom she loves. Their goal is to marry, but they are exploited by a local farmer and a rich city artist. The end is tragic.

*Miss Mary* (Argentina). 1986. The tale of the English governess, Miss Mary (played by Julie Christie), a wealthy family who lives and dies by tradition, and the broad political events and intimate personal dramas that carve their destinies: love and honor in Perón's Argentina.

*The Official Story* (Argentina). 1985. Alicia, the sheltered wife of a businessman, discovers that her adopted daughter may be a *desaparecida* stolen from a young couple who were "disappeared" after being imprisoned for political reasons. Winner of the Academy Award for Best Foreign Film.

*Retrato de Teresa* (Cuba). 1979. Teresa, mother of four, textile worker, and member of a dance group, faces a lack of understanding on the part of her husband, a television repairman who believes that a woman's place is in the home.

*Tango Bar* (Argentina). 1935. An honest man is tormented by the discovery that the woman he loves is a professional thief. Moved by his love, she gives up her life of crime to be with him, but he cannot believe in her again. With Carlos Gardel.